Books by
FAIRFAX DOWNEY

Our Lusty Forefathers
Laughing Verse (*Collection*)
Cavalry Mount
Army Mule
Jezebel the Jeep
Dog of War
War Horse
Reunion in Print (with William A. James)
Indian-Fighting Army
Disaster Fighters
Portrait of an Era, as Drawn by C. D. Gibson
Richard Harding Davis—His Day
Burton, Arabian Nights Adventurer
The Grande Turke
Young Enough to Know Better
When We Were Rather Older
Father's First Two Years
A Comic History of Yale

OUR LUSTY FOREFATHERS

OUR LUSTY FOREFATHERS

Being Diverse Chronicles
of the Fervors, Frolics,
Fights, Festivities,
and Failings of
Our American Ancestors

By
FAIRFAX DOWNEY

Illustrated by
JOHN C. WONSETLER

CHARLES SCRIBNER'S SONS, NEW YORK
CHARLES SCRIBNER'S SONS, LTD., LONDON
1947

To my aunt
ELIZABETH DAVIS HODGES

CONTENTS

FOREWORD

Oᴜʀ forefathers drank deep, ate hearty and lived lustily. They downed draughts of stone-wall, a mixture of rum and hard cider with an impact meriting its name. They relished meat four times a day and engulfed 12-inch oysters. They frolicked at corn-husking bees and enjoyed wheelbarrow kisses. Half an alphabet of scarlet letters, not just an "A," was worn on bosom or sleeve to signify their sins. Toward matters spiritual or political their attitude, anything but indifferent, rose often from fervent to fanatical.

Warm-blooded human beings with human failings along with their virtues—such were these forebears of ours and so these chronicles strive to show them. Too often have they been pictured as lay figures against a background of epic events. Intimate and revealing details have been suppressed, partly through prudery, partly as a form of ancestor-worship. As Charles Francis Adams put it in his notable essay, *Some Phases of Sexual Morality and Church Discipline in New England:*

> Like Shem and Japhet, approaching it [the past] with averted eyes, we are disposed to cover up with a garment the nakedness of our progenitors; and the severe looker after truth, who wants to have things appear exactly as they were, and does not believe in the suppression of evidence,—the investigator of this sort is apt to be looked upon as a personage of no discretion and doubtful utility, —as, in a word, a species of modern Ham, who, having unfortunately seen what ought to have been covered up, is eager, out of mere levity or prurience, to tell his "brethren" all about it.

Charges of indiscretion and inutility are hereinafter cheerfully risked in the hope that these reconstructions of the ways of our grandsires succeed in some measure in revivifying them —in redeeming them from the remote unreality to which they have been relegated. Perhaps these sketches may fill sundry gaps or may animate certain episodes, obscured in conventional history-books. They will not have been written in vain if they restore a sense of kinship with the once-lively bearers of names in our genealogical tables.

"As to our ancestors," wrote Doctor Henry Reed Stiles in his *Bundling: Its Origin, Progress and Decline in America,* "we must take them as history shows them to us—'men of like passions with ourselves,' and 'in all respects tempted as we are,' yet neither worse, nor, again, very much purer or better than ourselves."

FAIRFAX DOWNEY

New York City, 1947

OUR LUSTY FOREFATHERS

SWIPSY OR SOBER?

The Supervisor of Drinking Does His Duty

17th-18th Century

Not drunk is he who from the floor
Can rise again and still drink more,
But drunk is he who prostrate lies
Without the power to drink or rise.
Anon.: Good Old Madeira

ALICANTE
CALABAGUS
EBULUM
CONSTANTIA

"**M**ingle me a flip, Landlord,"
the guest ordered.

The tavern-keeper glanced doubtfully toward the stout,
red-faced man in brown homespun. Already he had drunk
enough to be rated as blue, perhaps even damp. And he
seemed bent on drinking right down the list posted beside the
bar.

"Alicante * . . . Calibogus . . . Constantia . . . Ebulum . . .
Flip." He had successfully reached the F's, but there was
trouble ahead. "Kill-devil . . . Metheglin . . . Mumbo . . .
Rumbullion." He might well manage metheglin, a strong,
sweet drink made of fermented honey and herbs, which was
mead, the draught of the Druids and Vikings. But kill-devil
and rumbullion were straight Barbadoes and New England
rums, branded by reformers as "hot and hellish liquors" but
beloved by imbibers as banishers of care, woes, and ills.
Kill-devil, they declared, really did kill devils or at least
knocked them unconscious until next morning. On top of the

*Alicante and Constantia were sweet red wines from Spain and
Africa, respectively; calibogus—cold rum and beer; ebulum—elder-
berry wine; mumbo (short for mumbo-jumbo)—rum punch; switchell
—a mixture of molasses, water, vinegar, and rum.

3

foundation already laid, straight rums might stagger even a seasoned toper. And the end of the list was not yet.

"Switchell . . . Spiced Syder . . . Stonewall." Surely if the guest survived to order them his sibilants at least would be slipping, and the effect of the last-listed, a potent mixture of hard cider and rum, would resemble a head-on collision with the structure for which it was named.

"A flip and make haste." The second demand was louder and more importunate.

The red-faced man was a traveler, a stranger. Consequently his name was not upon another list affixed to the wall behind the bar: a roster of known drunkards to whom the sale of liquor was strictly forbidden. Reluctantly acknowledging the order, the tavern-keeper nodded to his tapster. From a shelf containing an imposing array of tankards, beakers, punch bowls, flagons, posset-cups, jugs and mugs, the tapster took down a four-quart flip glass. He filled it two-thirds full of strong beer, sweetened it with molasses and several pinches of dried pumpkin. Then he poured in a generous gill of rum and set the concoction down before the drinker.

That worthy rose and strode a bit unsteadily toward the great open fireplace. Its warm glow turned his rubicund countenance redder still. Deep within it burned a back-log, so large it had been necessary to drag it in by a chain hitched to a horse. On the hearth various dishes were cooking, filling the taproom with savory odors. In a long-handled skillet a bear steak sizzled. A roast of beef, a large wild turkey which must have weighed close to fifty pounds, and a haunch of venison revolved, browning, on a spit. It was turned by the mechanism of a treadmill on which a small, leashed dog walked endlessly, his mouth watering as the meat juices dripped in the pan beneath the spit. They would be sopped up by diners with hunks of rye-and-Injun—bread made from rye flour and corn meal. In a brass kettle, swung from the crane, simmered a soup or a pudding.

No attention to the contents of pots, pans, and kettles and the alluring spectacle presented by the skewered roasts was paid by the flip drinker, a grave error on his part. The hard and steady drinking, so prevalent throughout the American Colonies, usually was accompanied—and its effects mitigated —by as hearty and simultaneous eating, especially of meat.

The rubicund gentleman, however, was concentrating on assuaging a thirst. He bent over the hearth and from a bed of coals drew the short, small poker called a loggerhead or flip-iron or flip-dog. Whistling and holding it like a torch, he carried it back to his table and plunged it, hissing, into his creaming glass of flip. He grasped the great glass in both hands and drained it, smacking his lips over the scorched, puckering taste which made flip a favorite drink of the day.

"Ahhh!" he sighed gustily. A beatific but somewhat vacuous grin wreathed his face. He might now fairly be described as slightly fuddled. A few more and he would be decidedly haily gaily. Others of the company, watching him, glanced apprehensively around the taproom.

"Tapster," roared the red-faced one, peering over at the list of drinks, "bring me a mug of kill-devil and tarry not."

"No more!" a stern voice decreed.

The drinker swung around on his bench to glare up at the lank and lugubrious individual who had suddenly appeared at his elbow. An uncomfortable silence was broken by the red-faced man's bellow: "And who might you be, Master Nosey, to interfere with my pleasure?"

"I am the Supervisor of Drinking," the owner of the commanding voice identified himself. "It is my duty to visit the inns and ordinaries of this town and prevent drinking to excess. If I lay eyes on any man who has ordered a drink too many—more than he can soberly bear away—I am empowered by ordinance to countermand it."

All the company in the taproom nodded in mournful confirmation. Strict regulations and restrictions on excessive drinking had been in force in most of the Colonies since the middle of the Seventeenth Century. Taverners were fined or lost licenses if any frequenters were found "disguised with drink" on their premises; even if they allowed a guest to tipple more than half an hour or to drink after 9 o'clock in the evening, or consume more than a limited amount at other than meal time. As liquor became more plentiful and cheaper—in Boston in 1686 the Reverend Increase Mather had declared that the poor and wicked could make themselves drunk for a penny—punishments multiplied in number and variety. Drunkards were disenfranchised and forbade holding office. They were fined, flogged and put in work gangs. In 1638 in Virginia two married couples were chastised for intoxication by being confined in stocks during church service. As an erring sister might be sentenced to wearing a scarlet "A," so might a bibulous brother be ordered to "weare about his necke, and so to hang upon his outward garment a D made of redd cloth and set upon white; to continyu this for a yeare, and not to have it off any time he comes among company." New Yorkers, caught in their cups, were forced to drink three quarts of salted water laced with lamp oil. Yet always the aim of the authorities was to restrict drunkenness, not drinking.

"Very well, Master Kill-joy, you have the power," the red-faced one ungraciously conceded. "But how do you know when to exercise it? How do you determine I've had one too many as you maintain?"

"By my own good judgment," the Supervisor affirmed.

The other sniffed. "So you presume to settle a moot question that has been agitated for centuries. Sages have vainly attempted to settle whether a man be swipsy or sober. Who are *you* to say?"

"I have had no little practice hereabouts," the Supervisor affirmed. There was a shuffling of boots, and a series of rueful grins ran around the taproom. "And," he continued, "I am informed as to the various statutes and tests applied in this and other Colonies. Both Maryland and Virginia define a drunkard as one who has been intoxicated thrice."

"You have no knowledge of how oft I've been fuddled, Master Nosey."

"None, Master Jorum," the Supervisor admitted, giving him the name of a drinking-bowl. "But when I behold the number of drinks you have encompassed, I will hazard that the occasions have not been seldom. Now Maryland specifies that drunkenness is: 'Drinking to excess to the notable perturbation of any organ of sense or motion.' You might try repeating that though I doubt you are able. My own favorite test is this: When the same pair of legs which carried a man into a house cannot bring him out it is a sufficient sign of drunkenness.

"But my duty, sir," he continued, "is to nip it in the bud —to prevent anyone becoming bereaved or disabled in the use of his understanding. And I shall never be a popular man," he finished sadly.

"Bah!" Red-face exclaimed. "You are but a bigot. I doubt not that you drink only water or at best small beer."

"You shall see!" The Supervisor was justly indignant at so monstrous an accusation. "Tapster, a flip."

The drink was quickly placed before him. He plunged a hot loggerhead in it and drank. Supervisor and Red-face resumed their argument. It became more heated. Shaking flip-irons in each other's face, they were, as the saying went, "at loggerheads."

Gleefully the company in the taproom hunched forward over their tables. They came to the tavern not only for meat, drink, and warmth and because they were lonely but for relief from boredom. In the tavern (the equivalent of the community center of much later days) were held court sessions, musters, elections, and entertainments—showings of wax-works and freaks, performances by ventriloquists and trained animals, dances, concerts, lotteries. Scarcely second to these, was a good, rousing argument like the one now developing. Everybody sat back to enjoy it.

The Supervisor still held the floor. "Tests to determine when the limits of sobriety are passed were established by the Bishop of London himself," he declaimed. "It is highly regrettable that they had to be devised for the clergy of Virginia, given to roistering. His Grace decreed that any clergyman might be proven to be drunk simply if he stayed an hour or longer in the company where they were imbibing

ardent spirits and in the meantime drinking healths or otherwise taking his cups as they came 'round."

"Had I a drink before me," interposed Red-face, "I would
propose a health. It might even be yours."

The Supervisor ignored him. He continued: "The Bishop
also made mention of such signs that a minister was swipsy
as: Striking, threatening to fight, or laying aside any of his
garments for that purpose. Also staggering, reeling, vomiting,
or incoherent, impertinent, obscene or rude talk."

"Amen for the Bishop," the other rudely interrupted. "Far
more revealing are the stages of intoxication as described
by a good Parson Weems in his pamphlet entitled, *The
Drunkard's Looking-Glass*. They should assist your endeavors
greatly, Master Nosey. Let me name them for you." He ticked
off on his fingers. "Stage One—a Drop in the Eye. Two—
Half-sleeved. Three—a Little on the Staggers. Four—Capsized.
Five—Snug under the Table with the Dogs. Six—Able to Stick
to the Floor without Holding on."

A roar of appreciation echoed through the taproom. Everybody ordered another drink, including the Supervisor. Somebody slipped one to the deeply grateful red-faced man. It
went unnoticed by his argumentative opponent who was
bursting with a retort.

"All very diverting," he caustically observed. "Mirth, like
wine, maketh glad the heart of man, as the Psalmist declares.
But we are discussing a serious question. Far more useful
than the Weems whimsies is this enumeration of the symptoms of drunkenness by the celebrated Doctor Benjamin
Rush of Philadelphia." He drew a broadside from his pocket
and began to read, glancing up after each item at Red-face.

" 'First symptom: unusual garrulity,' " he read. " 'Second,
unusual silence.' No one could convict you on that score,
Master Jorum. 'Third: captiousness and a disposition to quarrel.' Now there I have you."

Everybody laughed, Red-faced louder than the rest, and
everybody ordered another drink. With extra relish the Supervisor read the next items:

" 'Succeeding symptoms: uncommon good humor, and an

insipid simpering or laughing. Profane swearing and cursing.
A disclosure of their own or other people's secrets. A rude
disposition to tell persons what they know of their faults.
Certain immodest actions—particularly by women.' "

Somebody called for three hearty cheers for the last-men-
tioned symptom. They were given with a will. Everybody had
another drink. The Supervisor read on with greater gusto:

" 'Ninth: a clipping of words. Tenth: fighting. Eleventh:
singing.' "

The company seized the occasion to raise a jolly drinking
song until the rafters rang. When it ended, the Supervisor
and the Red-faced one were clapping each other on the back.
The latter scanned the broadside lying on the table and
exclaimed:

"Shay, ol' friend, here's shymptom you forgot to read.
'Shympton Number Twelve: Imitating noishes of brute animals.' "

"Aye," the Supervisor acclaimed. "Bes' shymtom of 'em all.
Woof, woof!"

THE GOVERNOR GOES A-WOOING

The Swashbuckling Courtship of Nicholson of Virginia

1699-1705

Hasten to Lucy young and fair.
Fly to her soft Engaging air.
Say to her vertuous Self so rare

Wast not yor youth in Coy disdain
Think not yor beauties Pleasing reign
By wayes of Rigor to Maintain

For tho^h to Queens we homage owe
And to the Goddesses with incense goe
'Tis for the Blessings they Bestow

Neither do they require that we
Should to their Courts and Altars flee
But for our own felicity

Thus if before it be too late
You bless me wth y^r Marryed State
In love you them will imitate

And I to you shall Constant prove
With Sacred Pledges of true Love
Which Age nor time shall ever move.

Francis Nicholson: *To Lucy Burwell* (c. 1701)

Lucy Burwell was barely six-
teen when the Governor wrote her a letter* on Valentine's
eve on the first day of spring of the year 1699. Just sixteen,
but then girls bloomed and married early in Virginia. Any
who lingered unwed on the parental vine until she was as old
as in her twenties risked being dubbed an "antient maid" or
an "antique virgin." **

Now Colonel Francis Nicholson, Royal Governor of the
Province of Virginia, was forty-four. But it was spring, and he
was sorely smitten and he penned his love letter without an
inkling in his mind that he might be called—if anybody dared
—an antique bachelor. Humbly but ardently he addressed
Lucy, "so divine a lady," begging that he receive pardon for
his presumption "from your own most beautiful lips."

Upon this spring freshet followed a flood of poems, missives
(tender and otherwise), memoranda, menaces, and memorials
—many of them, ink scarcely faded, preserved in the archives
of Williamsburg today. And thus began a courtship extraordinary, a romance rather one-sided but definitely ripsnorting,
an affair of the heart which would make American history.

Naming the cast, let it be gentleman, not lady first this time.
Francis Nicholson was a Royal Governor and is entitled to

*The Nicholson letters, poems, and memoranda, quoted in this
chapter, were purchased by Colonial Williamsburg, Inc., from a
large collection of Nicholson papers, preserved by the Society for
the Propagation of the Gospel in Foreign Parts, London. Photostats
were made available through courtesy of the documents' owners.
Photostats and transcripts may be consulted in the New York Public
Library and the Library of Congress.

**Col. William Byrd referring to his daughter Evelyn. Said the
Colonel: "Either our young fellows are not smart eno' for her or she
seems too smart for them." However the case, the lovely Evelyn died a
spinster.

13

precedence. Soldier of the King—in the course of his career
Lieutenant Governor or Governor of five Colonies, no less—
founder of Annapolis and of Williamsburg, and of twenty-
eight churches in America. Quite a man, Colonel Nicholson.
Able and arrogant, brave and overbearing, queer and can-
tankerous. A vessel of wrath, a pot of red pepper. It was evident all over town when the Governor presided at the Council—you could tell it by the bellowing. An Indian who once
saw him in one of his wild frenzies of rage declared he must
have been "born drunk." Some of the Virginians he gov-
erned called him a bastard, literally and figuratively, but the
evidence of a bar sinister in his escutcheon is inconclusive.
The Governor, for his part, roundly informed members of the
opposition that they were dogs and their wives were bitches
and he would beat manners into them and, failing that,
muster a standing army and put halters around the necks of
all rebels.

He swaggered and he swashbuckled, did the Colonel, but
it was not blustering bravado. In all weather he rode the
rounds of wilderness outposts to review his ranger companies.
He could and did storm French forts and scuttle a whole
fleet of pirates after an all-day battle on Chesapeake Bay.
And he could and did put passion into poetry, and passages
of his love letters to Lucy were so warm they smouldered. Not
a man any girl could easily ignore, Colonel Nicholson.

There is no record of any portrait of Lucy Burwell; it is a
fair assumption, however, that some painter missed a golden
opportunity. Colonel Nicholson declared her beautiful and
singled her out from her sisters * which was no mean feat.
For it is reliably recorded that Major Lewis Burwell of the
Manor of "Fairfield," Gloucester County, by his two marriages "had a whole houseful of blooming daughters"—
nine of them, along with six sons. Undoubtedly Lucy was one
of the fairest flowers of Southern womanhood, whose reputa-

*Several historians have erroneously stated that Nicholson's in-
amorata was Martha Burwell, Lucy's younger sister, who married
Henry Armistead. The statement is disproved by the Governor's
letters to Lucy.

tion for charm had been well established before the end of
the Seventeenth Century. Indeed she must have been super-
abundantly lovely so quickly and completely to have bowled
over the Governor, who was no callow swain but had been
around considerable.

Her disposition? One revealing glimpse is supplied by an
inscription on the fly-leaf of an old book, scrawled there perhaps by some beau, driven utterly distracted:

"Lucy Burwell is the devil. If not the devil, she is one of
his imps." *

Most certainly Lucy bedeviled or at least bewitched Governor Nicholson, though he kept calling her his "Vertuous
Soul," "Dear Saint," and "Fair Angel." He fell madly, fervently, rapturously, publicly in love.

The season was, as has been observed, spring, and the
very air of Virginia may have had something to do with it.
There had been much marrying and giving in marriage in the
Colony ever since the importation from London in 1620 of a
cargo of "young, handsome, honestly educated maids, of
honest life and carriage"—ninety of them, homesick and seasick but willing—each having her choice from among at
least three suitors. Other shiploads followed, and there were
weddings, right and left. It is not good, say the Scriptures, for
man to live alone. Widows and widowers seldom remained
long in lonely solitude. For the same person to marry three
times was not unusual. The redoubtable Colonel John Carter
of Virginia had five wives. There were even instances of
six undaunted ventures into matrimony, including the case
of a Virginian dame named Elizabeth whose maiden name—
not surprisingly—has been lost from the records.

So it was small wonder that Colonel Nicholson felt that
way. He was, he wrote Lucy from Jamestown where duty had
called him, her ladyship's Adorer and Admirer—with capital A's.

". . . And tho [he added] my very great misfortune at
present is to be debarred yᵉ unspeakable happiness and

*Cited by Mary Newton Stanard in her *Colonial Virginia; Its
People and Customs.*

hono"r of se°ing and hearing yor Ladys^p in reality (to which
nothing in thys world can be comparable; & hoped, wished
for, or desired more by me; because I should be then near
to ye object of my vows . . . So Madam, if what I think and
dream of very often were but substantial ours, I should be
ye most happy mortal alive."

Absence had made the gubernatorial heart fonder, if that
were possible. But love languishes on distant longing. They
met again, and the Governor was utterly enchanted. Picture
him—a fine figure of a man, brave in camlet coat, its sleeves
ending in ruffles of fine lace; a Turkey-worked waistcoat of
blue, broadcloth breeches, shoes with polished silver buckles;
a cocked hat, glistening with gold lace, doffed with a flourish.
And Lucy perhaps with a mantle of crimson taffeta, thrown
back from her shoulders; tendrils of curls peeping out from
beneath a sarsanet hood; her petticoat trimmed with silk lace
and over it a dainty flowered gown, its green satin bodice cut
fashionably and alluringly low.

A bow. A graceful curtesy. Who will doubt that bright
eyes sparkled flirtatiously above a fan? It was not every maiden
that had a Royal Governor at her feet—as this one so obviously was at Lucy's. Why shouldn't her young heart beat
faster with triumph, whether she wanted him or not? Who
could blame Lucy—the imp—if her glance, the curve of her
smiling lips, and the tilt of her head were just a touch in-
tentionally provocative?

Something certainly provoked the Governor into dipping
his quill deep in devotion and the inkwell to pen poems to
her.

> Vertuous pretty Charming Innocent Dove
> The only Center of my Constant Love
> Your hard-heartedness to me is Shewn
> By taking other Councills than your own
> Which theirs ten thousand times does far Exceed
> this makes my heart incessantly to bleed
> Least any harm to you should chance to be
> W^ch by your being cruel and refusing me
> yet I pray good heaven may not permit

Because you do So much resemble it
Therefore fair Angell be So Justly kind
As for to have me often in yor mind
For you in mine I do at all times find.*

Not bad, not bad at all for a governor and a soldier, more accustomed to writing dull documents such as decrees, orders, and reports. It must also be taken into account that the poems were not products of long leisure. Colonel Nicholson had a good many other things to occupy him besides penning and polishing poesy to a maiden fair. He was busy removing the capital of Virginia from Jamestown to a new site which he named Williamsburg in honor of the King. Accomplished courtier that he was, he first planned its streets be laid out to form a W and an M, the initials of his Sovereigns, William and Mary, but abandoned the idea as too difficult.** He was busied also in the building of "stately Fabricks," including the halls of William and Mary College, which had been founded in 1693 by Dr. James Blair, Commissary of the Bishop of London, in Virginia.

Indeed the Governor was occupied, yet Williamsburg could not hold him long from Major Burwell's not-distant Manor of "Fairfield." Had he himself not written

Hasten to Lucy young and fair.
Fly to her soft Engaging air . . .

Most certainly he had so written. To horse!

Journeys, if we can believe the Bard and the Colonel, end in lovers' meetings. The fair Lucy at least listened to her suitor's avowels. Did she give him any encouragement, any solace? Or did the Colonel's declarations (in a subsequent

See also Nicholson's poem to Lucy quoted at the beginning of this chapter.

**If only a Henry or an Edward had graced the throne of England at the time, the Governor could have managed nicely. One regrets today that he was forced to forego his W and M streets. They would have made a striking view from the air, and surely John D. Rockefeller, Jr., would have restored them as magnificently as he has the rest of Colonial Williamsburg.

letter) of his "extasie" spring from the glowing imagination, the wishful thinking of a lover? In any event, Lucy assured him of her determination to lead a single life, and home he rode in the depths of discouragement. So distraught was he that he sat up into the small hours writing her a long, per-fervid letter. Let the copy of it reposing in the Williamsburg archives be quoted in default of the original, whereabouts unknown. (Maybe Lucy burned it—or it burned her.)

> Williamsburgh Decr 30th ab^t 2
> aclock in ye morning [1700]

My Dove

I hope in God that you are not so melancholy as when I had the happiness or misfortune of waiting upon you last; for if I was anyways the cause thereof, then it was one of my unfortunate days, but what if I fancy that the place & other company were the real occasions thereof for pray Madam give me leave to put you in mind what trouble & concern you were under when a certain Gen-tleman appeared, or at least after his coming where I had ye honour to be with you—either at play or alone. It ought not to be in ye least wondered at that I do with so much eagerness & attention observe all yor heart & soul, and when I am so unlucky as to find you to be in ye least discomposed, melancholy, or seemingly angry, that I am in an agony of sorrow & grief &c, but when you are merry, pleased & so consequently with a cheerful countenance brisk & airy, look pleasant, & give me the innocent freedom of telling you of my extraordinary & exceeding passion of Love, affection, honour, esteem, respect & veneration, wch I solemnly & most cordially profess to have for you, or when you give me leave to kiss yor fair hand, yor pretty mouth, charming eyes & ravishing breasts, then I am in extasie of joy & satis-faction & rapt up in pleasure, nay I even pleased myself, when I recollect how many hundred nay thousand times I have done it.

For Heavens sake let this last day but one of the year

put an end to yor saying that you will live a single Life
and why may not I then hope that the new year may
be propitious to me, being I am sure that I do most
heartily pray & wish that it may be so to yor self and
that you may be one of the happiest & most fortunate
woman alive, nay even tho I were a real sufferer thereby;
for I thank God I have so far composed my thoughts
concerning you that I am in hopes of bearing it patiently
if I should not obtain you, and that my actions will
demonstrate it VIZ neither by leaving this Country
nor doing any violent act of any sort when I hear any
person courts you or is married to you but whether
that will be, before I am so, God Almighty best knows,
as likewise that is best for us both. But pray vertuous
Lady give me leave most earnestly to recommend to
you to consider & weigh well & take yor own advice &
follow yor own inclination in this most important affair
of yor Life.

Pretty innocent Creature I take yor Case to be thus
VIZ if please God you should refuse me & marry another
& he not prove a very Loving, kind, indulgent husband
in all respects, will it not be a trouble to you, when you
may be assured I would have endeavoured by all ways &
means to have been such a one to you, but if he should
prove, (wch God forbid) passionate, illnatured, illhu-
mored, poorish unsatisfied, discontented & Jealous, then
what a horrour & confusion will it be to you, when all
these or any one of them happens to you, especially
when you consider that you were only fearful that they
would have happened to you if you had married me, &
when please God I am ever so, wch I don't know but may
be very shortly, I am very certain tho I should meet with
but a very indifferent sort of a woman either for person,
quality, or fortune, yet I should make her a very good
husband in all respects, but when so what a very extraordinary tender, kind, indulgent & affectionate one
should I have made to you, to put you in mind of what I
have so often spoke & written to you, wch I hope I need

not here repeat to you, and I think it is not possible for your father to marry you to any man that will love you may be a thousand part so well as I do, My guardian Angel. But oh with what anguish of soul, horror & confusion of thought, destraction of mind, and all the dismal & melancholy ideas of my past Courtship &c to you, do I labour under; when I am almost certain or at least fearfull or apprehensive that any the least misfortune, may happen or befall you on my acco^{tt} expecially concerning yor marying or Living single, and if I were in the least conscious to myself that I have or shall be anyways wilfully the cause thereofit would be worse than death to me wch I hope in God I should face and meet the in the most terrible manner whatsoever with much less fear & concern then I do this my greatest misfortune & unhappiness of not being like to marry you. But I pray God that may never happen to wch I am fearful and apprehensive will, as I have formerly told & written to you, if you either live single or marry any other.

Innocent Dove being I am forced to conclude this letter (but it is with ye greatest reluctancy that ever any mortal man did) because I am fearful & apprehensive that it is like to be ye last, I beg of you, & that with all the passion &c of a real Lover & friend & that you would be pleased to take yor own choice of a husband for I know you have as much if not more good sense & understanding as any of y^r own relations, & friends, & as for good nature, humor, & disposition affableness & vertue I think you far exceed them my most entirely beloved mistress. The last things that I presume once more to recommend to you are, VIZ that you would be pleased to avoid, as much as possible talking & reflecting in company, Never to avoid the publick service of God Almighty in general, but particularly on ye Sunday at Church, to receive ye most Holy Sacrament at Easter next & to continue so to do at all publick times. to hear of these things will in some measure allay my grief, sorrow &c wch at present I am prest with, because I am forbid to make

any further application to you on the acco^{tt} of Love &c
but I think I shall never cease to be

Yo^r most entirely affectionate friend
& faithful humble serv^t whilst......

Enter now a deadly rival and hard on his heels the green-eyed monster.

Edmund Berkeley, a successful tobacco planter, had paid court to Lucy Burwell previously but had been for some time absent from the lists. His reappearance filled Colonel Nicholson with gloomy apprehensions and he told Lucy of them in a short undated letter, written probably some time in 1701.

> My dear Saint
>   I fancy tho it would be very ominous to us both, if when I saw you lately, should be our last meeting as Lovers, for you went down the back stairs & I went away from you very melancholy & concerned, & found with yor Father a certain person who I have reason to fear he preferred much before myself . . ."

If that was the way of it, then let the attack be shifted to Madam Lucy's parents. With epistles and memoranda, delivered by aides, Nicholson commenced bombarding both Major and Madam Burwell. He called the Major "Colonel." He nominated him for the Council. He dropped a hint that he might be of service in regard to the French refugees settled on the Major's lands. "Sir," the Governor wrote, "be pleased to give me leave to make my adress to yor daughter Madam Lucy: who by her beauty, many extraordinary vertues and rare accomplishments &c hath charmed me to a degree beyond expression &c.

"The person who pretends to her I am sure cannot really be in love with her any otherwise than for his own Interest; for certainly he would never have been so many days from seeing her, when it was in his power so to do, for which one Act alone I think he hath justly deserved to be debarred the honour & happiness of waiting upon the Lady: and by the strong and mighty Law of Love he hath most justly forfeited any promises made either by yoʳself, or the young Virgin" . . . And then in a postscript which bears all the earmarks of a mean crack at Berkeley—"If you and Madᵐ Lucy are resolved upon my ruin I pray God forgive you; but for his sake, Dear Sʳ, be pleased to have a good Settlemᵗ made for her, wᶜʰ to hear of will be a great satisfaction to". . . [F.N.]

This was asking father with a vengeance. Next the Governor advanced on Lucy's mother.

"Madam for Gods sake," he wrote her, "be so charitable as to pity this my present unhappy circumstances and use yoʳ Interest to make me one of the most happy men alive: and from my Soul I do assure you that if I did not fully design and endeavour by all honest Lawfull ways and means possible to make Madam Lucy so too, I would never have pretended to her: for I hope that both you Madam, and that most vertuous and fair Lady believe, or at least think that it is all powerful Love alone that causeth my passion for her: and I hope in God (for I have very often pleased myself with the thought of it) that she will be the principal means of governing my other passion, especially in her presence, in which I shall always [hope?] to be. I should never leave Virginia without she had a mind to it. . . ."

Major Burwell was in no comfortable position. Virginians were free men, and Royal Governors, checked by their Councils and answerable to their Sovereign, were no despots, but they could come perilously close to being such by stretching their powers—as several had. The Major, however, was not to be browbeaten. To Colonel Nicholson's animadversions on the hateful rival, Berkeley, Major Burwell stoutly retorted that the decision properly belonged to daughter Lucy. He wrote:

". . . Neither am I guilty in the least of any of these things you charge me with in relation to my forcing my daughter to have Mʳ Barkley, nor to my inviting you from Glowster Court to my house on purpose to affront you. Yoʳ Excellᶜʸ must remember that I have often told you that I left my daughter to make her own choice as to a husband, and

as for my inviting Mr Barkley on that acc^tt who ever told you
that Story, I do aver its a notorious untruth, for he nor I
have not had one word in relation to any such thing this
18 moneth, nor would I be guilty of such a horrible piece of
cruelty (for to gain a kingdom) as to force my daughter to
marry ag^t her will to the best man alive. . . ."

Spoken like a man and the father of nine daughters,
Major!

And so Major Burwell concluded, he entreated that in the
future the Governor would not give himself the trouble of
writing or sending any more messages on the subject, and his
Excellency would avoid any fancied affront by the simple
expedient of not again darkening the door of the manor
house of "Fairfield."

Colonel Nicholson took an appeal to the court of last
resort. He wrote Lucy a letter in which are blended piety,
naiveté, and fond, half-despairing yearning.

W^msburgh Janry 7th 1702/3

Madam Lucy
Vertuous Soul

God allmighty bless keep protect direct & guide you
in all y^r ways intentions designs and undertakings whatsoever & make you one of the happiest & fortunatest
women in all respects, and after you have had as long as
you please here, may you be conducted by yor lesser
Angels to that eternal mansion of bliss & glory. And if
please God that I should be so happy & fortunate as to,
be any ways the least instrumental in yor attaining those
things, it would be most acceptable to me in this world,
. . . [phrases lined out here are repeated later in the
letter]

For that these blessings may befall you are my hopes
and wishes & prayers & that with all the earnestness
sincereness & [?] possible, and I do them with all the
powers & facultys of my heart & soul. And thefore
Dear Madam why may not I repeat them for my meeting
of you in Abrahams bosom, being I'm now debar'd by

y^r father the hon^r & happiness of meeting you in this
world. The most cruel & hard piece of bad fortune
that ever befell me. & I think I have no way Justly
deserved it of him: and besides the hardness of my
fate is that he hath believed or too much Credit to
what hath been said ag^t me, pretty & charming Creature

You who I love & with a passion &c beyond the power
of words to express y^em give me leave to . . . [copy
incomplete]

Lucy's answer seems to have been a final, unequivocal "No."
She would not meet him in Abraham's bosom or short of it.
She refused to help him govern any of his passions. She
would not be his and was all too likely to be another's.

Virginia had known no fury like a Governor scorned. Good
folk took one look at the raging Nicholson and declared that
one might as well pretend to describe a hurricane to one
who never saw it as to describe the brutality and savageness
of the gubernatorial passions. Lucy Burwell had flatly rejected him, the Royal Governor—and everybody knew it—
and he loved her still. He raved and he ranted. He vowed
that if she married anybody else, he would cut the throats
of three men: the bridegroom, the minister, and the justice
who issued the license. He sent word to Lucy that he would
be the death of her father and brothers.

The noise of the Governor's roaring reached all the way
to London whence a friend hastily wrote, warning him: "It
is not here as in some barbarous countries where the tender
Lady is often drag'd into the Sultan's arms, just reaking in
the blood of her nearest relations & yet must strongly dis-
semble her aversion. But English women (you know) are
the freest in the world & will not be won by constraint but
hate them who use them or theirs roughly. Well, your ends
as to that Lady cannot be obtained, & you must submit to
your fate, & to the natural issue of unhappy conduct."

Warnings, in the Governor's state of choler, were equivalent to telling him that faint heart ne'er won fair lady. He

persisted in dispatching messages to the Burwells, and when they were refused wrote a furious memorandum:

> To go to Major Burwell's in the morning and tell him that the refusing his excellencys message is such a piece of inhumanity, barbarity, and ill breeding that no body would ever have offered the like to any Gentlemen, much less to him who is their Governor: but several of his family have not refused presents, tho his Excellency doth not value them, and they might have refused to accept them also, and then they would have done him Justice and saved him a great deal of charge, trouble, and loss of time.+ That his Excellency is resolved to see Madam Lucy either before or after she is married, and if he cannot be at home, he will find an opportunity to see her somewhere else, and if possible in a publick place (and hopes she has not forgot, since she came hither at a publick time and afterwards also) and perhaps tell her what she will not be willing to hear. That his Excellency expects an answer from the Major to what he has sent him and also from Madam Lucy under her hand concerning his Letters. That he is sensible there hath been a great many false, scandalous, and malicious Stories told both to the Major, Madam Burwell, and especially to Madam Lucy concerning him, but he trusts in God that truth will prevail at last, and he also, over his enemys of all sorts as (thank God) he hath hitherto done. Since his Excellency last saw Madam Lucy he has desired nothing but what he thinks ought to have been granted him: and neither the Parson can make Atheism or impiety of it, the Lawier make it high nor petty Treason, nor the Collonel cowardice or breach of honour, from all wch he says, Good Lord deliever him.
>
> +and he thinks if they had pick'd his pocket or broke open his house it had been by much a fairer and honester way of dealing with him.

Sensing that the sentiment of the Province ran against him, the Governor lashed out. He branded the clergy a pack of scandalous fellows, the gentlemen of the country a parcel of rougues, villains, Newgate birds, beggars, cheats, and cowards, while as for the gentlewomen, they were jades, jilts, baggages, and worse.

Name-calling was by no means left to the Governor. Assorted epithets began flying in his direction—"great monster of immorality"—"strange lewdness"—"malice, false, gross lies, and calumnies"—"more prone to perpetrating a rape than obtaining a consent." Most people now were afraid to speak to him in one of his tempers. From the safety of anonymity a minister blasted him with this scathing letter:

"It is said & sneered at by the meanest of those who have lately come in that you prosecute your amours without the least hope of success; that on this account you are so enraged toward the young ladys friends that you swear you will cut their throats, not sparing her Father's, and use such furious threatenings as to render you odious and hateful to all; that your passions are so very furious and frequent & you are wont in them to swear and curse most horribly, & at best high vociferations are your ordinary language; fourthly, it is now in many peoples mouths that you are abandoned to lewdness; fifthly, it is high scandal that notwithstanding such dreadful habits of sin, you are constant at prayers, which they cannot but think must be an abomination to the Lord."

"It was not the first time in history," observes a sage sadly, "that the mind and maners of a sensible man were distorted by an obsession for a charming woman."

Now the Governor in his jealous mania began to see a rival in every bush. The Reverend Stephen Fouace was warned that as the minister of the parish where Madam Lucy lived he might be in the line of fire. Persisting nevertheless in performing his duties, he was returning from a visit to Major Burwell, who was ill, when Colonel Nicholson rode out of the woods toward him shouting. The poor parson was so stricken by the Governor's fulminations he was able later to report them verbatim.

"I command you in the King's name and upon your Canonical obedience as I am your Bishop not to go to that house" —pointing to the Burwell manor—"except you be sent for, not to speak to the young lady," the Governor bawled at him.

"Why, Sir," begged the minister, "what is the matter? Does your Excellency take me for your rival? I can assure you I have not that foolish presumption to think to be preferred to your Excellency. I never spoke or acted anything that could justly give you any such jealousy."

"Hold your prate, Sirrah!" Nicholson thundered. "I have taken good notice of you and you are an impudent rogue, a villain, a rascal. You are insolent and proud now but I'll humble you and bring down your haughtiness. When you came hither, you had more rags than bags."

Meekly the parson answered that it was no shame to have been poor and that it was nothing to the Governor's ill usage and that whatever his circumstances might be now, they had been better if he had been less zealous in his Excellency's service.

That soft answer failed to turn away wrath. The Governor bellowed "Impudent rascal!" and "Scoundrel!" at him and leaned over and pulled his hat from his head, demanding how he had the effrontery to ride covered in his presence. All Parson Fouace's attempts to induce calm were futile. When the Governor seemed to be preparing to ride him down with his charger, the minister set spurs to his own mount and galloped for his life. He did not breathe easy until, concealed in the hold of a ship bound for England, he was well clear of Virginia and her terrifying Governor.

Next suspected of rivalry was the brother of President Blair of William and Mary College. "Sir, your brother is a villain, and you have betrayed me!" Nicholson roared at him.

But the Rev. Mr. Blair, sturdy Scot, was not to be over-awed. He was of stern stuff like his wife, Sarah Harrison, who when they were being married was told thrice by the clergyman to promise to obey and each time answered "no obey" —and stuck to it. So the College President imperturbably faced down the Royal Governor when Nicholson again thundered, lifting his hands and eyes toward Heaven:

"Mr. Blair, I vow to the Eternal God I will be revenged on you and all your family!"

How better could revenge be wreaked on the Rev. Mr. Blair than through his beloved college. Stealthily, craftily, the Governor took measures.

About midnight one night President Blair, who was lodged in the college, heard the boys driving great nails to fasten and barricade the doors of the grammar school. Promptly he mustered several servingmen and advanced to impose discipline. He had almost broken down one door when there was a fusilade of pistols. One of the servants yelped, as a wad hit him in the eye. This was no mere frolic but a regular riot. One of the boys called out to the President:

"For God's sake, Sir, don't offer to come in, for we have shot and shall certainly fire at anyone that first enters."

President Blair beat a strategic retreat, puzzled on how his scholars proved so well supplied with munitions. Next morning he returned with reinforcements of masters and workmen. Before assaulting, Dr. Blair in a parley offered the boys pardon if they would open the doors and tell the truth. His terms were accepted; and a ringleader climbed down a ladder and confessed.

Aha! The Governor was at the bottom of it all. The student leader declared that Nicholson had sent for him, given him money to buy victuals, drink, candles, powder and shot and lent six of his own pistols. A fine state of affairs when the Royal Governor stooped to foment a college rebellion! Stout Dr. Blair ordered the culprits to report direct to the Governor. Angry at the misfire, his Excellency refused to allow the boys to leave early for Christmas vacation, commanding that they continue at their books. This decision made the boys "very angry & they wondered what he had made all that to do for, when they were not to be dismiss'd one day sooner than ordinary for their pains." *

*Blair's Memorial against Governor Nicholson.

Dr. Blair, when someone—he was almost certain it was Nicholson—tried to break into his bedroom at night, decided that enough was enough. He and other leading Virginians sent memorials against the Governor to England. The Council petitioned the Throne for relief from maladministration. Nicholson did not lack loyal partisans, but Queen Anne, though the Colonel had flatteringly named Annapolis after her, ordered his recall in 1705.

It is not of record that Madam Lucy, the innocent—well, fairly innocent—cause of it all, so much as waved good-by. She had already married the hated rival, Edmund Berkeley. Before her death in 1716 she bore him two sons and three daughters. Whether she ever gathered them at her knee and told them the story of Mother and the Governor, we do not know. Anyway, history would do it for her.

The Governor had left his mark in Virginia and not only as a man who had loved not wisely but too well. Lest it be forgotten he had founded Williamsburg, he had named two streets for himself: one Francis and one Nicholson. And it was in the Old Dominion that he (one of the very first to do so) had proposed a scheme for mutual defense, approved and recommended by King William. Colonial assemblies were cold to it but later came to consider it quite a good idea. It was a union of the American colonies.

One wonders how soon the Governor—so sorely smitten had he been—recovered from his infatuation. Evidently he had determined to cease wasting in despair by 1710 when he led the expedition which captured the Acadian Port Royal from the French. Subsequently he was appointed Governor of Nova Scotia, then of South Carolina, was knighted and promoted to high Army rank. In 1728 died Lieutenant-General Sir Francis Nicholson, full of years, honors, and—perhaps—memories of Lucy.

BEAR AND FOREBEAR

Wives, Widows, Maids, and Thornbacks

17th-18th Centuries

We, the maids of New-York City,
(Maids, good lack! the more's the pity,)
Do humbly offer this petition
To represent our sad condition,
Which once made known, our hope and trust is,
That men of *parts* will do us justice.
Now you must know—ah! can't you guess
The subject of a maid's distress?
(Plague on the widows that compell us
Thus to petition for young fellows,)
But we were saying, you must know,
(Tho' blushing we declare our woe,)
A virgin was designed by nature,
A weakly and imperfect creature,
So apt to fall, so apt to stray,
Her wants require a guide, a stay.
And then so timorous of sprites,
She dares not lie alone at nights;
Say what she will, do what she can,
Her heart still gravitates to man;
From whence 'tis evident as light,
That marriage is a maiden's right;
And therefore it's prodigious hard
To be from such a right debarr'd. . . .

Hutchins Improved Almanac, 1801

Deborah's husbands had differed about her education. One was doubtful about it but tolerant. Another definitely disapproved but ignored it. The third decidedly liked it once he recovered from his amazement at a female with learning.

She realized she had no right to it. Parents refused to waste money educating daughters in the American Colonies during the Seventeenth Century, nor was there much change in that attitude after the turn of the Eighteenth. Some girls were taught a little of the three R's at home. Music and dancing lessons were provided in well-to-do families. But it was only such useful arts as spinning, sewing, and cooking that most girl-children were taught.

Deborah, in a way, stole her education, driven by her eager curiosity, her thirst for knowledge. When she was still quite little she followed her brothers to school, sat outside on the doorstep and never missed a word of their lessons. When it grew so cold the door was closed, Deborah was seen listening shiveringly at a window and was invited in out of pity. She sat quietly in a corner and bothered no one. Summers when the boys went fishing, the kindly schoolmaster conducted classes for her and a few other girls. Always she avidly read every book she could lay hands on.

But there had been a long, distressing interval after she reached maidenhood when she herself became almost certain that schooling was a sad mistake for a girl. Perhaps she showed off her learning overmuch. The young men, becoming aware

of it, avoided her like the plague, though in all the township there was no comelier girl than the blooming, buxom Deborah. She was put down as queer.

" 'Tis said she reads books lying abed," the lusty young fellows of the neighborhood told one another. Whereupon they guffawed, passed a coarse jest or two and went off a-courting other girls.

By the time she reached her nineteenth birthday unwed, Deborah was positive she was doomed to be a thornback—a spinster—all her life. After a younger sister's marriage, she threw her few precious books out the window—though retrieving them later. Was there any more dismal a spectacle than a superannuated maid in the midst of much marrying and giving in marriage? Most girls were married before they were her age. In the southern colonies they wedded in their early 'teens or younger. North Carolina girls married so young that grandmothers twenty-seven years old were far from rare.

Her plight was all the more distressing to her since she knew that there was strong pressure of opinion and even of law upon bachelors to marry. In other communities—though not hers—men who persisted in remaining unmarried were fined or otherwise penalized. One frugal township, where crops had been suffering from the depredations of birds, sentenced each of its bachelors to kill six blackbirds and three crows. In a number of towns bachelors actually were registered as "suspected criminals." Hartford, in Connecticut Colony, taxed "lonemen" twenty shillings a week "for the selfish, luxury of solitary living." Under such circumstances, thought Deborah, burning with shame, men would marry almost any woman. But none seemed to desire her in wedlock.

And wives were always in demand in the Colonies. Whole shiploads of maids had been imported to Virginia, and ardent prospective husbands had willingly paid the Emigration Company one hundred and twenty pounds of leaf tobacco, or eighty dollars, for a bride. Two cargoes of maids had been shipped as wives to Louisiana. Although the eighty girls in the first batch had been taken from houses of correction in

France, there was no lack of husbands to bid for them. A later and more proper company of maidens was supplied by the French Government with caskets of clothing to carry to their new homes, and they were called *filles à la cassette* to differentiate them from their predecessors, the *filles de correction*.* Deborah always wondered why the correction-girls had not as much need to be decently clothed as the casket-girls—perhaps even more.

Men were not only ready and willing to lay out considerable sums of money to purchase wives for themselves; that is, to pay a girl's passage from Europe. They would redeem a bondwoman or buy the indenture of a serving-woman, if they could not have her otherwise—or if they could. There was also a most wicked practice, adopted from usage in England, which rated women as mere goods for barter. Deborah still remembered the shocked horror with which she had read an account in the Boston Evening Post **

"Boston. The beginning of last Week a pretty odd and uncommon adventure happened in this Town, between 2 Men about a certain woman, each one claiming her as his Wife, but so it was, that one of them had actually disposed of her to the other for Fifteen Shillings this Currency, who had paid only ten of it in part, and refus'd to pay the other Five, inclining rather to quit the Woman and lose his Earnest; but two Gentlemen happening to be present, who were Friends to Peace, charitably gave him half a Crown a piece, to enable him to fulfill his Agreement, which the Creditor Readily took, and gave

*Louisiana families, stemming from the *filles à la cassette,* take considerable pride in their descent. Those sprung from the *filles de correction* are not so much concerned with geneology.

**Issue of March 15, 1736. Quoted by Alice Morse Earle in her *Colonial Dames and Goodwives,* p. 28. Mrs. Earle adds that as late as 1858 a wife-sale in England was cried by the town bellman, the woman being led through the streets with a halter around her neck and advertised to be "taken with all her faults." Even in 1887 a Sheffield wife was sold for five shillings.

the Woman a modest Salute, wishing her well, and his brother Sterling much Joy of his Bargain."

In the long-protracted scarcity of wives in this new land, was it to be wondered at that the settlers took women where they found them? Deborah, her ears always open, knew well enough that the fur traders and many others venturing into the wilderness cohabited with Indian women. It was the sort of loose alliance which appealed to a man's roving fancy: a winter in a wigwam, warmed by a young squaw—then a light leave-taking when the snows cleared with never a thought of meeting again nor of the child to be born. Some of the Colonies had passed ordinances providing banishment for life for any white man or woman, bond or free, who intermarried with an Indian, Negro, or mulatto. But penalties were little enforced—except upon white women who transgressed. Such laws, concluded Deborah, were made by men to be obeyed by women.

Certainly the marriage of John Rolfe and Poccahontas had been given royal approval in England, but then she was an Indian princess. William Byrd, a Virginia planter, had gone so far as privily to advocate matrimonial alliances between white men and red women, declaring:

"Morals and all considered, I can't think the Indians were much greater heathens than the first adventurers, who, had they been good Christians, would have had charity to take this only method of converting the natives to Christianity. For from all that can be said, a sprightly lover is the most prevailing missionary that can be sent among these or any other infidels. Besides, the poor Indians would have had less reason to complain that the English took away their land, if they had received it by way of portion with their daughters. . . . . Nor would the shade of the skin have been any reproach at this day; for if a Moor may be washed white in three generations, surely an Indian might have been blanched in two."

Yet the demand for wives appeared not to extend to learned

ones. Could it be a lingering of the superstition that women with too much knowledge were witches? Deborah, recalling tales of burnings and hangings of poor creatures convicted of witchcraft, shuddered.

One day the unhappy Deb was visiting with her friends, the Tuttle girls, when their brother Jacob strode into the room. He was often away trading with the Indians or fighting them. Deborah hardly knew this stalwart young man with a way to him, nor he her. If he had heard about her handicap of learning, he ignored it now. He saw before him a pretty girl who was plainly languishing. Her cheery-red lips beckoned. Jacob took the proper action. He swept up her gloves, which she had laid on a table, and would not return them when she stretched out her hands for them. He demanded a kiss as a forfeit.

What followed had best be described as testified to in court. For the sisters tattled, and Deb's father heard about it and forthwith he haled Jacob before a magistrate. The tale of the paying of the forfeit was thus told.

"Whereupon they sat down together," affirmed the witnesses, "his arm being about her; and her arm upon his shoulder or about his neck; and he kissed her, and she kissed him, or they kissed one another, continuing in this posture about one-half an hour."

(That was false testimony—that part about continuing half an hour, Deborah privately thought. It simply could not have been that long. But perhaps she had been unaware of the passage of time. She had forgotten everything else during those blissful moments, her education included.)

When Deborah's father charged on the basis of this evidence that Jacob had inveigled his daughter's affections, the magistrate demanded directly of Deborah: "Did he inveigle you?" And she in a clear voice answered, "No."

The judge dismissed the case against Jacob but lectured Deborah sternly and called her a bold virgin. But then she had been a bookish one so long. No wonder she was bold.

Despite Deborah's denial, it developed that there had been

considerable inveigling and it was mutual. She and Jacob were married. Her dowery was a featherbed. She did not read in it.

"Lo, children are an heritage of the Lord: and the fruit of the womb is his reward. As arrows are in the hand of a mighty man, so are children of the youth. Happy is the man that hath his quiver full of them."

So proclaimed the Scriptures. By the time she had borne her sixth child Deborah began to entertain fleeting thought that Jacob's quiver was full enough. Such thoughts, however, she quickly dismissed. Hers, she realized, was but a small brood. Numerous progeny were welcomed in this empty land.

Families of ten or twelve children were common. A household of from twenty to twenty-five was not even remarked upon. One Massachusetts woman was the mother of twenty-seven. She was surpassed by a South Carolina woman who bore thirty-four children, with only one pair of twins among them.

The pious and laudatory verses on the maternity of Mrs. Sara Thayer often ran through Deborah's mind:

> Also she was a fruitful vine,
>   The truth I may relate,—
> Fourteen were of her body born
>   And lived to man's estate.
>
> From these did spring a numerous race,
>   One hundred and thirty-two.
> Sixty and six each sex alike,
>   As I declare to vou.
>
> And one things more remarkable,
>   Which I shall here record;
> She'd fourteen children with her
>   At the table of our Lord.

Deborah never could decide whether those verses sustained or appalled her. There was another side to being a fruitful vine. Gravestones grimly illustrated it, like the one in the Plymouth burying-ground: "Here lies Anne Blank with twenty small children." That was what happened. So many of the poor little ones died, followed by their worn-out mother.

That was why so many men had three or four wives. A man's first wife, exhausted from childbearing and household labor, passed on to her reward. He married a second who, though young and sturdy, also succumbed. The third wife's lot was easier. By that time there were so many children from the first two broods around the house that she had plenty of help.

Help was needed, goodness knew, in the never-ending household tasks. The cooking and the washing. Churning and cheese-pressing. Spinning and weaving. Sugaring and soap-making and candle-dipping. Planting the garden and feeding the stock. Pickling, salting meat and fish, gathering herbs for medicine, brewing and cider-pressing. All these and more were laid upon women. All very well was the praise written of one housewife: "Her pride was to be neat and cleanly and her thrift was not to be prodigal, which made her seldom a non-resident of the household." Such an encomium failed to lighten the daily, monotonous, back-breaking drudgery which with frequent child-bearing was the death of so many women. Deborah had determined what her epitaph would be——

A loving wife and tender mother,
Left this base world to enjoy the other.

But it was not always the husbands who survived. Deborah could not deny that many of them worked hard—and lived hard. The wars or some ailment or another or reckless habits killed off plenty of them. So did exposure to the rigors of the elements, and not a few perished facing perils consequent to

their livelihood. Such was Jacob's fate. He never returned
from one of his trading expeditions. A comrade brought back
his scalp together with that of the Indian who had taken it
and been surprised in the act by Jacob's partner. He told
Deborah he was sure she'd want them for keepsakes. She
thanked him but buried them.

Now she was a widow, Deborah made a discovery. It
had not simply been her learning that had kept her unwed
so long. It was also because she was a maid. And all the men
went wooing widows.

They were most assiduous in their courtship of a "warm"
widow, as they termed a rich one.* But widows who were
still young and pretty—almost any widow indeed—never
lacked for swains. Small wonder maids everywhere complained
that widows gave them never a chance. It seemed a marvel
how any maiden managed to wed the first time and reach
the enviable state of widowhood.

Deborah was no warm widow but she was a comely one.
Soon beaux flocked around her, and now it mattered not a
whit that she was learned. She waited a decent interval of
five months. (She disapproved of the woman who after only
ten days of widowhood had married the Governor of New
Hampshire; on the other hand, the Pennsylvania law, requiring the widowed to wait a whole year before remarriage
seemed somewhat severe.) Then she accepted a rich merchant named MacDuff.

The canny MacDuff was taking no risks. Deborah's former
husband, said he, might well have left some debts, and claim
for payment of them might well be made on the man who
espoused Jacob's relict. Nothing so untoward would happen
to a MacDuff. The merchant insisted on a smock marriage.
Deborah, intrigued, agreed.

A new husband could avoid legal liability for a former
husband's debts if the bride were nude or clad only in a

*The wealthy Widow Custis brought George Washington a mar-
riage portion which included a fortune of fifteen thousand pounds
sterling and one hundred and fifty slaves. Franklin, Jefferson, and
Madison married widows.

eucumbrances from her old. Some widows rewed shivering in a sheet on the public highway. Deborah stood naked in a closet and thrust out a well-rounded arm through a hole in the door to her cautious but amorous bridegroom. She smock or shift at the wedding ceremony. Thus she was considered to be entering into her new marriage free of any had pierced a peephole through which she watched, giggling audibly, the difficulty being experienced by the young parson in keeping his mind on his task of joining Merchant MacDuff in wedlock to an unseen but unclad dame.

Now Deborah led a life of comparative ease. Some of her children were old enough to help her with the new babies and the household tasks, and she had a serving-maid besides. She might have had more except that her husband was not over-free with his money. But neither her fine house, nor leisure to read, nor the journeys to other Colonies on which the merchant occasionally took her could compensate her. MacDuff, a gay dog, soon began letting his lawful wife sit home alone while he spent his evenings carousing with wanton wenches and willing wagtails.

Deborah knew well enough the penalties which would be meted out to her should *she* be taken in adultery, but as she already had learned, the same law applied differently to men and women.

Her case was less tolerable because MacDuff was the sort of rakehell who makes boasts of his conquests. He reminded Deb of the warriors of the Mandan tribe of which Jacob once had told her.

"The chief business of those young gallants is to try their fortune with the maidens and women, and they do not meet many coy ones," Jacob had related with a grin. "In this manner do they mark the number of their successes. As a token of each conquered beauty a warrior carries a peeled osier twig, painted red at the tip, some two or three feet long. They pride themselves on thick bundles. Or they carry a stick longer still, painted with alternate red and white stripes to show how many doxies they have."

MacDuff, Deborah reflected, would like a stick of such

sort, did he know of the custom, and might even have planted one outside the house except for the chance that it might cause him to be mistaken for a barber-chirurgeon.

Yet the day came when Deborah got the upper hand of her errant spouse and thereafter kept him in order.

He had taken her on a journey to New York where he had business connections. At night he left her in the chamber at the inn and sauntered out, saying that he must call upon a brother merchant. When Deborah woke the next morning, he still was gone, but a message from him shortly arrived. He was in gaol. Would his good wife come and give him bail for his appearance at the Special Court of Sessions? Although entirely innocent of course, he had been involved in an unsavory affair, and being from Massachusetts, he was given slight consideration or credence here in New York but seized by the watch and thrown into durance.

An unsavory affair it was in truth. It seemed that a lieutenant of the garrison, finding a number of the soldiers detailed to his guard were absent from their post of duty, had set out through the town to conduct a search for them. He found them, together with several civilians—one of them Merchant MacDuff—involved in highly disreputable doings. All were arrested and held for trial. Deborah had a copy made of minutes taken in court in the belief that such a document would prove useful, as it did. The minutes proclaimed in part:

"Whereas Information hath been given to this Court by Charles Oliver—one of the Lieuts. of his Majesty's Forces . . . that last Night several soldiers being missed out of the said Garrison he the Depon't tooke some soldiers . . . and went in search of those missing . . . and there found two soldiers in bed in (Jannica Inmin's) house . . . found Elizabeth Stoaks and Isabell Aggott who . . . had been in bed also but had got from thence into the Cellar without Shoes and Stockings and also in another bed found A man with the children of the said Jannica Inmin And in a backhouse found one of the soldiers and Katherine Didlow together the soldier being in bed and she just got out from thence . . . and being Examined all made frivolous Excuses to the said In- formation . . . Ordered . . . that . . . (the women—being tyed upon a Cart or Carts and publickly Carted throughout all the Streets of the City and that they be afterwards dis- charged paying fees." *

As usual the females fared worst. A court martial punished the soldiers. Deborah saw to the punishment of MacDuff who was terrified his name would be published abroad. His business standing would have suffered greatly if it became known that he had been caught in a place so low as to be frequented by common soldiers. Deborah held it over his head the rest of his life.

That remainder was not long. Deborah was too honest to make any great show of mourning him.

Once more she was a "weed." As a warm widow, her opportunities to remarry were more ample than before. Every maid in town heaved a sigh of relief when the rich relict of Merchant MacDuff made a choice from among her many suitors.

She wed with an older man, a judge—stern when he sat as a magistrate but kindly and merry in his home. He had been married thrice before.

Their life together was long and happy. Again Deborah was the survivor. The pious admired the fervent manner in which the widow prayed at the grave, though they could catch none of the words formed by her lips.

This was her prayer:

"Dear Lord, there's my Jacob and MacDuff and the Judge, and the Judge's Anne and Constancy and Mary and me. What ever will happen when we all meet in Thy Heaven?"

*Ms. Minutes, New York Court of Quarter Sessions, 1694-1731. Quoted in *Law Enforcement in Colonial New York* by Julius Goebel, Jr., and T. Raymond Naughton.

THE OLD BLACK BULL AND THE MEETING-HOUSE

A Girl-Child Is Christened With a Name, Mete and Proper

17th Century

When the horn on Sabbath morning, through the still and frosty air,
From Spurwink, Pool, and Black Point, called to sermon and to prayer,
To the goodly house of worship, where, in order due and fit,
As by public vote directed, classed and ranked the people sit;
Mistress first and goodwife after, clerkly squire before the clown,
From the brave coat lace-embroidered, to the gray frock, shading down.

John Greenleaf Whittier: Mary Garvin

Staunch and strong-built were the walls of the old meeting-house. How stoutly it was now resisting the efforts of men tearing it down to make way for a new one! Deliverance Lynd, watching the workmen, knew it to be twenty years older than she, and she had lived long past her span of three score years and ten. Perched here on its hill-top—uphill like the way to Heaven—the old meeting-house might well have outlasted her.

Small wonder it stood so firm, Deliverance thought. When the elders and the deacons and the people first planned to raise it, they had written a wise old minister, once their pastor but since removed to a distant town, for his counsel. A letter from him soon was received. Reading it, members of his former flock were sure the screed had come to them by error and was intended rather for a man who was farming the minister's land.

"You will see to the fences that they be high enough and strong," the minister had written. "And you will take particular care that the Old Black Bull don't get into the pasture."

But Deacon Amos Shute had maintained that the letter was for them, and no mistake. "Brethren," he declared, "the parson is telling us to build our meeting-house strong as the stoutest fence around a pasture so as to keep out the Old Black Bull—the Devil."

And thus they had built it, its walls sturdy and secure. Even so, Deliverance was not at all certain but that the Old Black Bull had broken in now and again.

Trouble and tribulation had begun early—even as the meeting-house was being raised. The story of that day, as it was related to Deliverance Lynd, convinced her that the Devil was well aware the people were calculating to keep him out and so he bestirred himself to do all the wickedness he could while still he had the chance. Every man of the community came to give his labor at the raising, as the law required, bringing his own nails. According to custom, barrels of rum were broached—five of them, good Medford—along with a barrel of brown sugar and a box of fine lemons for those whose taste was for punch. The Lord's work was making swift and merry progress when suddenly two-thirds of the frame collapsed. A score of the builders working upon it fell and were sorely injured; one later died of his hurts. In the Devil's despite, the town held a second raising, and this time the framework of the meeting-house, annointed with less rum, stood.

Often enough Deliverance had heard rum called "the Good Creature of God," even by the clergy. It was not for her to question, but doubt had crept into her mind that day the parish celebrated the ordination of a minister. Portable bars had been set up right there at the doors of the meeting-house, and drinks served free, though it cost the parish a goodly sum. Beer, specially brewed for the occasion, flowed. Barrels of rumbullion and kill-devil, of cider, and of metheglin were no sooner tapped than they gurgled down dry gullets. Deliverance herself, a young girl then, had quaffed several ordination cups, compounded of Malaga and Canary wine, spices, and rosewater, and quite delectable they smelled and tasted. She had felt mightily uplifted and moved to raise her voice in sacred song until she was shocked into sobriety by the spectacle of two aged ministers plainly foxed and a third indecently excited.

Might it be possible for the Evil One to disguise himself as the Good Creature of God? The Reverend Increase Mather, who avowed that kill-devil ought to be called kill-man, could pierce its disguise, but evidently numerous other clergymen could not. No few New England parsons were said to have gone to their graves full of years, honor, simplicity, and rum.

Deliverance knew it was not by chance that the meeting-house stood so close to the Lion Tavern yonder. The elders had voted that it be so located for the convenience of visiting clergymen. Besides it was well to have the tavern nearby on bitter-cold Sabbaths when folk, fleeing the icy meeting-house after the morning service to thaw out before the afternoon devotions, warmed the outer man before the tavern's blazing hearth and the inner with the landlord's equally fiery spirits. If no tavern were near at hand, a congregation was driven to building a "fire-room," hard by the House of the Lord, and there draw warmth from blazing logs and mugs of flip.

Once indeed two inn-keepers had themselves raised a meeting-house, locating it between their taverns, as a sure device for bringing in considerable custom, but had later allowed it to sink into such disrepair that it was called "The Lord's Barn." Tap-rooms were busy spots on a wintery Sabbath. So heavy were demands upon Landlord Jenks and his tapsters that his exertions were said to have worn him out and brought him to an early grave. His death by no means closed the tavern, as his headstone in the burying-ground testified.

> Beneath this stone, in hopes of Zion,
> There lies the landlord of the Lion.
> His wife keeps on the business still,
> Resigned unto the Heavenly will.

Remembering long, congealing hours in the meeting-house on winter Sabbaths, Deliverance shivered painfully, even in this warm summer afternoon. Though the walls were built to bar the Devil, nothing had kept out the bone-chilling cold. The people, muffled in cloaks and shawls, sat hunched and miserable on their benches while the minister preached a sermon that turned the hour-glass thrice and prayed, the people standing, for more than an hour. The sacramental bread froze on the Lord's Table and rattled sadly as it was broken into the plates. On that frigid day when Little John Tuckerman was baptised, the minister had great ado to break the ice in the christening-bowl. Deliverance had wept when she saw how the babe shrank from the water yet uttered no cry, being too benumbed. Even when heating stoves were devised, the Elders would not permit them to be installed. It was sinful to be warm in winter meetings.*

Trust the Devil to see the chance the freezing weather gave him. Of a surety he must have slipped right into the meeting-house with the dogs.

'Twas the women brought them in first. Nothing served so well as a large, shaggy dog—and the larger and shaggier the better— to warm a worshipper's feet, so cold that, verily, they seemed about to drop off. Men in their heavy boots (throughout the service they stamped their feet for warmth) were in no such straits as the more lightly-shod women and girls. Some brought little foot-stoves, filled with hot embers, but those soon cooled. Old Rollo stayed warm and slept right through the sermon, Deliverance remembered, and so grateful for his comfort were she and her mother that they found it hard to chide him when, chasing conies in his sleep, he barked vehemently.

While some dogs were led in, others came of their own accord. Mastiffs, beagles, and hounds, they were all most ardent churchgoers. They would trot in through the doors of the meeting-house with the throng and sniff their way down the aisle, seeking their owners. Unfortunately their presence could not long be regarded as a manifestation of piety by

---

*When in 1783 the Old South Church, Boston, installed an iron stove, the *Boston Evening Post* bewailed:

> Extinct the sacred fire of love,
>   Our zeal grown cold and dead,
> In the house of God we fix a stove
>   To warm us in their stead.

dumb beasts. When a deacon blew his pitch-pipe and raised a psalm-tune for the people to sing, the dogs pointed their muzzles to the rooftree and bayed loud and long. Once a whole pack of hounds burst in, yelping and howling. Deliverance was certain the Devil was in their midst, for a pungent odor, as of brimstone, arose. 'Twas not the Fiend but only a skunk; nonetheless the congregation was forced to flee the meeting in haste. All too often, dogs—set on by the Devil, no doubt—engaged in snarling, growling, yelping fights, to the great delight of unruly little boys in the gallery. Decorum of worship was not restored until the congregation appointed and hired dog-whippers whose duties were to keep the dogs out of the meeting-house and the boys in till the exercises be ended.

Nor did the Devil seem to relax his efforts when the winter cold departed. The meeting-house waxed as hot in summer as it had been icy. The people grew drowsy as the sermon droned on and on, with the parson, expounding his text, reaching an, "And twenty-seventhly, brethren—." One listener after another dropped asleep—doubtless to the Devil's delight. But the congregation countered the Evil One by appointing a tithingman, armed with a long staff. Its one end carried a heavy knob to rap the pates of dozing men and boys; its other a fox-tail or hare's-foot to tickle awake the sleeping women. Once the tithingman erred and waked a slumbering matron with the knob-end, and what a commotion that had caused! And once a man, smitten on the poll, indignantly insisted that he had been wide awake and was only nodding approval of the minister's arguments.

But the tithingmen were busiest employed in keeping the wretched boys in order. Deliverance never had understood why the boys were seated all together in the gallery, away from their families' control. They wiggled, twisted, shuffled their feet and snickered. Full of original sin, they sported, made wry faces and threw pellets. They whittled the woodwork. Veritable "sons of Belial," during the psalm-singing they chanted impious catches under their breath.

> Noah built the ark,
> Shem he laid the floor,
> Japhet drove the geese in,
> And Ham he shut the door.
> Hey trixi rim! Hi trixi rim!
> I don't believe Old Noah could swim.
> Oh, nonny, nonny, no!

Whacks from a tithingman quieted them only for a time. They minded naught except when they were shamed by being led down to sit with their discomfitted mother on the women's side.

But neither dogs nor boys could match the disturbances caused by the Quakers. Sometimes they stood without the meeting-house, shouting direfully through the windows, "Woe! Woe! The Lord will destroy thee!" Or they thrust their way in and sat—in other people's pews—with their hats on and their coats covered with ashes. Female Quakers leaped up and screamed: "Parson, though art an old fool!" and "Parson, thy sermon is too long!" and "Parson, sit down. Thee has already said more than thee knows how to say well." Most shocking and scandalous of all was the Sabbath morn Lydia Wardwell, a young and chaste woman, though a Quakeress, walked into meeting wearing not one stitch of clothing, affirming that she came, naked as when she entered the world, to bear testimony against wicked priests and rulers. The Quakers declared that the Lord led them, and whipping never deterred them. No more did banishment to that sink of religions, Rhode Island, for they only returned. Quakers were hanged, even one of their women. So stubborn was Mary Dyer, she returned from exile, in spite of most solemn warning, to mount the gallows in Boston. There, while drums rolled to prevent any hearing her if she spoke, the noose was tightened around her neck, and soon her body swung against the sky. But hangings aroused too wide sympathy for the sect, as even the Reverend Cotton Mather had been compelled to concede. More effective might have been his scheme that "a shipload of the heretics and malignants called Quakers, with W. Penn, who is the chief scamp, be sold in the Barbadoes where slaves fetch good prices in rum and sugar."

"Parson, thy sermon is too long!" the Quaker women had cried. It was like to be true all too often, Deliverance thought. It was not only the boys who itched with impatience for the exercises to be ended. All the rigors and restraints bore heavily on the maidens and young men. Seated apart, they gazed across the aisle of the meeting-house and yearned for each other and lost hours. Was it to be wondered at that when the afternoon service was at last over, the young folk sought to make the most of the rest of a day free of toil? Cotton Mather had sensed peril and preached a sermon wherein he warned:

"The evening that follows the Lord's Day may not be prostituted into such Vile Purposes, as to spoil and lose all the Good of the Day; and that there may no more be such a Quick transition as there often is, from the Exercises of Godliness, to all Ungodly Vanities and Lewdness. It is complained that there is more Sin committed in that Evening among us, than in any Evening of all the Week beside. Young People, where were you, and what was it that you did last night?"

The young people were not moved to answer such stern ministerial quizzings. Yet sometimes events compelled them.

The wreckers had removed the roof from the old meeting-house, and now one wall was down, exposing the long-familiar interior to Deliverance's gaze. Her fancy peopled it once more. Yonder the preacher held forth in the pulpit. Foremost below him was the Deaf Pew, its aged occupants with their great ear-trumpets upturned. There sat the deacons, ranked on their bench. Worshippers possessed of prestige, position and worldly goods, held the rented pews; behind them sat the common folk. Up there in the furtherest corners of the galleries were "Swallows Nests," pens marked "B.M." and "B.W." for black men and black women—Negro slaves— and cribbed in with them sometimes, Indians. Deliverance never had been able to rid herself of the queer notion that

God might not have wished it so. Once she had read a verse, actually written by a black slave girl. How ran it?

> "Some view our sable race with scornful eye.
>   'Their colour is a diabolic die.'
> Remember, Christians, Negroes, black as Cain,
>   May be refin'd, and join th' angelic train." *

And there, full in view of all the congregation, was the Stool of Repentance. Images of the poor creatures who had sat there passed before Deliverance's mind's eye—men convicted as wanton gospellers, women who wore the scarlet letter.

But it was another scene that flashed most terribly before her, a scene long past but still vivid. How often had her aunt related it to her, though she, Deliverance Lynd, had played a chief part in it.

In the broad aisle of the crowded meeting-house stood a man and a woman, side by side, a babe, scarce a week old, cradled in the woman's arms. Their faces were white and strained and set with an almost desperate determination somehow to endure the ordeal before them.

"Stand forth!" the minister commanded. Grim, sombre in his black robe, he was no longer the priest but the judge, personification of the power and stern discipline of the church. No longer was the meeting-house a place of worship but a tribunal. With gaze piously averted from the young couple, he announced in a loud voice:

"Charity, the daughter of Brother Fales, now the wife of John Wynn, having been guilty of the sin of fornication with him that is now her husband, has presented a paper containing full acknowledgement of her great sin and wickedness."

The girl in the aisle turned even paler. The young man beside moved closer as if to take on his broad shoulders the weight of denunciation falling chiefly on her.

*Poems on Various Subjects, Religious and Moral. By Phillis Wheatley, a Negro slave. Published in London in 1773.

"Charity," the minister demanded," do you publically be-wail your disobedience to your parents, your pride, and your lapse from grace as cause for God to punish you? Do you warn all to take heed of such sins, begging the church's pardon? Do you beg that God humble you?"

The young wife whispered assent under the cold, hard stares of the congregation, humbling and humiliating her in the Lord's behalf. Yet there was veiled pity in the eyes of one matron who whispered to her neighbor: "Born one week later, yon child would have been a seven-month babe, and Charity need not have suffered this." Such indeed was the rule of the Puritan Church. Any child born seven months or longer after the marriage of its parents was presumed to have been conceived in wedlock.

The preacher was thundering on in his diatribe, merciless, unsparing,—castigating them for incontinence and unlawful cohabitation. Would he never have done? They were wedded now. Had they not made amends? Once the young husband, wrath rising up in him, made as if he would lead his wife out of the meeting-house, defying them all. But Charity with an anguished look drew his eyes toward the girl-child in her arms. For the babe's sake they stood and endured.

The minister was speaking of mercy now. The church council, he said, had compassionately decided to order neither whipping nor a fine but would content itself with a solemn admonition after public confession.

"Here before all the people do you confess to fornication?" he demanded.

Firmly the couple answered: "We do."

The minister turned to his clerk. "Write down 'Confessed Fornication,'" he ordered. On the records the clerk's quill scratched, "C.F." He knew well enough how to spell it. It was one of the five-syllable words he had learned to spell as a child from the *New-England Primer*. He could visualize it standing forth on the page of that lexicon now: For-ni-ca-ti-on. The clerk used an abbreviation only because he so frequently made the same entry.

"Search your heart," the minister charged Charity, "for ways to make thorough work of your repentance."

Buzzing as those do who have witnessed a spectacle, the congregation cleared the meeting-house. But the pair who had undergone punishment stood unstirring until most of the others had left. Then Charity hastened forward. Appealingly she held her baby toward the minister.

"Now," she besought him.

"Now that you have made public confession, the babe may be baptised," he granted. "Otherwise, as you know, baptism would have been withheld."

All too well Charity knew what that would have meant. Infant damnation. Torture for this little one of hers through all eternity for a sin committed before she was born. To spare her from that her mother and father would have suffered far more than the shame and humiliation they here had sustained.

"How will you name the child?" asked the minister, dipping a finger in the water of the christening-bowl.

The mother gazed tenderly down at her babe, saved now from a dreadful fate, and gave the chosen name.

"Deliverance," she said.

The walls of the meeting-house stood firm. That time the Old Black Bull had not broken into the pasture.

PARCHING THROUGH GEORGIA

Governor Oglethorpe's Preview
of Prohibition
1734-42

The antediluvians were all very sober,
For they had no wine and they brewed no October;
All wicked, bad livers, on mischief still thinking,
For there can't be good living where there isn't good drinking.
> Derry-down.

'Twas honest old Noah first planted the vine,
And mended his morals by drinking its wine;
And thenceforth the drinking of water decried,
For he knew that all mankind by drinking it died.
> Derry-down.

Benjamin Franklin: *Drinking Song*

James Edward Oglethorpe, soldier of the King, stood in a square of the town of Savannah, seat of the government of the colony he had founded and named Georgia in honor of his Majesty George II. He gazed about him and found good all he surveyed. Neat, clapboarded houses, each with its glebe of garden land, faced on the squares. The bright sun of this New World warmed the rich loam, mingling its earthiness with the fragrance of jasmine and the scent of pine needles, wafted from the deep forests.

Along the river sweeping past Savannah on its plateau were other settlements, regarded by General Oglethorpe with no less pride. For they were peopled by Germans, French, Piedmontese, Italians, Greeks, and Spanish Jews; and these men from foreign lands, numbering a good third of the population of this English Colony, were proof of its founder's broad tolerance. Georgia was open to all creeds (save only Papists), to all nationalities (excluding, naturally, the hostile Spaniards, glowering from Florida to the south), and to all races (with the exception of Negroes, who were not allowed to be brought hither as slaves, and of Indians, who, perforce, had been pushed westward).

He had conceived of this new colony, had Oglethorpe, as a refuge from poverty and a sanctuary for former inmates of the miserable debtor's prisons of England. Here, with every prospect pleasing and man industrious, need be no poverty, no debt. Importations of Negro slaves being forbidden as was the enslavement of the Indians, each colonist must live and prosper by the fruit of his own toil, and what could prevent him prospering in this fertile paradise?

One thing perhaps. In this earthly Eden the Serpent was proffering no mere apple but a cask of rum.

Sundry cases of sickness had been reported to Governor Oglethorpe. Upon their becoming more widespread, he had caused investigations to be made. Several deaths occurred and were declared due to too free use of the fiery potion which was the trade staple of the West Indies. Plainly rum was debauching the Indian tribes; with the savages it usually was a case either of abstinence or besottedness.

James Edward Oglethorpe was an idealist, possessing "strong benevolence of soul," as the poet, Alexander Pope, had declared in a tribute. He was also General Oglethorpe, man of action. He acted with the promptitude and energy with which he defended his southern marches against the Spaniards. Taking quill in hand, he penned a cogent letter to the Trustees of the Colony in England, setting forth the evil effects of rum on Georgia. Steps, he maintained, must be straightway taken.

Yet neither Oglethorpe nor the Trustees were given to sudden, drastic measures where moderate would suffice. Man, full of iniquity, could not be separated altogether from liquor. To dash from the lips of the colonists the cup which they and their fathers before them had quaffed would be unjust and unwise. Let it be filled with the milder draughts then. Leave but wine or beer within the cup, and they'd not ask for rum. So, after due reflection, determined those in authority over the Colony of Georgia.

Pipes of Madeira were imported. Tons of the best strong beer were sent over from England. Brew-houses were established. To each settler was allotted a supply of forty-four gallons of strong beer and sixty-four of molasses for brewing. Ships sailing to England carried the message: "Beer, being cheap, is the only way to keep Rum out of the Colony. Send more." The planting of vineyards was strongly encouraged. Nor was the proper education of the people neglected. Two hundred copies of the Reverend Stephen Hales' tract, *A Friendly Admonition to the Drinkers of Gin, Brandy, and other Spirituous Liquors,* were distributed, along with various religious texts.

But certain—and too numerous—Georgians resisted these kindly designs for their betterment. Some, who had essayed wine-growing, avowed that the grapes were small and unprofitable and the vintage sad stuff and bitter. Others would have naught to do with beer but imbibed strong drink copiously. Governor and Trustees deemed it time to take stern uncompromising action and banish rum totally and forever from the Colony of Georgia.

*   *   *   *   *

On Mount Olympus, Clio, Muse of History, grasped her stylus and began inscribing on her waxen tablets an account of these proceedings in a segment of the New World. The Father of the Gods glanced over her shoulder.

"Old stuff!" he snorted. "Forbidden fruit again. I can tell you what is going to happen. Why don't you just write 'Ditto'? Must you always repeat yourself?"

"Sir," Clio answered. "I only record. It is mankind that repeats."

*   *   *   *   *

The people of the Colony of Georgia stood amazed, reading and hearing read the novel and unprecedented law, statute, and ordinance which the Trustees had laid before his Majesty the King at the Court of St. James on April 3, 1735:

> May it Please Your Majesty
> The Trustee for establishing the Colony of Georgia in America in pursuance of the Powers and in Obedience to the Directions to them given by Your Majesty's Most Gracious Charter Humbly Lay before Your Majesty the following Law Statute and Ordinance which they being for that Purpose assembled have prepared as fit and necessary for the Government of the said Colony And which they most Humbly Present under their Common Seal to Your Most Sacred Majesty in Council for Your Majesty's Most Gracious Approbation and Allowance.

An Act to Prevent the Importation and Use of Rum
and Brandies in the Province of Georgia.

Preamble   Whereas it is found by Experience that the use
of the Liquors called Rum and Brandy in the Province
of Georgia are more particularly hurtfull and pernicious
to Man's Body and have been attended with dangerous
Maladies and fatal distempers and if not timely prevented will in all likelyhood ruin the said Colony and
frustrate Your Majesty's good and fatherly Intentions
towards such of Your Subjects as shall go to reside in the
said Province And Whereas We Your Majesty's most
dutifull Subjects the Trustees for Establishing the Colony of Georgia in America have received Complaints
from the Chiefs of Several of the Indian Nations Inhabit-
ing near to Your Majesty's said Colony of great disorders
amongst them Occasioned by the use of the said Liquors
and which are brought them by the Persons using and
carrying on the Indian Trade for Remedy thereof We
the Trustees for Establishing the Colony of Georgia in
America humbly beseech Your Majesty THAT IT MAY
BE ENACTED AND BE IT ENACTED that from and
after the four and twentieth day of June which shall be
in the Year of Our Lord One thousand Seven hundred
and thirty five No Rum or Brandys nor any other kind
of Spirits or Strong Waters by whatsoever Name they are
or may be distinguished shall be imported or brought
aShore either by Land or Water in any Ship or Ships
Vessell or Vessells whatsoever or in any Cart or Carts
Carriage or Carriages whatsoever either by man or horse
into any Port Haven Creek Town Village or other Place
whatsoever in the said Province of Georgia from any
Country Colony Province Place or Port whatsoever by
any Person or Persons whatsover either mixt or unmixt
and that all such Rum and Brandys Spirits or Strong
Waters either mixt or unmixt which shall be Imported
or brought into the said Province contrary to this Act
in whose hands and Custody or in what Place soever they

shall be found shall and may be forthwith publickly Staved and Split in the Presence of such Officer as shall for that Purpose be appointed by the Common Council of the said Trustees or by the Major part of such of them as shall for that Purpose be present and Assembled AND it is hereby further ENACTED that no person or persons whatsoever shall presume to save any of such Rum Brandys Spirits or Strong Waters so adjudged to be Staved and Split under the penalty of five pounds Sterling over and above the Value of the said Rum Brandys Spirits or Strong Waters AND BE it further ENACTED that every Person or Persons Indian Trader or other that shall from and after the said four and twenieth day of June in the Year of Our Lord One thousand Seven hundred and thirty five sell utter and retail any Rum Brandys Spirits or Strong Waters mixt or unmixt as aforesaid to any Person or Persons either English or Indian shall. . . .*

Readers and auditors glanced aghast at each other. Next followed penalties—fines. For the first offense—five pounds sterling. For the second—no less than £50. The statute went on to maintain that its operation would prevent "prophane Cursing and Swearing, Vice and Debauchery, too frequently occasioned by Tippling Houses and disorderly publick Houses." Yet its very reading occasioned not a little of said cursing. For it was no mere proposal. This Act, passed by Parliament, had received His Majesty's royal approbation and was thereby confirmed, enacted and ratified. Thenceforth, so far as concerned rum, Georgia would be dry as a desert.

But trials, troubles, and tribulations quickly commenced. Many a Georgian throat grew parched. It mattered little that the Trustees' store at Savannah was regularly supplied with wines and beer, and that magistrates were freely empowered to grant licenses for retailing beer and for brewing. Only spirituous liquors seemed capable of assuaging the increasing thirst. Colonists, who had cared little for rum, began to crave it, now that it was prohibited.

*Quoted from *Colonial Records of Georgia.*

Rum they would have and rum they got. Sutlers, licensed to sell wine and beer, secretly sold rum also, though well aware that if caught at it their licenses would be withdrawn. Hidden stills were operated. Spirits were slyly retailed in private houses (veritable nurseries of villainy) and in all the bye corners of the town. Servants were seduced from their masters, workmen from their tasks. Savannah folk drank long and deep in indignant defiance of the regulations.

Plying the river by night sped the boats of the Carolina rum runners, bound to slake—for a profit—the Georgian thirst. Some of these craft were forced to lay to and were boarded by Georgia law-enforcement bailiffs; their rum casks were staved and their crews imprisoned. Whereupon the Colony of Carolina lodged huffy complaint. But many a runner slipped past. They landed casks falsely labeled "Cyder" in secluded Georgia coves. More rum still was brought in by pack animals over the wilderness trails. When runners were arrested, they demanded a jury trial in Savannah and generally were acquitted, even when the judge instructed the talesmen to bring in a verdict of guilty.

The majority of the people simply refused to regard rum-drinking and rum-selling as criminal. No man would carry tales on his neighbor and enmesh him in the toils of the law. It became easy to bribe officials. Bailiff Henry Parker was plied with "his beloved liquor to keep him warm and steady" until his loyalty succumbed and he lay wallowing, drunken, in the mire. One night at Jenkins' public house, Parker and the landlord agreed over a bowl of punch to change places for the entertainment of the company. They stripped themselves and exchanged clothes. Immediately Parker in his capacity as landlord started to make free of the liquor, but Jenkins in the character of magistrate despotically forbade it. Then he called his host a drunken swab and other opprobrious names, chastised him and threw him down. Seldom had any tavern company been afforded such amusement.

Evading the Act was easy. James Carwell bought £205 worth of dry gods in the town and then made shift to convert them all into wet—and drank them up. The military roistered as soldiers will; Lieutenant Horton was forced to make report to the Trustees that his "regiment had lost from its rolls— thirty persons, including the women, who were hard drinkers." An increase in infant mortality was ascribed to the bibulous habits of expectant mothers. Revelers turned into roisters; when taken into custody by tithingmen and peace officers, they impudently refused to disclose where they had bought strong drink. Never had the magistrates—those who still strove to enforce the Act—been held in such disesteem by the people.

This sorry state of affairs was observed and candidly set down by John Perceval, Earl of Egmont, one of the Trustees, in his journal.

"The Rum Act is not at all regarded, and if any man has but a shilling he lays it out that way, not buying shoes or stockings. From high to low the magistrates drink it, and are unwilling to inquire what others do in it. This makes many idle persons, not even the servants caring to work above three hours, and then running to public houses and spending the rest of the day there. . . .

"Our Act versus Rum hinders not its being drunk in every corner of the Town of Savannah, but at the same time makes it so dear, that other Provinces cannot have it in exchange for their commodities. . . .

" 'Tis a mistake to think that the Inhabitants of Savannah have Rum. What they have is a poisonous spirit from the Islands; but it would be profitable if they might be allowed to import Rum, for then their lumber might be taken off in exchange, and the Rum they imported would be bartered with the Indians for their skins."

Thus had matters fallen out, and not even Governor Oglethorpe could gainsay it. The Act was totally disregarded in the Colony of Georgia. Its expected good effects had failed— the mischief remained. Georgians could sell none of their timber to the Islands unless they traded for rum. All the commerce in that "hot and hellish liquor" was being funneled through Carolina, and she was waxing rich on it.

Word was passed by the Trustees to Col. William Stephens,

president of the Colony of Georgia. Wink at the importation of rum and discourage all seizures thereof. Allow none to be drunk save in licensed houses. Hinder recovery of debts due rum sellers.

The Trustees were fighting a rearguard action, but there was no doubt about their retreat. Before long Colonel Stephens was writing them that less rum was being consumed in the Colony after its use was permitted than when it was obtained and drunk clandestinely. He added that he personally could recommend a beverage composed of 1 part rum, 3 parts water, and a little brown sugar as very fit to be taken at meals and more wholesome during the warm season than malt and liquors.

In 1742 Parliament repealed the Georgia Rum Act. Its epilogue was pronounced by that friend of America, Edmund Burke:

"The regulations were designed to bring about wholesome results but promulgated without sufficient appreciation of the nature of the country and the disposition of the people."

*   *   *   *   *

A little less than two hundred years later, Clio, Muse of History, grasped her stylus and began inscribing on her waxen tablets an account of National Prohibition in the United States of America. The Father of the Gods glanced over her shoulder.

"Old stuff!" he snorted. "Georgia again—only on a larger scale. I can tell you just what will come of it. Again I recommend ditto marks. For about the ten millionth time I ask you, must you always repeat yourself?"

Clio replied: "Sir, for about the ten millionth time I answer that I only record. It is mankind that repeats."

"Then," snapped back the Father of the Gods, "since man makes the same mistake over and over again and never learns, why do you go on recording it for him?"

Clio looked up startled. For a while she made doodles with her stylus on her tablets and could think of no answer. Finally she said:

"I guess it must just be habit, sir."

TIGHT COLLEGE YEARS

Pleasures Are Discovered to Be Rife at Yale

Mid-18th Century

Here's to good old Yale, drink it down, drink it down.
Here's to good old Yale, drink it down, drink it down.
Here's to good old Yale, she's so hearty and so hale,
Drink it down, drink it down, drink it down, down, down.

Anon.: Bingo

T utor Weedin was still fuming with indignation when, back in his room in South Middle,* he sank into a chair and snatched the hot wig from his grizzled pate. Yale College in New-Haven, Connecticut Colony, was a seat of learning, yet oftentimes that might well be doubted by any one who witnessed the behavior of the scholars. Were they devoted to storing their minds with knowledge? Not they! Tutor Weedin snorted. They were intent on filling their bellies. If it wasn't their bellies, their throats seemed incessantly to be dry and needing wetting. And if it wasn't their throats—well, they were always leaning out of windows (when they should have been at their books) to ogle those pert baggages of the town flouncing across the Green. How did the lads dub them? "Plump little partridges," adding—the young rascals—that it was high time they went a-hunting. *Lux et veritas* forsooth!

The source of Tutor Weedin's present annoyance was the riot in Commons he had assisted in quelling during dinner today. All week the long room, which served as chapel and lecture hall as well as dining room, had rung with the com-

*Later called Connecticut Hall and still standing on the Old Campus.

plaints of the scholars. Nothing served could please them, so it seemed. Given boiled beef, they had cried out that it was so tough and ancient it could only have been cut from the lean kine of Pharoah. Today the dish had been mutton which set the students to bleating and blattering and creating such a clamor as destroyed all decorum. They had even dared fling the roasts on the sanded floor. On tasting the butter—Tutor Weedin was assured it was only slightly rancid—Jeremiah Jessup, a reprehensible young rowdy, had shouted at the top of his voice, "Wheel Grease!" and hurled the whole firkin out a window. Haled up before the tutors, dining on their dais, to be reproved and reprimanded, the culprit had noted that food there was of somewhat different quality. Instead of standing in silence, the graceless scamp had hallooed:

"Down with tidbits for tutors! The same fare for one and all!" And the riot was on.

Beer mugs were banged on the table. Young wretches beat on the board and upon the large pewter pitchers with the knives, forks, and spoons with which they were required to provide themselves. Others set up a howling and whooping like so many Mohawk Indians. The frightful din drowned the scandalized admonitions of the tutors: *"Proh pudor! Proh pudor!" "Miserabile vulgus!"*

Flying food literally darkened the room. That rapscallion, Jeremiah Jessup, leaped on a table. Quoting from *The Frogs* of Aristophanes—in correctly accented Greek, Tutor Weedin grudgingly recalled—Jessup croaked loudly and raucously:

"'βρεκεκεκὲξ, κοὰξ, κοάξ.
βρεκεκεκὲξ, κοὰξ, κοάξ.'"*

Commons reverberated to the rafters as every rioting scholar in the hall, including the student waiters, took up the chant. They capered and cavorted through the hall. They

*Used as the basis of the Yale cheer by Joseph Henry Vernon, of the Class of 1885. The use in this reconstruction of a Commons riot is a fictional anticipation.

began leap-frogging one another. Jeremiah Jessup on his table perch leaned down and seized a larger pewter platter. Assuming the pose of Discobolus, he scaled the platter through the air. It landed with a tremendous crash full in the center of the tutors' table.

Tutor Weedin had sent the instigator of the riot up before President Stiles. Jessup would undoubtedly be expelled—or at least rusticated.

Would not the scholars who had so shamefully flung their food about in Commons grow hungry? Aye, as ravening wolves. And would they have to do without sustenance until supper? Not they! reflected Tutor Weedin bitterly. They would repair to the Buttery. Even now alarums and excursions could be heard below.

An ill day that, when the President and Fellows had permitted the establishment of a Buttery in South Middle. The Butler, usually a recent graduate of good repute, was awarded a monopoly on the sale within the College precincts of eatables, drinkables, and articles of daily use, it being recognized that the scholars would otherwise fare forth to the low taverns and other reprehensible haunts of New-Haven. The Butler dealt in tobacco, pipes, and cigars; in apples, pears, peaches, and water-melons; in raisins, almonds, nuts, loaf sugar and lemons (for punches), ginger, honey, eggs, biscuits, cakes, and pies. For the authorities had acknowledged that three meals a day at Commons, ample and tasteful as they were—though denied so to be by rebellious scholars—that such regular collation would in no wise sate the voracious appetite of youth. Also the Butler purveyed writing paper, quills, and wafers for the sealing of letters, pomatum for the hair; wash-balls and black-balls.*

And—*Io, Bacche!*—what an array of pitchers, bowls, mugs, decanters, glasses, and corkscrews crowded the Butler's shelves! These were furnishing for the service of his sizable stock of cider, beer, ale, porter, and metheglin—beverages thought to remove the temptation to indulge in strong drink.

*Soap and shoe-polishers.

These drinkables were ordered doled out on easy but limited
terms of credit, and the Butler employed a waiter to carry
them to scholars' quarters. The strength of every barrel of
strong beer, stocked by the Butler, was regulated by the Trustees of the College; ingredients must consist of one-half a
bushel of good barley malt, ground, or a bushel of good oat
malt, ground, or a peck of good barley malt, ground, and a
quart of molasses—all to be well brewed and hopped.

Such were the provisions and precautions, devised by the
authorities, against rum and revelry. But they availed little
with the present stiff-necked and stubborn generation of
youth, given to perversity and iniquity. "ורת," Tutor Weedin
muttered morosely in the Hebrew tongue. Was it for this
that Elihu Yale had made his gift of books and goods, endow-
ing the college? The tutor, recalled his own attendance here
as a scholar, decided that Yale now was not what it was in his
day.

How often flouted was the College rule: "None shall call
for any strong drink in a tavern within two miles of the College, except in company with his father or guardian. . . . Nor
shall any bring rum, wine, or other strong drink into his
chamber." Despite the fact that Yale was a godly institution,
with a goodly group among its one hundred and fifty scholars
candidates for the ministry, it lacked not "wine-bibbers among
riotous eaters of flesh." Why, ardent spirits were mixed, as
it were, with the very mortar of its foundations. It had been
necessary to ply workmen who raised this very building with
£67 worth of liquor, else South Middle never would have been
erected. Back in 1727, the legislature of Connecticut had
voted the revenue of the rum tax for one year to the support
of Yale College, its rector, and—yes, its tutors. Many scholars
were so bold as to keep wines and liquors in their rooms. And
once—*dies irae, dies illa!*—Tutor Weedin had witnessed a most
scandalous performance. A student had dispatched a freshman
(though freshmen were obliged to run only *proper* errands
for upperclassmen) to fetch a quart of rum into the College.
On the Lord's day when the bibulous one came to public
worship in the chapel, he carried in part of said rum in a

bottle or phial and gave it to some scholars, who then and there drank of it. Never had the like been seen unless it were the Sabbath evening when White, Tertius, a sophister of unbounded impudence, stood up and profanely mimicked the president at prayers.

Gambling in one form or another had fastened its grip on the student body. Lotteries were all the rage, nor was any better complexion put on them by the fact that the prizes offered were copies of the *Iliad,* the works of Virgil, Wilson's *Trigonometry,* and *The Compleat Letter-Writer.* In many a chamber of an evening, the midnight oil or tallow candle would be burned not for study but to light a card game, spiced with a stake. As Tutor Weedin aptly put it: "The muses of learning fled dismayed into the shadows of the night, and the goddess of chance reigned supreme over giddy youth." Upperclassmen, old in the ways of iniquity, did not scruple to seduce freshmen with money into wasting their substance. The devil's lure of card-playing had prevailed even over a scholar of rare promise and piety, young Timothy Dwight,* who at the age of four had been found seated under an apple tree teaching the catechism to Indians. Dwight, however, always refrained from playing for stakes.

Prayers must be attended twice a day, at sunrise and between four and five in the afternoon, besides the Sabbath exercises. Scholars being wont to stamp so loudly that President Stiles could not be heard, it was small wonder prayers did them little good. Offenses were punished by fines, public confession, public rebuke, and public expulsion. Nonetheless, Tutor Weedin in the course of his academic career had beheld the commission by wayward students of deeds ranging from monstrous impieties to acts of immorality. The stealing of hens, geese, turkeys, pigs, meats, and wood. Unseasonable night-walking (undoubtedly hunts for those "plump little partridges"). Breaking people's windows. Cursing, swearing, damning, and using all manner of ill language. Even beating tutors with clubs. *"Facilis decensus Averni!"* Tutor Weedin gloomily commented.

*The Rev. Timothy Dwight was elected President of Yale in 1795.

That evening word came of Jeremiah Jessup's interview with the President.

The President had condescended to explain to him that ever since the founding of Yale in 1701 it had been deemed essential that students gather as a family at a common table, obedient to common discipline. When the student body grew too large for the Rector's table, a Steward had been appointed for the dieting of the scholars. Meat was provided three times a week. The very ingredients of each apple pie were specified (one and three-quarters pounds of dough, one-quarter pound of pig's fat, two ounces of sugar, and one-half peck of apples). Beer, cider, and milk were furnished. Yet carping and complaints had been constant.

That young rogue Jessup had boldly replied with charges which were the veriest calumny. He maintained that the Steward's profit would bear looking into; he must be pocketing a pretty penny, charging as he did for such execrable sizings. As for the cooks, Jessup branded them as insolent, incompetent and "too lazy to exert themselves to cook clean for us." Furthermore, he accused them of selling Commons-baked apple pies outside in the town for their own gain. He declared that the tutors at their table were pampered and preferred. Finally he protested that students should be required to shell peas for the cooks. If the shelling of beans should also be exacted of them, as was now purposed, the result (he threatened) would be such revolt and rebellion as even Commons had not hitherto witnessed.

In spite of all this brazen asserration, reviling and railing, the President had merely rusticated Jessup for two weeks.

On his return from rustication, Jessup had reported to Tutor Weedin. He looked sleek and fat.

"No doubt you spent your time gourmandizing," Tutor Weedin sourly surmised.

"Aye, sir," the scamp admitted. "To make amends for the diet at Commons. We fare well at home. *Ummm.* Beefsteaks at least twice a week. Fresh veal stewed with a well-made crust. Stewed oysters for breakfast. Delectable apples—'Seek-no-farthers.' Roast turkey. Sausage and pancakes. Pies, puddings, and dumplings. *Ummmm*." He smacked his lips and rubbed his belly. Tutor Weedin, listening, commenced to feel somewhat sharp-set.

Jessup had been ordered by way of penance to recite the College rules every night for a month to his tutor—to recite them first in their original Latin and then render them into English, to make certain of his comprehension of them.

"Will you now hear our Lights and Perfections, sir?" demanded the young rascal with a grin. "The Gospel according to Eli. The very Urim and Thummim of Yale—אורים ותמים."

Eyes twinkling, he paused for effect.

Tutor Weedin forgave him his impertinence because of the apt citation of the Hebrew legend on the Yale seal. "Say on," he bade, and Jessup rattled off the rules.

"If any scholar shall be guilty of Blasphemy, Cursing, Robbery, Fornication or Forgery or any such atrocious crime, he shall be immediately expelled . . . Scholars are forbidden to wear women's apparel. . . . No damnifying College property . . . No singing, noisiness, rout, tumult or bellowing . . . Scholars shall not fire gunpowder . . . No association with vile, idle, dissolute persons. . . . Every student shall exercise himself in reading Holy Scriptures by himself every day that the word of Christ may dwell in him richly and that he may be filled with the knowledge of the will of God in all wisdom and spiritual understanding. . . . In Commons students shall behave decently, abstaining from all rude and loud talking, and keeping their places until thanks shall have been returned. . . ." (Of late, Tutor Weedin recalled, grace had perforce been curtailed to "God bless us for Christ's sake, Amen"—and even that had been punctuated by the explosion of squibs, set off under the table by young infidels). . . . "No scholar shall publicly cry nor attempt to sell his commons on the Lord's Day or the eve preceding or during study hours, on penalty of having them forfeited to the waiters. . . . Every student shall in his ordinary discourse speak in the Latin tongue. . . . No student shall undress himself for swimming in any place exposed to the public view. . . . Every scholar is required to show due honor and reverence, both in words and behavior, to the President, Fellows, and Tutors of this College."

Jeremiah Jessup finished in recitation with a respectful bow to his tutor. Then ostentatiously he cleared his throat. "Dry work, sir," he observed. Permit me to offer you some of the excellent cider I brought from home."

Before Tutor Weedin could refuse, Jeremiah had fetched a jug and two mugs and was pledging his health. Excellent cider it was indeed—tasty and aged in the cask. Tutor Weedin mellowed slightly toward the reprobate. Jeremiah now began to consult him flatteringly concerning subjects for debate at the next meeting of the Linonian Society. The two questions proposed were: 1. Aeneas and Dido, in what time did they live? 2. What thing is the most delightful to man in the world?

Tutor Weedin, quaffing his third mug, raised his brows quizzically and asked if there were any connection between the two questions. He had, he said, chuckling, reference to that occasion when Aeneas and Dido took refuge in a cave during a storm.

Jeremiah grinned delightedly, called him a gay dog, and refilled his mug. It was indeed most excellent cider. With such a satisfying beverage at hand, who could crave strong drink? Tutor Weedin demanded.

" 'Who hath woe?' " he quoted the Scriptures. "Who hath sorrow? Who hath contentions? Who hath wounds without cause? Who hath redness of eyes? They that tarry long at wine. They that go to seek mixed wine.' "

Promptly Jeremiah capped him. " 'At the last it biteth like a serpent, and it stingeth like an adder.' "

The jug gurgled. Cider so well aged as this could scarce be improved were it laced with rum, Tutor Weedin privately reflected. He voiced his appreciation of it aloud. Jeremiah nodded vigorously.

"How fortunate that we at Yale are so little beset with the problem of strong drink!" he remarked. "Now at William and Mary College, in Virginia, I am told that spirituous liquors are permitted, though rules require they be used 'in the moderation which becomes the prudent and industrious student.' "

"William and Mary!" sniffed Tutor Weedin. " 'Tis known that a father, with a son a student there, wrote one of the tutors: 'I hope my son does not get drunk by himself, because that would evince a total disregard of decency and decorum.' "

"And, sir, had you heard that at Harvard the entire class of 1760 has been suspended for drunkenness?" Jeremiah pursued.

"It does not surprise me in the slightest," Tutor Weedin responded, his *s's* slipping somewhat. "A pox on Harvard!"

"Plague take Harvard!" Jeremiah seconded loudly and loyally. They emptied the jug together and bade each other a jovial good-night.

Tutor Weedin was convinced that Jeremiah Jessup was a scholar of parts whom others had misled. But that was before he visited his bin in the cellar of South Middle next day. The lock was damnified and—*eheu fugaces!*—all Tutor Weedin's private stock of rum had been rifled.

JUST BETWEEN FRIENDS

A Quaker Wedding in Philadelphia

Mid-18th Century

"I've a ring worth twenty shillings.
  Oh, oh, oh, oh,
And thee may wear it, if thee's willing,
  Oh, oh, oh, oh."
"What care I for rings or money,
  Fol de rol de hey ding dido.
I'm for the man that calls me honey,
  Fol de rol de hey ding day."
      Anon: *The Quaker's Wedding*

Innocency Williams and Abel
Sterling had given notice, in accordance with Quaker marriage regulations, that they would appear before the next
Monthly Meeting and publicly declare their intentions of
matrimony.

Philadelphia acclaimed the news. The families of the young
couple were prominent and well provided with worldly goods,
and a wedding of Friends in William Penn's "greene country
towne," grown now into the greatest city in the Colonies,
was a great occasion for kith and kin and for guests from
near and far. It meant gala days, too, for the neighborhoods
in which the parents of bride and bridegroom dwelt, since
the neighbors, whatever their faith and degree, would share
in the festivities.

A fine-appearing pair, Philadelphia agreed. A young man
of worth and a well-inclined damsel.

Innocency, observed many another member of the Society
of Friends, must often have been at some pains to resist the
temptations of female vanity. She had been named from that
early pamphlet of William Penn's (a favorite with her
parents), *Innocency with Her Open Face*, and indeed there
was such charming candor in her countenance, though it was
not beautiful, that few could resist its winsome appeal.
Straight and slim she stood, as a young spruce. Because she
did not limit herself to dove-gray but loved bright colors in

her gowns and aprons and cloaks in blues, greens, and scarlets, some of the stricter Friends had felt impelled to labor with her. Citing the writings of Penn, they demanded of her, whether Eve, Sarah, Susannah, Elizabeth, and the Virgin Mary were wont to curl, powder, patch, paint, wear false locks of strange colors, rich points, trimmings, laced gowns, embroidered petticoats, shoes with slipslaps laced with silk or silver lace and ruffled like pigeons' feet. Innocency answered nay, they did not and neither did she, but she privately resolved some day to have shoes "ruffled like pigeons feet." They sounded most fetching.

Whence came the follies and fripperies of fashion? those laboring with Innocency asked, then themselves answered. Why, from such women as the infamous Clytemnestra, the painted Jezebel, the lascivious Campaspe, the most immodest Posthumia, the costly Corinthian Lais, the impudent Flora, the wanton Egyptian Cleopatra, and the most insatiable Messalina. Innocency thanked them for warning her with the words of the Founder, but reflecting that William Penn had, nevertheless, worn a sky-blue sash and taken pleasure therein, the Quaker maid did not greatly curb her own fondness for bright hues.

Innocency Williams had not lacked opportunity to marry another than a Quaker. There were rich merchants a-plenty and many a young officer in coat of scarlet or blue at her feet. But she knew that wedding any such would mean dismissal from Meeting, since the Friends deemed it impossible to discipline a mixed marriage. Nor had she ever considered a marriage out of Meeting; that is, taking vows before a justice or a "hireling priest"—a salaried minister of another denomination. Such unions also were frowned upon by Friends as having been used to cloak bigamy or illicit relations before marriage, or as a device to avoid the necessity of parental consent.

No, Innocency had rejected all suitors until stalwart, young Abel Sterling came to pay his court. A shipwright in his father's bustling yards and sometime shipmaster, Abel's demeanor was staid and grave beyond his years. God-fearing

he was but in fear of no man. He would have stood up as
stoutly as had George Fox, founder of the faith, when he was
haled before a magistrate during the savage persecutions in
England. "Tremble at the word of the Lord!" Fox thunderously bade the judge. Do you and your followers so tremble?
the judge demanded. When Fox acknowledged it, the magistrate had forthwith dubbed them Quakers.

Abel, while he obeyed the Quaker rule against waging war,
would fight in self-defense like many another Friend. Once
when his ship was attacked by pirates, he calmly and stub-
bornly led his crew in the bloody battle to repulse the buc-
caneers. Sighting a pirate swarming up a rope to board, Abel
slashed it with his cutlass and called down to the fellow,
fallen back on his own deck and clutching the coils of the
severed rope: "Friend, thee may have that." It was Abel
who disarmed the pirate captain in a fierce struggle on the
quarterdeck; then heaved the bearded rascal overboard with
the remark: "Friend, thee has no business here."

As quietly determined had been his courtship of Innocency.
Demure coquetry sparkling in her gray eyes, she begged when
Abel asked her hand:

"Pray tell me why does thee ask that I marry with thee,
Friend Abel?"

Soberly he ticked reasons off on his fingers.

"Love of thy converse. The desire of thy friendship. The
sympathy of thy way and humor with my spirit."

Her red lips began to pout at so contained an avowal.
Sensing her disappointments, Abel rose nobly to the occasion.

"And because," he said, reddening and breathing hard but
immensely earnest, "because Innocency, we are touched with
a secret unity."

There, that was better. There was even poetry and romance
in that. Innocency smiled and waited for more. "And because—" she prompted.

"And because," Abel warmly responded, all his soul in
his eyes, "because I can truly say in the fear of the Lord
that I have received a charge from him to *love thee.*"

"And is thee moved to obey that charge?" Innocency whispered.

"Strongly moved," Abel affirmed—and proved it.

Innocency, loving him, had taken him then. No sooner was Abel her accepted suitor than he ardently hastened to make arrangements for passing the Meeting which must be done twice. Application was made in writing, supported by the written consent of all surviving parents. At the first appearance of the betrothed, committees of Friends were appointed to inquire into the couple's clearness, character, and financial stability and make certain both were free from marriage entanglements. At the second Meeting, permission for the wedding was granted and overseers named whose duty it was to make certain that the ceremony was conducted in due form.

But the serious and farsighted young bridegroom had a preliminary provision of his own in mind. Having taken note of other marriages, both of contemporaries and elders, he drew up and dispatched an ante-nuptial agreement to the maiden of his choice.*

To Mrs. Innocency Williams,

Madam:

Seeing I, Abel Sterling, have addressed myself to thee upon the design of Marriage, I therefore esteem it necessary to Submit to consideration some particulars before we enter upon the Solemn Enterprize which may either establish our happiness, or Occasion our Inquietude during life.

I conceive the following Rules and particulars ought to be steadily observed and kept, viz.

1st. That we Keep but one purse, a Severance of Interest bespeaking diffidence, mistrust, and disunity of mind.

2nd. That we avoid anger as much as possible, especially with each other, but if either should be over-

*Based on the agreement made in 1751 between Jacob Spicer and Deborah Leaming.

taken therewith, the other to treat the angry Party with Temperance and moderation.

3rd. That if any misunderstanding shou'd arise, the same to be calmly Canvassed and accommodated between ourselves without admitting the Interposition of any other, or seeking a Confident to either reveal our mind unto, or Sympathize withall upon the Occasion.

4th. That in Matters of Religious Concernment we be at liberty to Exercise our Sentiments freely without Controul.

5th. That we use the Relatives of each other with Friendly Kindness.

6th. That if anything be omitted in the foregoing rules and Particulars that may Conduce to our future Happiness and welfare, the same to be hereafter Supplied by reason and discretion as often as Occasion shall require.

7th. [Abel had borrowed this clause; it was Law 28 from Penn's Frame of Government, written in England in 1682] That all children that shall be born to us, upon reaching the age of 12 years, shall be taught some useful trade, or skill, to the end that none may be idle, but that the poor may work to live, and the rich, if they become poor, may not want.

Thereto Abel and Innocency had set their hand and seals, promising to observe its rules and particulars.

Years later a son, coming across the document among family papers, had found a short verse penned in Innocency's handwriting on the margin opposite the last clause. It was the little litany which Edward Shippen, first Mayor of Philadelphia, had composed:

> From food when it is hash,
> From a young doctor when he is rash,
> From foe reconciled
> And from woman wild,
> Lord, keep this child.

There were older Friends who still found it hard to
credit the existence of all the carefree merriment, inspired
by the approaching wedding. It was not so many years ago
that Quakers were hanged, scourged, prisoned, or hounded
from their homes in England, Ireland, and Wales—aye, and
from Holland and Germany. Fleeing from persecution to the
American Colonies, they had scarce fared better in New
England—save only in Rhode Island. But they had come to
their own in Pennsylvania. Here had they prospered and by
fair dealing, even with the Indians. Shipowners, merchants,
armers, artisans, they were men of mark and powers in councils of state. The red-brick houses of Friends rose three stories
in their City of Brotherly Love, and if within there was no
dancing, playing at cards, or reading of novels, nonetheless
there was no lack of good cheer.

The homes of the Williams and Sterling families resounded
with it. Kinsfolk from distances packed all the spare rooms.
Feasting seemed never to cease. Once the Williams bid one
hundred and twenty to dine. There were few dinner guests
who could not be prevailed upon to stay to tea and supper.
For every repast there was a profusion of good things to eat.
Abel's mother wrote in her diary of a small dinner she gave
—only twenty-four sat down at table.

"Dressed two green turtles and invited only near relatives.
Had three tureens of soup, the two shells baked, besides several dishes of stew, with boned turkey, roast ducks, veal, and
beef. After these were removed, the table was filled with two
kinds of jellies and various kinds of pudding, pies, and pre-
serves; and then almonds, raisins, nuts, apples, and oranges."

Beneath that entry she had placed a telling postscript next
day:

"My husband passed a restless night with gout."

From all quarters came testimony to the quality of Quaker
hospitality. A wedding guest from out of town sat down, sighing with repletion, to write home:

"A mighty feast again. Nothing less than the very best of
claret, Madeira, & burgundy. Ducks, hams, chickens, beef,
and pig. Tarts, creams, custards, jellies, fools, trifles, floating

island, sweetmeats, whipped sillabubs, and twenty sorts of flummery. Beer, porter, punch, wine &. Of a surety these plain Friends with their 'thees' and 'thous' live well." *

Meanwhile such generous distributions of meats, cake, and punch were being made to the neighborhood that whole streets took on a carnival air. Was it not commanded in the Scriptures? "When thou makest a dinner or a supper, call not thy friends, nor thy brethren neither thy kinsmen, nor thy rich neighbors; lest they also bid thee again, and a recompense be made thee. But when thou makest a feast, call the poor, the maimed, the lame, the blind; and thou shalt be blessed for they cannot recompense thee." The Williams and Sterling families followed this generous wedding custom without ostentation, for it was the practice of Friends in providing for the poor to give alms so secretly that it was never known beyond those immediately concerned.

Quakers were pledged to temperance in all things, but the drinking at the home of the bride, if not excessive, was deep and steady for days. Products of those breweries and wineries, established by William Penn, were by no means neglected. Friends, declared their guests, were as free with beverages as an appletree with its fruit on a windy day. Most seemed content to let the excellent water from Philadelphia pumps be used for the purpose for which it was famed; boiling greens. There was no need to drink it.

"Punch and cider for lunch," a New York visitor set down in his journal in somewhat shaky handwriting. "Rum and brandy before dinner. Punch, Madeira, port, sherry at dinner. Punch and liqueurs with the ladies. Wine, spirits, and punch till bedtime. And all in punchbowls big enough to have swimmed a half a dozen young geese.

"I groped my way to where I lodged after having butted against some posts on the sides of the pavements, which kept me in the road. I got at length to bed where I inclined to let myself rest until morning.

"They should follow here the custom of the Dutch families in New York town who take up a collection for the poor at

*From the diary of John Adams.

their wedding receptions. After the fourth or fifth round, all subscribe richly."

Abel and Innocency knew that the wedding would put no period to the gaiety and frolicking. Custom would require them to hold receptions and large tea parties in their own home for sometime after the marriage, with the bridegroom ladling punch on the first floor and the bride, on the second, being enthusiastically kissed by gentlemen callers at the rate of some one hundred and fifty a day.

Came the wedding day, and the clans gathered in the meeting-house. Silence and solemnity reigned, as the parents of the bride and bridgroom entered and seated themselves on facing benches, the Williams opposite the Sterlings. Then Abel and Innocency accompanied by groomsmen and brides-maids walking arm in arm, moved down the aisle, parting at its end, she joining her parents, he his. Admiring glances followed the bride, her bright eyes shining, dainty lace cap set proudly on her chestnut curls. Her gown of soft blue, so full-gathered as to stand out around her like a hoop-skirt, abetted a close-fitted bodice in displaying her slenderness. Over her skirt she wore an apron of apple-green. Matching it were green stockings of thin worsted encased in tiny slip-pers which—oh, vanity!—were ruffled like a pigeon's feet. Abel, who had lost his self-consciousness at his first dazzling glimpse of his bride, wore a full-skirted coat of dark blue camlet with gleaming gold buttons, small clothes, stockings, and pumps. His stock was of fine white linen and his hat the broad-brimmed headgear favored by Quakers. He and the other men wore their hats throughout the meeting except during times of prayer.

Now silence again, the deep, impressive silence of Quaker meetings. Then the bridegroom and bride rose and advanced toward each other. Abel knew he would never forget the sight of Innocency coming toward him and the light which shone in her eyes. He took her right hand in his and held it tight, looking down into her glowing open face.

Was it fitting that passages from *The Song of Solomon*

should keep coursing through his head? Perhaps it was not, yet he could not prevent them. "Behold thou art fair, my love . . . Thy lips are like a thread of scarlet, and thy speech is comely; thy temples are like a piece of pomgranate within thy locks. . . . Thy two breasts are like two young roes that are twins, which feed among the lilies. . . ." Enough! Abel sternly recalled his mind to the ceremony. Together he and Innocency faced the assemblage. Most earnestly he recited, gazing into her eyes:

"In the presence of the Lord and of these our friends I take thee, my friend, Innocency Williams, to be my wife, promising through divine assistance to be unto thee a loving and faithful husband until death shall separate us."

A little tremulously, her upturned face rosy, Innocency repeated the vow, pledging herself to Abel. Both signed their names to certificates of marriage. Then they sat down together, hand in hand. Again silence, long and meaningful, time for reflection on vows given and taken, time for taking thought of the past and of the present and of the future. It was upwards of half an hour when an appointed Friend arose and announced: "This is perhaps a suitable time for the wedding company to withdraw."

They trooped out of the quiet meeting-house. There was gay chatter and happy laughter as the young couple were escorted to their new home through the tree-lined streets of William Penn's "greene country towne."

TAVERN IN THE TOWN

Black Sam Fraunces and His
New York Inn

1762-1785

There is a tavern in the town, in the town,
And there my true love sits him down, sits him down,
And sips his wine with laughter free,
And never, never thinks of me, thinks of me.

Song

There is, in fact as well as in song, a tavern in the town. It stands near the lower tip of Manhattan Island, New York City, restored much as it appeared in the 18th Century. If you feel the need of some restoration yourself, you can step up to the bar and appropriately order a "Manhattan". It should be drunk as a toast to the shade of Samuel Fraunces.

Around you in Fraunces Tavern a ghostly company will raise their glasses, too—glasses of old Madeira, bumpers of sangaree, mugs of flip. "To Black Sam!" they will echo. "The finest host in New York! Spy on the redcoats! Friend of poor devils of prisoners in the hulks! Father of the fair Phoebe who saved General Washington's life! Steward to the first President of the United States!"

Drink hearty. Black Sam deserves it.

He came from the West Indies, born there about 1722, of French extraction. It was his swarthy skin, tanned by tropical suns, that gave him his nickname of Black Sam. Affable, hospitable, a connoisseur of food and drink, he was a born tavern-keeper, and, after emigrating to New York, in due course he found the ideal tavern in a house at Pearl and Broad Streets. It was the home Stephen De Lancey built in 1719, and as capacious and comfortable as a Dutch burgher.

Sam bought it for £2,000 in 1762. He arranged its kitchen where countless roasts would brown on spits turned by boys or by trained dogs on treadmills. He stocked its cellar with wines and spirits which would wet the gullets of the notables of the town, the American and British armies and the Continental Congress. With pride he surveyed its handsome Long Room on the second floor, and his pride proved better justified than he imagined. History would be made there.

Indeed it was in the making there on the night of April 22, 1774. An excited company was gathered in the Long Room—Sons of Liberty and the Vigilance Committee. Tea was frequently mentioned but nobody ordered it. There was a British tax on it and true Americans were pledged not to drink it. Black Sam, smilingly serving stronger stuff, listened patriotically and discreetly. The room rang with angry words. It was soon apparent that George III, as Patrick Henry suggested, might profit by the example of Caesar and Charles I, but not by a tax on tea.

Down at the East India Company's wharf nearby lay the newly arrived tea ship, *London*. Something ought to be done about the tyranny of taxation without representation. In Boston a little while ago patriots disguised as Indians had boarded a tea ship and dumped the tea in the harbor. What a pity the New York tea ship had been delayed by the storm, allowing the Boston Tea Party to be given first. Just the same, it was a good idea, the Sons agreed. To the wharf!

Out of Fraunces Tavern they streamed. It was as well no British patrol encountered that determined mob. They hailed Captain Chambers of the *London,* demanding whether he had tea aboard. Not a leaf, Chambers declared. The Sons expressed impolite disbelief. They swarmed over the side, dragged eighteen cases of tea from the hold, broke them open and emptied them into the harbor. Plainly, Americans preferred their tea, as long as it was taxed, with neither cream nor lemon but with plenty of salt water.

Ensued trouble and plenty of it, during which Black Sam found himself in the line of fire. His tavern was becoming known as a hotbed of rebellion. John Adams and the Massachusetts delegation to the Second Continental Congress on their way to Philadelphia put up at the tavern, already known to Adams for serving the best dinner he ever ate. A month or so later (August 23, 1775), Sons of Liberty and Columbia students, among them a young fellow named Alexander Hamilton, began removing cannon from the Battery out of danger of capture. Captain Vandeput of the British man o' war *Asia* in the harbor cleared for action and opened fire on the party and the lower part of the town. The result is best described by the patriot-poet Philip Freneau:

"Scarce a broadside was ended, till another began again.
By Jove! it was nothing but Fire away, Flannagan!
Some thought him saluting his Sally's and Nancy's,
Till he drove a round shot thro' the roof of Sam Francis.
At first we suppos'd it was only a sham,
Till he drove a round ball thro' the roof of Black Sam;
The town by the flashes was fairly enlightened,
The women miscarry'd, the beaus were all frightened.
For my part, I hid in a cellar (as sages
And Christians were wont in the primitive ages)."

Sam kept open for business during repairs, and business was excellent. The bloods of the town flocked in to drink his proverbially fine Madeira.*

Sam's cooking was also famous and he carried a toothsome line of eatables to be taken out: "portable soup", catchup, bottled gooseberries, pickled walnuts and mushrooms, sweetmeats, jellies and "pickled and fryed oisters, fit to go to the West Indies". In June, 1776, he spread his tables for one of the most splendid banquets of his career, the party thrown by the Provincial Congress for General Washington, his staff and the officers of regiments in and around New York.

The Long Room glittered with lights, which later showed

*A bottle brought $38 in 1860, and in the museum rooms of the Tavern a bottle of it survives to this day.

up on the bill along with the glassware broken in the course
of the evening. Around the festive board sat the General and
his officers in blue and buff and the more soberly attired
members of Congress. Host Sam marshalled his serving-men
who advanced with a procession of steaming dishes. All, it
may be hoped, partook heartily, for ballast would be needed.
Tapsters established a virtually endless chain from the cellar.
Madeira, port, porter, cider, spruce, sangaree, punch, and
bitters flowed and glasses clinked. Toasts began, getting off to
a good start with healths to Congress, the American Army
and Navy. The company then drank to Mr. Burke and other
friends of America in Parliament. Somebody bid for Irish
support with the proposal, "May the generous sons of St.
Patrick expel all the venomous reptiles of Britain." Somebody else proposed the praiseworthy but vain wish, "May
placemen and pensioners never find seats in America's Senate." Freedom was heartily approved. They drank to the
Governor of South Carolina without mentioning the Governor of North Carolina, for it definitely was not a long time
between drinks.

Thirty-one toasts, no less, were quaffed that night. They
missed a few good ones of the day, such as, "May the enemies
of America be turned into saltpetre and go off in hot blasts",
and "The daughters of America—in the arms of their brave
defenders only". But not many were neglected. Along toward
the end of the evening toast Number 31 was given. It was,
believe it or not, "The civil and religious liberty of all mankind", and perhaps it was actually pronounced, "Th' shivil
an' relishous liberty 'fallmankinsh".

At the door of Fraunces Tavern that night there may have
been a waiting line of wheelbarrows.* If so, there is no evidence of how many of them were needed, as there was in
the case of a later New York dinner, attended by 120. Its
bill lists as its final item, "Coffee for eight gentlemen", which
indicates the number of survivors.

However, banquets did not interfere with serious business.
There was a war on and the Americans held New York against

*The taxicabs of the time.

the British fleet and army eager to capture it. George Washington had come to entertain a high opinion of Samuel Fraunces who, with his family, was devoted to the General. On that simple fact—the loyalty of a tavern-keeper and one of his daughters in particular—depended for some breathless hours the course of mighty events.

It is a little-known story, since it is one of the might-have-beens of history. Had the plot come off—and it was a near thing—it would have meant the ruin of the American cause or at least a tremendous setback. The plot, said to have been hatched within the British lines by Governor Tryon of New York, involved Mayor Matthews and, as an American put it, "a number of villains possessed of fortunes and who formerly ranked with gentlemen". Cannon defending the town were to be spiked and powder magazines blown up. The crowning blow was to be the assassination of Generals Washington, Putnam, Greene and others. As a mode of warfare this was hardly cricket, but it promised to be effective.

Washington's headquarters was in a house on Richmond Hill, isolated by a fine stand of trees. On duty with the General's bodyguard was an Irishman named Thomas Hickey, who, as a deserter from the British Army and a trained soldier, had been welcomed into the American service. This man, aided by the fifer, drummer, and several others in the guard, was to kill the General when the plot was sprung. His position gave him excellent prospects of success.

It happened, however, that Washington, impressed by Black Sam's culinary skill and surmising it must run in the family, had appointed Sam's daughter, Phoebe, housekeeper at headquarters. The General lived well. So did his bodyguard. Thomas Hickey fell in love with Phoebe. As for the girl, she was hardly unreceptive. Those June nights the moon shone through the trees on Richmond Hill. It was wartime and Phoebe was eloquently courted by a stalwart fellow at once a soldier and an Irishman, an almost irresistible combination. But when, like Irishmen and men in love, Tom Hickey talked too much and told of the plot, the idyll ended. Love failed to conquer all. Phoebe knew what she ought to do and what her father would have her do. She told the General.

The Americans moved fast, arresting Hickey, the faithless fifer, the dastardly drummer, and quantities of Tories. It speaks well for patriots, enraged by "a hellish plot against the best man on earth", that the trial of the conspirators was fair. The American Commissary General remarked that he prayed "the villains may receive a punishment equal to a perpetual itching without the benefit of scratching". But no drastic penalty was imposed except in the case of Hickey, who was sentenced to death.

Details with fixed bayonets from the American battalions reported at jail on June 28, 1776. They were hanging Thomas Hickey in the morning. With dead march and muffled drums, they haled him to Bowery Lane where a concourse of 20,000 was gathered around the gallows. Hickey brazened it out until the chaplain grasped his hand and bade him farewell, when tears gushed from his eyes. Scornfully then he wiped them away with the back of his hand and paid his disrespects to the fair Phoebe with the remark that keeping company with lewd women brought a man trouble. His last words were a defiance to American officers, "We'll get you yet!"

They strung him up. So died one who so nearly robbed a young nation of the leader who was to be its salvation.

The Americans intensified their preparations to defend New York. Windows of Fraunces Tavern suffered as its roof had. All the lead sash-weights were taken to be moulded into bullets. Sons of Liberty pulled down the leaden statue of George III on Bowling Green. Somebody with a feeling for history or a desire to insult royalty made a count which showed that the effigy supplied 42,088 shots at His Majesty's myrmidons. In spite of that, the Americans lost the city after the Battle of Long Island.

Now in British-held, Tory-filled New York, it was up to Sam Fraunces and others to do their best under cover for the American cause. Along with such men as James Rivington, unsuspected since he was the editor of *The Royal Gazette*, Black Sam became a spy. He kept the tavern running full blast, and British officers made it a favorite resort. The military secrets they babbled in their cups were passed on by Black Sam to General Washington. Notable, too, was Sam's aid to American prisoners of war, confined in the noisome jails and in the leaky, rat-infested hulks in the harbor. Thousands of them suffered and died under the inhuman treatment given them by Provost Marshal William Cunningham whose cruelty was enhanced by the fact that he was a renegade son of Liberty. Cunningham packed his victims in so tightly that when they lay down to sleep on the damp, dirty straw it was impossible for any man to shift from one side to another unless a command of right or left turn was given for the whole floorfull. He sold their food and gave them only muddy water to drink. It came to be his boast that he had killed more enemies than all the British armies.

Black Sam was able to lighten the misery of the prisoners, to smuggle in food and clothing, perhaps to arrange escapes. What he accomplished in their behalf during the long years of the British occupation is not specifically recorded, but its value is testified to by a grant of £200 by Congress and the New York legislature to Samuel Fraunces for his kindness to American prisoners, and other services to the patriot cause.

When the war was won, General Washington met British officers to arrange for the withdrawal of their troops from New York. Sam catered for their dinner which cost £500, but that was in depreciated paper money. At last, on November 25, 1783, arrived the great occasion of Evacuation Day. Out marched the redcoats; in marched American troops through a wildly rejoicing town which showed the effect of an iron hand. Houses of rebels had been reduced to rack and ruin, and many a fine shade tree cut down for firewood for Hessian officers. A few minor disturbances occurred. An American officer was insulted by a British son of Bellona (as the press euphoniously put it) who promptly received a horse-whipping and a half-dozen *coups des pieds au derriere*. Provost Marshal Cunningham, after tearing down several prematurely hoisted American flags and "pronouncing some scores of

double-headed Dams, besides the genteel epithet of Rebel
Bitches", prudently boarded a British ship; subsequently he
was hanged for forgery in London. The British had left their
flag flying with cut-away halyards on a greased pole, but an
American sailor nailed cleats, climbed up and hoisted the
Stars and Stripes.

The celebration also called for many a drink to be hoisted,
and Black Sam never spent a busier day. General Washington
made his headquarters at the Tavern, and that night Governor Clinton gave a dinner there for the General and his
officers. While the toasts drunk were to the Original States,
which limited them to only thirteen, the evening was a
grand one.

December 4th saw the most famous scene in this already
historic setting. Then Sam's Tavern was done such honor
as he must have remembered to the end of his days. Washington, about to retire as Commander-in-Chief of the Army
and return to Mount Vernon, summoned his officers to meet
him in the Long Room and say farewell. A hard-riding cavalryman, Colonel Benjamin Tallmadge, wrote of that affecting moment in his diary:

"We had assembled but a few moments, when His Excellency entered the room. His emotion, too strong to be concealed, seemed to be reciprocated by every officer present.
After partaking of a slight refreshment, in almost breathless
silence the General filled his glass with wine, and turning to
the officers he said, 'With a heart full of love and gratitude, I
now take leave of you. I most devoutly wish that your latter
days may be as prosperous and happy as your former ones
have been glorious and honorable.'

"After the officers had taken a glass of wine, General Washington said, 'I cannot come to each of you, but I shall feel
obliged if each of you will come and take me by the hand.'

"General Knox, being nearest to him, turned to the Commander-in-Chief, who, suffused in tears, was incapable of ut-
terance but grasped his hand, when they embraced each other
in silence. In the same affectionate manner, every officer in

the room marched up to, kissed and parted with his General-in-Chief."

Such was that affecting leave-taking of comrades-in-arms who had fought and won the war for American Independence. Nor can the General have neglected to say farewell to Sam Fraunces. He, too, had served.

Certainly Washington did not forget the tavern-keeper he esteemed so highly for his own and for his daughter's sake. He wrote Sam in 1785, asking a favor in the following letter:

"As no person can judge better of the qualifications necessary to constitute a good housekeeper, or household steward, than yourself, for a family which has a good deal of company and wishes to entertain them in a plain, but genteel style, I take the liberty of asking you if there is such a one within your reach whom you think could be induced to come to me on reasonable wages. I would rather have a man than a woman, but either would do, if they can be recommended for honesty, sobriety and knowledge of their profession, which, in a word, is to relieve Mrs. Washington from the drudgery of ordering and seeing the table properly covered and things economically used . . .

"The wages I now give a man . . . is about one hundred dollars per annum; but . . . I would go as far as one hundred and twenty-five dollars."

Whether Sam found a steward is not stated. Curiously, four years hence he was filling the job himself, but not in Virginia. George Washington had been elected President, inaugurated in New York, and had established his "White House" at No. 3 Cherry Street. Black Sam ran the household with his accustomed skill, and probably no President since has given state dinners better cooked and served. Still the household budget had to be balanced, and it was made clear that no over-lavishness should be tolerated. That point was clinched when Sam served up a fine shad, the first catch of the season, for breakfast one morning.

"What fish is this?" demanded the President.

"A shad, Your Excellency."

"It is very early in the season for it. How much did you pay for it?"

"Two dollars."

"Two dollars! I can never encourage this extravagance on my table. Take it away. I will not touch it," said the economical Father of his since more spendthrift Country.

The steward took it away and relished breakfasting on it himself.

Black Sam was still in the position the following year when death claimed the famous keeper of a famous tavern in the town.

THEIR EARS WERE RED

Corn-Husking Bees and Other Frolics

1755

For each red ear a generous kiss he gains,
For each smut ear he smuts the luckless swains,
But when to some sweet maid a prize is cast,
She walks the round, and culls one favored beau,
Who leaps the luscious tribute to bestow.

Anon.

Being the new schoolmaster, Jack Ramble * was of two minds whether to attend the corn-husking at Aunt Nabby's. A schoolmaster, especially a young one, must maintain his dignity. Likewise decorum would be expected of him as a graduate of Harvard College—by those unacquainted with Harvard College. Thirdly, this village of Kingston, New Hampshire, was his mother's former home, and there would be critical eyes upon him.

Might a corn-husking prove *infra dignitatem* then? It might well. Master Ramble remembered them from his farm-bred boyhood. Some of them were bacchanals, veritable saturnalia, scenes of riotous revelry. Old Ned Ward, the London publican who visited New England and wrote a scurrilous book about its people, had declared:

"Husking of Indian-Corn is as good sport for the Amorous Wag-tailes in New-England, as Maying amongst us is for the forward Youths and Wenches. For 'tis observed there are more Bastards got in that Season, than in all the Year beside; which Occasions some of the lesser Saints to call it Rutting Time."

Some farmers called the bees "husking entertainments" and, grudging their cost in food and liquor, would not have bid the neighborhood to come help if they could have accomplished the task otherwise. They complained that even the vigorous young swains feigned to be unable to carry in the husks until the rum bottle enlivened them. Then all the work

*"Jack Ramble" is a character in the verse of Jacob Bailey. This narrative is based on an episode in Bailey's early career, used by him as a verse theme. The verses herein quoted are his. A few years later, Bailey took orders in the Church of England and became a noted frontier missionary. A Loyalist, he emigrated to Nova Scotia at the outbreak of the Revolution.

was done in a trice, and after a hearty meal about ten at night they and the maidens went to their pastimes.

But there was some exaggeration in such tales. For various reasons it was incumbent upon him, Master Ramble felt, to take part in these communal undertakings. Theirs were the spirit of neighborliness and good will. They were the very fabric of America. Many willing hands made quick work of tasks scarce to be done at all by a few pairs. A man helped his neighbors in their need, and they helped him in his. Most of the meeting-houses, houses, and barns in New England would never have gone up if it had not been for good folk gathering from all over the countryside for the raising. People hayed and threshed each other's fields. They worked together on the minister's wood spell. By united effort winter roads were broken out after a snowfall. It was stone-bees that cleared the fields and built all the stone fences hereabouts. The covering on Jack's bed was the product of a quilting bee. A heavy chore was lightened when neighbors were called in for an apple bee: paring, coring and stringing them up to dry. There was hard work a-plenty when the maple sap ran, but host and helpers forgot arms aching from carrying pails at the sugaring off, when they sampled the tasty wat, or froth, and munched delicious snowballs, dipped in the warm syrup. Making a husking, though, was the most rollicking fun of all. You could not rightly stay away, reflected Master Ramble.

Then if truth be told it seemed rather dull in the New Hampshire backwoods after four merry years at Harvard. Here, Jack had found, almost the only pleasures were books, ink, and quill. To be sure those also had been available at Harvard, but no lively lad need be reduced to them alone. The recently-graduated scholar sighed as he recalled those bygone days. Song and jollity—week-night dances—logs rolled down stairways to frighten the tutors out of their wits—hours spent pouring down liquor on high quarter-days. *Haec olim meminisse juvabit,* as Vergil had it.

Another reason for attending. Would not a corn-husking furnish a most excellent subject for the verse-making of which

Master Ramble was so fond? Already he had devised a beginning—

> The season was cheerful, the weather was bright,
> When a number assembled to frolic that night . . .

Finally it could not be denied that the bee's powers of
attraction were due somewhat to the schoolmaster's recent
encounter with a maiden fair. Most certainly Tabitha was
not just one of the village girls—none of your Pollys and
Kates of whom he had versified.

> Their courting is simple; they tumble all day
> With Roger and Damon in winrows of hay.

No, Tabitha was different. She could inspire a man to
poetry. Indeed, she had, and Jack had penned several fervent
couplets to her.

> She is the chief of all my joys,
> And none but she my heart employs.

> Bright as an angel, clear as light,
> Fair as the snow's unspotted white.

"Fair as the snow's unspotted white." Not a bad line at all.
Tabitha was the sort of girl a schoolmaster could court with
propriety and—considering her chaste beauty and her well-
turned arms and graceful ankles—with enthusiasm. Assuredly
she was no bold creature like that minx Dolly who almost
had taken him in.

Jack had met Dolly after a quilting bee. When a girl gave
a quilting, her female acquaintances always came immediately
after dinner and worked like spirits to get the quilt out before the young men arrived. When the girls had finished
and had their supper, in trooped the beaux. It amused the
sophisticate from Harvard to see how they all sat about at first
like a parcel of ninnies, the girls at one side of the room, and

the boys at the other. But soon they mixed together, dancing
or playing chasing the squirrel or other games so lively that
they were finally ready to sit around and rest. Jack chose
Dolly to talk to—she seemed far less forward and fidgety than
the other girls who were always hopping up and running
about like pismires.

Dolly told him that he looked tired and pale; that he
worked too hard at his schoolmastering. What he needed was
a quiet day out-of-doors. Why didn't he come up some day
and go blackberrying with her and her folks?

"We live beyond Hampton village," she told him. "Father's
fields are all walled in, and the pasture is surrounded by a
good hedge-fence, and there the blackberries grow as thick
as mustard. You can't think how delightful they look hanging
on the bushes, all black with them. You can get as many as
you please. I very often go out after I get my skeins off and
stint done. Pray come and pick and eat the berries and some
of our good brown-bread and milk with them. Depend on it,
you will feel stronger and have more color in your face."

Jack, trapped by the solicitude of a designing female like
many another man, went. Somehow that day Dolly's family
were unable to help, and she and he picked berries alone in
the pasture hidden by the hedge-fence. They began talking
about his studies at Harvard but somehow soon shifted to
other subjects.

" 'Tis the time now for blackberries," Dolly chatted on.
"They'll soon be gone. Good things last so short a time in
this world. How runs the maxim: 'Soon ripe, soon—'? Dear
me! But we've picked enough now to show. Let's sit and rest,
Jack, and blacken each other's faces with berry stain till we
look like Indians."

The schoolmaster had made haste to escape from a situa-
tion which seriously threatened his dignity and he knew not
what else.

That hussy, Dolly! But Tabitha was different, and since
Tabitha would be at the corn-husking, Master Ramble decided to attend.

Jack trudged toward Aunt Nabby's in the late afternoon. The husking would be held as near to early candlelight as the chores allowed. How clear and fresh the fall air felt! Along his path the foliage was aflame. Plucked apples in rosy heaps dotted the orchards. Pumpkins and squash gleamed orange and gold in the fields. Matching their hue, a great, full harvest moon would rise tonight.

Already there was a goodly gathering at the big barn. Aunt Nabby was a widow woman, and people were even readier than usual to turn out and help. Jack hastened to make his manners to the older women as a young schoolmaster should and had to stay and listen to a deal of dull women-talk—all the uses they made of husks. Some used them for mops or mats or to stuff mattresses, and some even scrubbed the children with them. One dame avowed she always burned cobs for saleratus; another insisted she made middling good molasses out of the stalks. One good wife took it upon herself to instruct the schoolmaster in weather signs. Said she: "There's a skunk under our kitchen I cal'late the winter's going to be uncommon hard."

Jack escaped to a group of young people. Somebody handed him a jug. He took a long and grateful swig, a draught which would have been deeper still if the jug had not been so heavy to lift and tilt. Laughing, they showed him why: to limit deep drinking the bottom of the jug was lead. On its side was scratched a verse which Jack read with glee.

> Women make men love;
>   Love makes them sad.
> Sadness make them drink,
>   And drink sets them mad.

Lofts of the big barn were full to the rafters with fragrant hay. Candles in tin lanthorns, hung on pegs, shed soft, twinkling light. Men still were breaking the ears of corn from rustling, brittle stalks and heaping them in great piles for the huskers. All about were baskets in which the golden ears would be carried to the crib.

Yonder a group lifted young voices in a tuneful ballad,
New Hampshire John:

> In Boston there did live
> A merchant by trade
> Who had for his servants
> A man and a maid.
>
> A New Hampshire boy
> He had for his man
> And for to do his business.
> His name it was John . . .

Jack Ramble saw Dolly among the singers, but the girl
of the blackberries ignored him, much to his content. For
now Tabitha, aloof and lovely in blue, swept in. Her golden
tresses were combed back from her forehead and secured at
the nape of her neck with a hair spring, thence floating in
rich waves to below her waist. Instantly Jack was at her side.
She graciously consented to be his partner and took her place
on his right when belles and beaux ranged themselves alter-
nately in circles, seated around the husk heaps.

As the husking started, the frolic * began in earnest. It
was plain that kisses and drams already had set more than a
few virgins aglow. Talk was bold and free, love-making open
and ardent. Now and again couples paying too much attention
to each other and not enough to husking were targets for
ears of corn, shied by laughing companions.

Jack admired the way Tabitha's nose tilted up at all such
rowdy goings-on. She told him she thought it would be far
nicer if they played games while they were husking. "Com-
parison," for instance.

"Let's you and I play it," she invited her partner. "I'll

*The word frolic, so far as the meeting of a large number of ac-
quaintances at the house of a neighbour is concerned, meant what
the word party means now; but otherwise it was quite a different
thing. It was not a place where young ladies with false curls stuck
full of turtle-shell, met to talk nonsense and retail scandal.—*The
Yankee,* April 2, 1828.

show you how. Now I think of something, and you have to guess what it is, so you ask what it is like. Say my secret subject is a watch. You ask, 'What's it like?' I say, 'A carriage.' Then you bid me tell you why and I answer, 'Because it has wheels.' Or it's like a person because it has a face and hands." Tabitha's laugh was silvery. "Do you understand how it's played?"

Jack said he did. Privately he thought it excessively dull. He welcomed an uproarious interruption which now took place. Some lad had husked a blackened ear and exercised his privilege of smuting other men's faces with it. To Jack he gave a particularly good blackening. The schoolmaster felt Dolly's merry eyes on him. She called across the circle:

"I could have done better with blackberries."

Tabitha sniffed and bridled and went on talking of games. "Some think 'Philanders' fun," she said. "Of course we could not play it while husking, but this is the way of it. All take hold of hands excepting one who is seated in the middle of the room. All march around this one in a circle singing the while, 'Come, Philanders, let us be marching. Every one speaks from his heart strings. Come, choose your true love now or never and be sure you choose no other.' The person in the chair, if a boy, chooses a girl from the circle and kisses her."

Tabitha blushed a little. Jack moved closer to her. This game sounded better. The girl chattered on.

"Then they are considered married. All dance merrily around and sing: 'Now you are married, you must obey, or else you'll have a fine to pay. I am too young, I am not fit to go and leave my mamma yet.' "

" 'Fit' and 'yet' do not rhyme," observed the poet severely.

Tabitha, paying no heed to such a technicality, continued: "Then the girl sits down in the chair and chooses a boy from the circle and kisses him and so it goes on. Do you like that game?"

Jack gazed into her eyes. "I do—the kissing part. Could we not leave out all the rest of it?"

Tabitha regarded him coldly and tossed her head. "How

silly!" she sniffed. "It's not that I think kissing any such abominable thing, but if it must be done, I like to see it done decently."

"How may it be so done?" Jack impudently inquired.

"Well, none of those wheelbarrow kisses they ask for in some games," she answered indignantly. "I was once shut up in a dark closet half an hour for a forfeit because I wouldn't kiss a man wheelbarrow-fashion."

"A wheelbarrow kiss? What is that like?" Jack demanded with unconcealed interest.

Tabitha frowned. "You are better off not knowing," she told him severely. "I vow such kisses are all of a piece with field-beds and bundling and red-ear kisses."

Just at that moment, as fate would have it, Tabitha stripped the husk from a red ear.

It was the first of the husking, and all had been eagerly awaiting it. A wild chorus of shouts and screams arose, demanding she follow the old husking custom. "Choose your beau, Tabby!" "Kiss him, kiss him!" "The schoolmaster's waiting, Tabby."

But Tabitha, flushing with annoyance, scrambled to her feet and raced from the barn.

Poor Jack sat there, the picture of utmost discomfiture. Every one was looking at him and howling with mirth. He was wishing most heartily that he could sink through the floor when he was suddenly and dramatically rescued from his plight.

Dolly had husked the second red ear. She jumped to her feet and skipped straight across the circle to Master Ramble. She tapped him on one shoulder with the red ear. He scrambled up, and stood before her.

"I heard you ask about a wheelbarrow kiss," she pertly declared. "Did they never teach you that at Harvard?"

Jack shook his head, grinning.

"The schoolmaster is about to be taught!" Dolly cried, while the company roared.

Facing him, she clasped his hands. Then, pirouetting, she whirled him about also, their hands still clasped, so that they stood, back to back and arms around each other. Dolly leaned her head back on his shoulder, and as Jack turned toward her, their lips met.

"And that, sir," said Dolly, "is a wheelbarrow kiss * and a red-ear kiss, all in one."

The schoolmaster flung dignity aside and responded with gratitude—and stronger emotions. Here was a maid with warm blood in her veins. Let Tabitha go—"fair as the snow's unspotted white." Aye, and as cold. He put his arm around Dolly, and they sank back into a heap of husks. By the by, the older women had forgotten to mention corn-husk beds as a use for husks.

Several ears of corn were tossed at the lovers and perforce they started husking again. Lines of poetry about Dolly were beginning to run through Jack's head now.

> She baffles description. The fire in her eyes
> Can be likened to nothing on seas, earth, or skies.

At last the husking was done, and it was time for supper. Aunt Nabby and her helpers carried in great trenchers of food—pots of baked beans, hams and chickens, roasting ears giving off clouds of steam, doughnuts, pumpkin and apple pies. Month-old cider with maple syrup added, rum and molasses, a barrel of dandelion wine. The ravenous huskers fell upon the refreshments. It reminded Jack of the end of a quarter or a fast-day night at Cambridge, with scholars vigorously attacking the roast beef and pudding. He began rhyming to himself.

Vide "New England as It Was. A Frolic." In *The Yankee,* April 2, 1828:

. . . You would then see a fine, well-formed young man, and a beautiful, half-blushing—half-laughing girl, with 'long loose hair' meet on the floor; close their right and left hands, on both sides; and with a whirl as quick, and mysterious as the lightning's flash—almost—turn through their arms, bring the back of their shoulders in contact—each with the head resting upon each other's right shoulder, their mouths meeting with as much precision as the points of a pair of scissors. It was considered very ungenteel to err in the performance of the manoeuvre, either in time or point.

The girls in a huddle stand snickering by
Till Jenny and Katy have fingered the pie;
Then on it like harpies with hunger they fall,
Or rather like scholars in old Harvard Hall.

A fiddler struck up a reel. The big barn was filled with a turmoil of stamping feet and rising clouds of dust. Wilder and more and more rowdy waxed the frolic. The schoolmaster, forgetting his dignity, swung Dolly off her feet.

The chairs in wild order flew quite round the room;
Some threatened with firebrands, some brandished a broom,
While others, resolved to increase the uproar,
Lay tussling the girls in wide heaps on the floor.

Jack thought: Mother Dilly's in Boston could scarce match this scene. Abruptly he recalled his position in the community as schoolmaster. Breaking away from the reel, he seized the breathless Dolly by both soft shoulders and made her look at him.

"My dear, do you consider that all this is fitting?" he demanded of her chidingly.

"Nay," she answered, "but 'tis fun," and kissed him fervently.

"Nonetheless, it is time we left," he declared sternly. "Come, we'll go," he ordered and she followed. As the last lines of his poem on the corn-husking would declare:

Quite sick of confusion, dear Dolly and I
Retired from the hubub new pleasures to try.

But since every proper poet, even when his theme is such a riotous frolic as a husking, should introduce a note of pensive melancholy, Jack would end his verses thus:

But, alas! it was transient. All human delight
Is like birds that we read of forever in flight.

SCARLET LETTERS

Crime and Punishment by Aid of the Alphabet

17th-18th Centuries

No room for mirth or trifling here,
For worldly hope or worldly fear,
  If life so soon is gone.
If now the Judge is at the door,
And all mankind must stand before
  The inexorable throne.

No matter which my thoughts employ,
A moment's misery or joy;
  But, oh, when both shall end,
Where shall I find my destined place?
Shall I my everlasting days,
  With fiends or angels spend?
                Charles Wesley: *Hymn*

Stern-visaged though he was, Justice Brand of the General Court of Massachusetts Bay Colony was yet a handsome man, still in his prime. He stood tall and straight in peaked hat, long cape, and garb of sober hue. Not arrogantly but with the mien of one who wields the power of life and death, he strode through the streets of Boston town. Men and women watched him pass, some with awe, others with fear scarcely concealed.

By the Justice's side today walked a friend, newly come to the Colony from England. As they entered the Common, culprits confined in the stocks and pillory eyed the judge apprehensively but not bitterly. Better to sit shivering, locked in the stocks, or stand long cramping hours with head and hands pilloried than take twenty stripes at the whipping-post yonder whither they might have been sent. All Boston said of Justice Brand that while departing not from the letter of the law, he tempered it when he could with mercy.

The newcomer nodded toward the men in stocks and pillory. "A sight no less familiar at home," he observed.

"Aye, Friend Dickson," the Justice answered, "And mark how yon instruments of punishment flank the meeting-house. Thus they stood anciently in the day of the Prophet Jeremiah, hard by the house of the Lord, and so we place them. You will comprehend why 'tis so when you know Boston better.

117

"Our statutes in 1641 demanded death for twelve crimes—
mercifully today reduced to three. Capital punishment, in
each case sustained by the Scriptures, was imposed upon
those convicted of"—he ticked them off on his fingers—
"idolatry, witchcraft, blasphemy, murder (wilful, guileful,
or in passion), sodomy, buggery, man-stealing, false witness
to take away life, treason, and . . . and adultery."

"And men convicted of all such crimes were hanged?"

"Aye, and women, too. The day is not long past—God be
thanked that I sat not then as a Justice—when twenty persons,
chiefly women, were executed as witches, with all the Colony
inflamed to madness by the sermons and writings of our
minister, Cotton Mather ——." He abruptly broke off and
looked cautiously about him. Obviously none had been close
enough to overhear. Justice of the General Court though he
was, he looked vastly relieved.

"It is not we, the magistrates, who are really feared by
the people but the clergy," he continued in lowered tones.
"It was the ministers who demanded enactment of our strictest laws. They it was who clamored for the harsh, implacable
punishments of the Old Testament."

"How else may crime be halted?"

Justice Brand answered gravely: "Wickedness stopped by
strict laws, like streams damned from running quietly in
their own channels, breaks out where it gets vent. Thus declared William Bradford, Governor of Plymouth Colony two
score years ago. His are true words. There are some among
us now—and I am one—who believe that laws too numerous
and too cruel serve but to drive poor sinners into the Devil's
talons.

"Death was formerly always inflicted both here in Massachusetts Bay and in Plymouth Colony according to the Law
and the Prophets. In Governor Bradford's day occurred a
crime of foul nature.* A youth of 17 was detected in lewd
practices with a mare, a cow, two goats, five sheep, two calves,
and a turkey. Haled before the court, he confessed and de-

*Bradford, William. Bradford's History "of Plimoth Plantation."
Boston, 1899.

clared which beasts were partners of his guilt. Then was he condemned with them, and that befell which is required in Leviticus, the twentieth chapter and the sixteenth verse: 'And if a man lie with a beast, he shall surely be put to death; and ye shall slay the beast.' First the mare and then the lesser cattle were killed before the youth's face and then he himself was executed."

"Just desserts!" Dickson indignantly exclaimed.

The Justice fell silent for some moments, then resumed: "Come let us turn to more pleasant reflections—the punishment of scolds."

Dickson eyed his friend covertly. He strongly suspected why the reflections Brand mentioned would prove pleasant to him. Was not the tongue of Mistress Brand sharp and always clacking?

" 'Tis one of our most wholesome laws," the magistrate observed as they strolled on. "If any turbulent woman be troubled with an unruly member and uses it to defame anyone or to the disquiet of her neighbors, upon complaint she is ordered gagged and must take station at her own door as many hours as the court sees fit, there to be gazed at by all passersby."

"In Old England," said Dickson, "we use the brank, sometimes called the scold's bridle. It incloses the woman's head, like a helmet, forcing an iron bit between her teeth. That stills her tongue, I warrant you."

"We employ also another method," Brand returned. "If we make haste toward the pond at this end of town, we shall be in time to witness the ducking of a scold."

A jeering jostling crowd was gathered at the pool. Town sergeants were binding a buxom, red-faced dame in a seat on the end of a plank, laid over a trestle like a seesaw.

" 'Tis Goody Applegate, a termagant in very truth," Justice Brand declared. "She spent all day constantly and continually scolding her goodman and children. Then she turned to and reviled her neighbors. Thereafter she railed at the dog and the poultry. At night she opened the window and bawled imprecations at the watchman. Why, when she stood trial before me, I was compelled to order her tongue pinched in a cleft stick, so fast did it wag."

The sergeants swung the plank out over the water. Twice they submerged the woman on its end. Each time she came up sputtering and ranting wildly in her rage. Dickson gleefully quoted:

> "She mounts again and rages more
> Than ever vixen did before,
> So throwing water on the fire
> Will make it but burn up the higher.
> If so, my friend, pray let her take
> A second turn into the lake,
> And rather than your patience lose,
> Thrice and again repeat the dose.
> No brawling wives, no furious wenches,
> No fire so hot but water quenches."

Twice more they ducked Goody Applegate before she cried out, "Let me go! By God's help I'll sin no more."

"Untie the ropes," Justice Brand ordered, "and let her walk home in her wetted clothes, a hopefully penitent woman."

Strolling back toward the town, the judge remarked to his companion:

"In earlier times yonder scold would have been tied to a cart-tail and flogged all the way to the pond. Such need not be. The ducking sufficed."

Dickson smiled to himself. Again he thought: A ducking with all the rest would well serve *your* wife, Friend Brand. Never have I encountered so unquiet a woman nor one with so bitter and biting a tongue. A harried life she leads you at home with her shrewish nagging. Yet you dare not send her to the ducking stool, nor will any other since she is the wife of a judge. In truth, the bench is no easy seat. 'Tis plain why you are so staunch an advocate of mercy and mildness, Friend Brand. Sore need have you of them at home.

"The ducking sufficed," Brand was repeating. "We need not resort so often to the whipping post. Why, 'tis said that all inhabitants of the town of New Haven—all above the age of 14—have been whipped for some misdemeanor or other. All, that is, excepting two."

Dickson, grinning, spoke up: "And I doubt not yon two exceptions are: the minister and the justice of the town."

Justice Brand nodded assent.

"Too many laws," he mused. "Our courts are hard-pressed trying violations of the Sabbath alone. Be advised, Friend Dickson, now you are come among us, that on the Lord's Day none shall dance, play at cards, make mince pies nor play upon any instruments of music save the drum, trumpet, or Jew's-harp.

"Take note, too, that on the Sabbath no married couple may embrace in public under penalty of a fine or a flogging. Not long since a sea captain of this town, returning from a long voyage, met his wife upon the street and bussed her heartily. Unhappily, 'twas the Sabbath. He was fined, but only 10 shillings, circumstances being taken into account."

"A silly ordinance," Dickson scoffed. "Why, in Old England on any day a man may, without legal penalty, not only kiss his own wife but other men's, too. Ha, Ha!"

"The law is the law," Brand declared sternly.

"On second thought," Dickson pursued, still chuckling. " 'Tis an excellent law. By forbidding lovers to embrace publicly on the Sabbath it persuades them to make the most of their time in private. A good-humored lass, to make amends, should kiss me all the kinder in a corner."

A ghost of a smile curved the Justice's lips but he held up a hand in a warning gesture. "There is recent record," he said, "of a couple sentenced to whipping for Sabbath kissing —she to twenty lashes, he to thirty. Chivalrously he made a plea that he be allowed to take all fifty, and it was granted him."

"Humph!" the other sniffed. "Since public kissing and single fornication are fined alike if detected, I know which I should choose for my money. Yet I do not deny that the law must punish some shameful and unchaste acts," he finished lightly.

"That it must," the Justice austerely agreed. "Come now with me, and I shall reveal a punishment we inflict. A punishment of seeming mildness, yet more to be dreaded than banishment—mayhap even more than death. A punishment which seeks out the most secret sins and publishes them to all mankind in the broadest light of the noonday sun."

Grimly, he led the way to a house hard by the Common. Its door was opened to his knock by a little old woman who bobbed a stiff and creaking curtesy as she gave him welcome.

"This is Goody Gregory," the Justice introduced. "A sewing-woman employed by the General Court upon a certain task."

"The letters are ready, Your Worship," the old woman announced. "Come, see. How like you them?"

She motioned toward an oaken table on which was spread an array of letters of the alphabet, neatly cut from scarlet cloth. Some were two inches high, others larger. The Justice's gaze rested sombrely on the *A*. His deep voice recited:

" 'And if any man shall commit adultery,' declared our court, 'the man and woman that shall be convicted of such crime before their Majesties' justices shall be set upon the gallows for the space of an hour, with a rope about their necks, and the other end cast over the gallows, and on the way from thence to the common gaol shall be severely whipped, not exceeding forty stripes each. Also every person and persons so offending shall *forever after* wear a capital *A,* of two inches long; and proportionate bigness, cut out in cloth of a contrary color to their clothes, and sewed upon their upper garments in open view.' If any shall be found without the letter, they shall suffer fifteen stripes more."

"What if the woman alone shall be taken?" Dickson asked.

"Then shall she suffer the penalty alone," the judge declared inflexibly.

He pointed to the various letters, explaining them. How the *B* must be worn by those convicted of blasphemy, burglary, or of bastardy; in the case of the third-mentioned, the woman also was whipped and fined, but the man sentenced only to contribute to the illegitimate child's support. *D* was the stigma for drunkards who must wear it a year and might in addition be disenfranchised, forbidden to hold office, flogged and given a term in a work gang. *F* was the brand of forgery or of fornication, and *I* of incest, guilty ones being also whipped on a gallows.

"We deem it incestuous," the judge explained, "when a man has carnal knowledge of his wife's daughter or sister, equally as of his own."

"You can't trust 'em no-ways," mumbled Goody Gregory.

"A scarlet *P* signifies a poisoner," Brand broke in. "*R*, one who has committed rape. *T* marks a thief, and *V* those guilty of vulgarity or viciousness—a man being held vicious if he has attempted lewdness with divers women."

"Here lies my rarest bit of scissoring," boasted the old woman. She showed them the clearly recognizable silhouette of an Indian warrior, cut from red cloth.

"A white woman must wear yon image a twelve-month upon her right arm if she cohabits with one of the red savages," Justice Brand expounded.

As the two men took their leave and stepped out upon the stoop, Dickson remarked:

" 'Tis curious, though I have been a fortnight long in Boston, that I have not yet beheld any such scarlet symbols."

"Then use your eyes now," Goody Gregory cackled from the doorway behind them. "There she minces, the hussy! Her the Justice here sentenced himself!"

Across the Common a young woman came toward them, a small boy trudging at her side. The hooded cloak of gray she wore was thrown open despite the chill air. As she approached, a scarlet letter *A* gleamed on the breast of her gown.

"The whore!" Goody Gregory snapped. "Wouldn't tell who 'twas begot that brat on her. Said he was married, and she would not be his ruin. But you dealt with her proper, Your Worship."

The woman was comely, Dickson saw. Her hair was fair

under her hood, her gray eyes lustrous though sad, her lips alluring, firm-compressed as they were. Evidently she had recognized the Justice who condemned her, yet she made no effort to avoid him by taking another path.

"Behold!" Dickson gasped. "See how she has bordered the scarlet token on her breast with golden thread! Yon *A* she wears might mean Admirable—anything rather than Adultress." *

The wearer of the scarlet letter paid no heed to the speaker. She only grasped more tightly the hand of her handsome little son. But proud and unashamed, she looked straight into Justice Brand's eyes as she passed—a look which held no resentment but rather compassion and something deeper still.

"Did you not see how she had edged yon letter with gold?" Dickson indignantly cried. "Why, she sports with her infamy! What say you to that?"

The Justice's answer came at last in a strangled voice.

"What say I? What One once said upon the Mount long ago: 'Judge not that ye be not judged.'"

Dickson gazed curiously at him. "These New-Englanders!" he muttered under his breath. "Ned Ward was right in what he published in London of them after his sojourn here in Boston. They can neither drive a bargain, make a jest nor scarce give any answer without a text of Scripture on't."

---

*See Nathaniel Hawthorne's story, "Endicott and the Red Cross" in *Twice-Hold Tales*. Boston, 1851. This story was originally published in the Salem Gazette in 1837, thirteen years before Hawthorne wrote "The Scarlet Letter."

WHEN CO-EDS WERE RED

Goings-On at the Indian Charity School of Eleazar Wheelock, circa 1766

I

Oh, Eleazar Wheelock was a very pious man.
He went into the wilderness to teach the Indian
With a *gradus ad Parnassum,* a Bible, and a drum,
And five hundred gallons of New England rum.

Chorus

Fill the bowl up, fill the bowl up.
Drink to Eleazar,
And his primitive Alcazar,
Where he mixed drinks for the heathen
In the goodness of his soul.

II

Eleazar and the big chief harangued
          and gesticulated.
They founded Dartmouth College, and the
          big chief matriculated.
Eleazar was the faculty, and the whole curriculum
Was five hundred gallons of New England rum.

Richard Hovey: *Dartmouth Lyrics*

I, John Smith, merchant of Boston dealing in furs, have made a journey to the town of Lebanon in Connecticut and there did visit the Indian Charity School conducted by the Reverend Eleazar Wheelock. All that I beheld at that extraordinary institution and all that befell me I hereby inscribe in my journal in this year of Our Lord Seventeen Hundred and Sixty-six.

Word of the school had spread throughout the Colonies and drawn many to see it—ministers, schoolmasters, and laymen such as I. Unless they set eyes upon it few could credit the existence of an endeavor to impart learning to red savages and return them to educate their brethren in turn. Yet exist it does, this chain of knowledge, and flourishes. Its student body has grown to comprise twenty-nine Indian boys and ten Indian girls—Delawares, Mohawks, Oneidas, Montauks, Mohegans, and Narragansets—and seven English boys as well.

Graduates of the school go forth as missionaries to the tribes. It must, I considered, determining to inspect it, indeed be a most pious and praiseworthy undertaking and not without effect, good or ill, upon the fur trade.

Mr. Wheelock himself, decent in black gown and powdered periwig, received me. Of fine appearance and harmonious voice, his countenance bears the mark of a strong will that likes not crossing. He is a man of considerable learning

though he attended Yale College. No doubt our Harvard was too far distant from his home. He is also a preacher of such fervor as has convinced many of the blackness of their sins. He is, they say, scarcely less moving than was our own Jonathan Edwards, able in his prime to persuade the wicked that it were better to cut their own throats than to continue to live in iniquity. So eloquent is Mr. Wheelock reputed that once he was followed through the street by a band of children who demanded for themselves a sermon with which he promptly obliged.

But that was ere he launched his school, being fully persuaded, so he informed me, that Indians have souls and that they might be saved. Nor did he doubt that the savages would welcome salvation more warmly than many of the stubborn and stiff-necked generation composing his own congregations.

"So it happened," he said, "that I resolved to teach the Indians—to suckle the tawnies. Yet when I first asked subscriptions for an Indian school from my own church, what think you I found to be the sole deposit in the collection basket? A bullet and a gun flint."

Nevertheless he persisted and raised goodly sums from other sources and began this school. Here come the Indians direct from their wigwams. All their clothing, if you except a pair of old blankets and stockings, is not worth sixpence, and they are very lousy. They are able to speak no word of English. Yet shortly are they cleansed and clothed, and in six weeks they can read, and write a little. Thence they proceed to the study of theology. Ere long they are conning Latin, Greek, and Hebrew.

I betook myself to the schoolhouse when the bell rang at five o'clock in the morning. There sat the good Eleazar like a loving and affectionate father in the midst of his tawny family. He named the chapter in the Scriptures for the day and called upon an Indian pupil who read three or four verses. *"Proximus,"* said the master, and the next pupil took up the reading until all had read. After Mr. Wheelock had offered up a prayer, the red scholars parsed verses and entered into disputations propounded them in the arts and sciences. It was no less than amazing.

Here were youth, who not so long ago had been untutored savages, discoursing learnedly in English. In former times our missionaries made no attempt to teach the tawnies to read the Scriptures in English, much less in Hebrew or Greek, but translated for them into their own barbarous tongue, like Eliot who thus rendered a verse of one of the Psalms:

> *"Kesuk Kukootumshteaumoo*
> *God wussohsumoonk*
> *Mamahehekesuk wumahtuhkon*
> *Wuanakausnonk."*

Evensong was attended by all. First chosen was a hymn composed by Samson Occom, an Indian graduate of the school in whom Mr. Wheelock takes great pride. 'Tis said that Occom will one day publish a hymnal all his own.* He has preached hundreds of sermons, notably one delivered at a hanging which is widely admired.** For this hymn of his, entitled *Awaked by Sinai's Awful Sound,*** an Indian youth set the time and the rest followed, singing the tenor and the bass.

*Occom did so in 1774.

**A sermon preached at the execution of Moses Paul, an Indian who was executed at New-Haven on the 2d of September, 1772, for the murder of Mr. Moses Cook, late of Waterbury, on the 7th of December, 1771. Preached at the desire of the said Paul. By Samson Occom, minister of the gospel, and missionary to the Indians. New-London, Printed and sold by T. Green. (1772). (A liberty with chronology has been taken in the premature reference to this sermon in the text. F. D.)

***The hymn was still frequently sung 100 years later. As a commentary on its title line, the Rev. Edwin M. Long in his *Illustrated History of Hymns and Their Authors* (Philadelphia, 1876) piously observes: "Mr. Thorpe, with a group of scoffers tried to mimic Whitefield [one of the early revivalists]. One and another stood on a table to try their skill. Thorpe opened the Bible and read, 'Except ye repent, ye shall all likewise perish.' It was 'Sinai's awful sound.' He trembled, wept, ran from the room, was converted and became a useful preacher."

"Awaked by Sinai's awful sound,
My soul in bonds of guilt I found,
And knew not where to go;
Eternal truth did loud proclaim,
'The sinner must be born again,'
Or sink to endless woe."

And on they sang, rendering all seven stanzas with remarkable gravity and seriousness.

For more than one hundred years, I knew full well, there had been missionaries in this land of ours who went among the Indians, preaching and teaching. There had long been hundreds of praying Indians in New England. But this school of Mr. Wheelock's I deemed unique and accordingly desired of him that he tell me its ends and purposes in his own words. Thus he answered me:

"I train and send forth my pupils on missions to recommend to the savages a more rational and decent manner of living than that which they are in. Thus is removed the impediment hitherto in the way of all our missionaries, namely the constant rambling about of the Indians—which they can't avoid so long as they depend so much on fishing, fowling, and hunting for their support."

"If they ramble not, how shall they take furs?" I reflected but I contented myself with asking, "How shall they live then?"

"By husbandry,"—Mr. Wheelock replied. "I teach them by employing them upon my farm. There are those, including the father of one of my Indian scholars, who complain that such instruction is but an ingenious method of accomplishing my own farm chores. But they profit by labor and the sweat of their brows. Lacking physical exertion, they fall ill like one promising pupil named Pumpshire who sickened and died of overeating."

"Now, sir," I inquired, "what of the ten Indian girls in the school? As yet I have seen none."

"They are instructed in whatever is necessary to render them fit to perform the female part—as housewife, school mistresses, tailorettes, and so forth. One day a week they are taught reading and writing in the school. For the greater part they are taught housewifery in the home of neighbors."

Thereupon Mr. Wheelock took me to see one in the house of a farmer. "Here," said he, "lives one of my Indian girls who was, I hope, converted last week." And calling to the farmer, he, unperceived, brought the young girl to our sight. The pleasure was exquisite to see the savageness of an Indian moulded into the sweetness of a follower of The Lamb. And I doubt not that she was willingly trained in housewifery by the farmer's spouse who thus gained a serving-maid free of wages.

"For what are those learned Indian maidens destined?" I asked Mr. Wheelock who made answer:

"They are being fitted to go as consorts with the Indian youths when they return to their tribes on the business of their missions. There they make a decent home which prevents them turning savages again. 'Tis hard to live without a Rib. One of my pupils, sent back to his people as a missionary, was captivated by a young female and fell from grace back into the wild life."

Such events might easily occur, as I was well aware. Many of my fur traders, going among the tribes, are captivated by young females and neglect their business.

Had I then left Lebanon, I might have been convinced of the lasting success of the school. But I remained longer and must set down sad tidings in this journal.

In the absence of Mr. Wheelock at Norwich, I witnessed a fierce altercation among his scholars. After what I had seen of their godly and sober demeanor, I was sore distressed. They might have been so many brawling Harvard students.

Furthermore, one of the participants was a son of the Rev-

erend Eleazar, John Wheelock.* There had been words between him and one of the Indian pupils dubbed great William. John had ordered William to saddle his horse for him,
and William had refused, saying that he was a gentleman.
What is a gentleman? demanded John, and William straightway answered: A gentleman is a person who keeps race-horses
and drinks Madeira wine; and that neither you nor your father do. Therefore saddle the horse yourself.

They fall to calling one another names. With prudence,
John then challenges William to fight another Indian youth
named Johnson, calling him speckle-face white eye which
Johnson repeats. William advances up to Johnson and offers
to fight. Whereupon they both strip off their waistcoats and
prepare for the encounter. All the other schoolboys gather
around.

Johnson calls great William an Indian devil and a son of
a bitch. In retort William might well have dubbed Johnson a
bastard, for he is no less, being the natural son of Sir William
Johnson, got upon a squaw. They come to blows until they
are breathless. They then go at it again with more fury till
they tear the shirts off each other's back. Through the day
they and others fought on. Studying there was none.

More scandalous still were the goings-on at the tavern.

I was lodged above the taproom there and had retired early
one evening only to be aroused by a fearsome noise. Not
doubting it was soldiers and other rakehells, I peered down
through a hole in the floor. To my dismay I beheld the Indian
boys and girls of the school engaged in a full-fledged frolic.

All were quaffing deeply of spirituous liquors. Between
drafts they lifted their voices in song. I fear that I recognized
snatches of *Awaked by Sinai's Awful Sound,* and in truth it
was an awful sound but most certainly not Sinai's. I recognized Hannah Nonesuch and Sarah Weogs, two Mohegan
girls of the school, not uncomely wenches. They were dancing and displaying such carnal enticement that had I been

*He became the second president of Dartmouth College, succeeding
his father.

younger—but enough. Mary Secuter, a Narraganset, was undeniably intoxicated and was conducting herself in a lewd and very immodest manner among the Indian lads. All tarried in the tavern and reveled to an unseasonable time of night. The devil was in them, one and all.

Written confession was later made by the girls to Eleazar Wheelock. Yet theirs was not the first nor the sole transgression. When I called upon him to bid him farewell, he was melancholy.

"Alas," said he, "for rum. I believe in its moderate use. I buy it for my own table and once though with a trembling heart, even purchased sufficient to set up a tavern keeper in his business, since taverns are necessary to travelers. But with the Indians there is no such thing as moderation."

He spoke truth. I have myself seen how if a quantity of liquor be distributed among a party of Indians and there is not enough for a debauch, they will draw lots to determine which shall drink it and be dead drunk. (Yet in barter with the Indians, liquor must be employed. In the fur trade, 'tis either rum or ruin.)

Furthermore, Sir William Johnson, powerful among the Six Nations of the Iroquois, was at odds with Mr. Wheelock on matters of doctrine and had withdrawn his favor from the school. There were increasing local difficulties. Yet was Mr. Wheelock ready to give over? Nay, he was preparing to expand! He planned soon to move his school to what he termed a more suitable location: to wit, the New Hampshire wilderness. Generous subscriptions already had been obtained by Samson Occom and Nathaniel Whitaker, journeying abroad: more than nine thousand pounds sterling in England and, credit it or not, 2,500 from Scotland.* In especial a goodly gift has been promised by the Earl of Dartmouth after whom the good Eleazar purposes naming his new school.

"My nephew soon will haul my household goods north to the town of Hanover in New Hampshire," Mr. Wheelock

*Occom, the first Indian preacher to visit the British Isles, drew immense audiences and during a year's sojourn delivered 400 sermons.

said. "Those goods will include a cog of wine, a quantity of apple brandy, and a barrel of rum.* Doubtless I shall have tavern trouble there also,** but I shall still suckle the tawnies."

"Will you have Indian girls in your new school?" I asked.

"Nay," replied the good Eleazar firmly.

---

*By poetic license the barrel overflowed into the "five hundred gallons" of Richard Hovey's song.

**He did.

SINGING SCHOOL WAS SOCIABLE

"Young Virgins All With Beauteous Voice, Make Music Harmony Your Choice"

1770

The psalms of David in the singing-seats
Of the meeting-house, bass-viol, flute,
And tuning-fork, and rows of village-girls,
With lips half-open; treble clashed with base
In most melodious madness; voices shrill
Climbing for unreached keys, grave burying soft
In solemn thunders; fugues that rush and wait
Till lagging notes find the accordant goal.

Lucy Larcom

There was dissension in the congregation, and music was the cause of it all. So Deacon Briggs said, and everybody, even the minister, listened when the old deacon held forth, not daring to do otherwise. To be sure there were others, mostly young people, who whispered, logically enough, that there would be less discord in the church if there were more harmony in the singing. But nobody ventured to tell that to Deacon Briggs,—least of all his fair daughter Sophia, one of the secret rebels. For it was the Deacon who not only lined out the psalms but sang countertenor in the choir.

Some vowed there never would have been any music at all if the old Deacon had prevailed. He had subscribed to the belief of earlier days when music was regarded as an evil device of the Tempter. In Old England the Puritans had banned it, destroying music-books and organs, dissolving choirs and chasing players of instruments from the organ gallery. Here in New England strict tenets had been relaxed. Had not Moses permitted horns in the Temple, and David played upon the harp? The Scriptures were further cited to show that some, at least, of the psalms were intended to be sung.

The dour adversaries of music failed to maintain the ban. Soon psalms were being sung right out in meeting. From London were brought over copies of the Sternhold and Hopkins *Book of Psalms*, "set forth and allowed to be sung in all the churches of the people together, before and after Morning and Evening Prayer, as also before and after Sermons; and, moreover, in private houses, for their godly solace and comfort, laying apart all ungodly Ballads, which tend only to the nourishment of vice and corrupting of youth." But for years such psalm-books were few, nor could many members of the congregation read. Therefore it fell to someone—usually a

137

deacon—to "line out" or "deacon out" the psalm; that is, to sing every line in turn so that the congregation might catch the words and tune of each and sing it after him.

When that duty was proffered Deacon Briggs, he first disdained, then reluctantly accepted it. Before long he was performing it with enthusiasm he could not altogether conceal. On the minister's announcing the psalm, a long, lank figure would pop up from the deacons' bench. Briggs would blow a blast on his pitch-pipe, snort, clear his throat and bellow:

"MakeajoyfulnoiseuntotheLo-ord, all ye la-a-a-ands—." . . .

The people would give him back an antiphonal echo, and the Deacon would vigorously continue, beating time like a windmill.

Yet not everyone, by any means, was contented by the performance. One day Sophy and her best friend Emily found some scurrilous verses scratched on the back of one of the pews. When they read them, they could scarcely suppress their shocked titters. Somebody—likely that scamp Elijah Cushing—had traced with a knife-point:

"Could poor King David but for once
To Salem Church repair,
And hear his Psalms thus warbled out,
Good Lord, how he would swear!" *

Psalms had been the entering wedge for music. Next strong sentiment urged the formation of a choir. Deacon Briggs opposed it mightily. A choir to sing hymns, not taken bodily from Holy Writ like the psalms, and sing them in part-harmony! "Next comes popery!" he direfully warned. But the demand was too insistent, even for him to block, and he was compelled to yield though not without reservations and restrictions. He would still line out the psalms, he would sing in the choir himself, and he would select the hymns to be

*Printed in the American Apollo, Boston, April 20, 1792, with the title: "Lines written, rather out of temper, on a Pannel in one of the Pews of S——m Church."

sung. On those points the old curmudgeon was adamant, and the Elders and others of the deacons stood with him.

So a choir was formed and placed in a singing-gallery—the men and the women seated separately, of course, with an aisle between them. Glances exchanged by the young men and maidens were even more frequent and ardent, now they were singing together. There was no swain whose gaze did not stray from his music toward the two pretty girls standing side by side in the front row, especially when sunbeams streamed through a window to make Sophy's fair hair glisten like gold and Emily's titian tresses gleam like burnished copper. Nor were the two maidens altogether attentive to psalm or sermon; least so, certainly, when Elijah Cushing was home on vacation from Harvard College. Although Emily was her best friend, it piqued Sophy decidedly that whenever Elijah looked toward them, Emily would assume a seraphic expression and shift to soprano from alto, her proper part. You could attract more attention singing soprano, particularly if you came in a little ahead of the beat. It was ridiculous how some females made fools of themselves over men. And surely no maid with red hair, striking though it was, should try to look seraphic—not in Sophy's opinion.

The choir sounded forth the praises of the Lord with vim and volume but, alas, with little else. Fresh and young some of its voices were, but they were untrained, and few of the choristers had more than a remote idea of how to read their parts. Then there was Deacon Briggs' distressing determination upon singing counter-tenor. Reaching for that high-pitched part, designed for boys' voices, he emitted a series of falsetto shrieks which wrought havoc with the harmony and almost destroyed decorum. Once, leaving meeting, Sophy dared murmur to Elijah; "Father sounded like one of the damnèd souls he makes us sing of so oft," and the handsome student almost choked with laughter.

Indeed the Deacon persisted in choosing only the gloomiest and most dismal of hymns. Sophy and Emily could not restrain a few shudders when they had to sing such of the Deacon's selections as Hymn 44: *Hell, or the Vengeance of God.*

With holy fear and humble song,
The dreadful God our souls adore;
Reverence and awe become the tongue
That speaks the terrors of his power.

Far in the deep where darkness dwells,
The land of horror and despair,
Justice has built a dismal hell,
And laid her store of vengeance there.

Eternal plagues and heavy chains,
Tormenting racks and fiery coals,
And darts t'inflict immortal pains,
Dipt in the blood of damnèd souls.

Tremble, my soul, and kiss the Son!
Sinners, obey thy Saviour's call,
Else your damnation hastens on,
And hell gapes wide to wait your fall!

Yet sometimes the minister came to the choir's rescue and called, Deacon Briggs regardless, for less doleful anthems such as Watts' *Creation* and *Rocky Nook*. Favored, too, by the singers were hymns written for fuguing, where one part stated the theme and continued in counterpoint while the other parts at intervals gave the answer. Fuguing, thought Sophy, was fun, and even her father betrayed a fondness for it, especially in selections where the counter-tenor was featured.

But it was fuguing that caused all the tribulation upon a certain disastrous Sabbath.

The fatal fugues were embodied in an anthem in praise of the Lord's mercy. One verse was rendered and the second well launched without the slightest foreboding. Sang the choir:

He careth for the fatherless,
He feeds the hungry poor,
And in the pious He delights. . . .

The score then called for fuguing, based on the third line, and various parts proclaimed:

> And in the pi-
> And in the pi-
> And in the pi-ous He delights.

Mistress Goodale, whose mind was on the mince pie she planned to bake next day, looked up startled. But nobody else seemed to notice anything odd. On coursed the choir, and now the basses stated a theme and were answered:

> We'll catch the flee-
> We'll catch the flee-
> We'll catch the flee-ting hour.

Still nothing ludicrous struck the congregation. Nobody even scratched. It was not until the women's voices earnestly chanted a following passage that the dreadful debacle took place. Slowly but fervently sopranos and altos trilled:

> O for a man-
> O for a man-

Sophy and Emily, who both happened to be bestowing a sidelong glance on Elijah as they sang, stopped singing suddenly on the second "man-." Both blushed hotly. Emily giggled. At the same moment Elijah caught it. He was utterly unable to smother a whoop of laughter. In the ensuing confusion, hardly anyone heard the choir finish the fuguing with:

> O for a man-sion in the skies.

Naturally such unseemly levity and lewd mirth could not be tolerated in the house of the Lord. Forthwith—Deacon Briggs saw to it promptly—the choir was abolished, and his daughter was forbidden to see anything further of Master

Elijah Cushing. Duly chastened, that young scalawag returned
to Harvard where, perhaps, such godless goings-on were con-
doned.

No more unfortunate moment could have been chosen
for starting a singing-school in Salem than the week following
the frivolous fuguing. Yet how was Samuel Wadsworth to
know of the choir catastrophe? The singing-master had taken
quarters in town and published his announcement before he
heard of the ill favor in which music had come to be held by
Deacon Briggs and other authorities.

Master Wadsworth was not one to beat a retreat. He made
it known that he would conduct a singing-school, willy-nilly,
for four weeks, collecting a small fee from each student. His
advertisement was craftily phrased.

SAMUEL WADSWORTH

Begs leave to inform the Publick, but the Female Sex in
particular, that he has opened a SINGING-SCHOOL for
their use at his Dwelling-House near the Town-House,
to be kept on Tuesday and Friday Evenings, from 6 to
9 o'clock. If any of the Sex are desirous of being instructed in this beautiful Science, they shall be instructed
in the newest Method.

> Ye Female Sex, I pray draw near,
> To Music sweet pray lend an Ear;
> Young Virgins all with beauteous Voice,
> Make music Harmony your Choice.

Philo Musico

Well Master Wadsworth knew that it would suffice to enroll the maidens in his singing-school. A burning interest in
song would shortly thereafter develop among the young men.
Thus experience had taught the itinerant teacher in all his
journeying about the country.

The angry opposition of Deacon Briggs quickly manifested
itself. No good could come of a singing-school, he declared.

How could it improve the choir? No longer was there a choir. This frivoling could only lead to profane song and devilment of divers sorts. He had heard that singers nowadays actually were being hired to sing at funerals in New Hampshire and, to boot, provided costly entertainment of rum, brandy, cider, pies, fried nuts, cheese, and tobacco.

Master Wadsworth retorted that he was a friend and disciple of William Billings, highly esteemed in Boston for his compositions of sacred music. Some of them were said to have been humbly scored upon leather hides, for Billings was a tanner. The singing-master had brought with him copies of Billings' newly-published collection entitled, *The New England* Psalm Singer; or, American Chorister, containing a number of Psalm tunes, Anthems, and Canons. In four and five Parts (Never before published), Composed by William Billings, a Native of Boston, in New England. Matt.xxii.16: 'Out of the Mouth of Babes and sucklings hast thou perfected praise.' James v. 13: 'Is any Merry? Let him sing Psalms!' *

"Is any Merry?" That was the keynote. The young people of the town and the surrounding farms longed to be merry together. There was so much hard work and so little frolicking. And you could be merry singing—even psalms. That they had found out in the choir. The maidens and young men wrought on their parents with persuasions. Master Wadsworth moved mightily to the attack. In Deacon Briggs' favorite tavern, the singing-master rose one evening and hurled an encomium of his friend Billings' on the power of music full in the teeth of the doughty old deacon.

"Great art thou, O Music!" he declaimed. "And with thee there is no competitor. Thy powers by far transcend the powers of physic, and the reception of thee is far more grateful than the nauseous drugs of the Apothecary; thou art as early as the Creation: for when the foundation of the earth was laid, the morning stars sang together and shouted for joy.

"Thou art able to extract the poison from the venomous bite of the Tarantula, which baffles the skill of the Physician.

*Boston, 1770. Printed by Edes & Gill.

Thou canst make stammering people pronounce distinctly and without hesitation."

Deacon Briggs had grown so furious that he sputtered in his mug of flip, striving vainly to speak.

"Deacon," Samuel Wadsworth offered, "let me but enroll you in my singing-school, and yon impediment in your speech——"

Waiting to hear no more, the raging deacon stormed out into the night.

An effective flank attack was launched from Cambridge. Elijah Cushing, hearing of the singing-school controversy, unearthed a musty document in the Harvard Library: William Byrd's *Psalms and Sonnets and Songs of Sadness and Piety*, printed in 1588. He had broadsides struck off of its preface, which set forth these reasons for learning to sing:

1. It is knowledge easilie taught and quicklie learned when there is a good master and an apte scholar.

2. The exercise of singinge is delightfulle to nature, and good to preserve the health of man.

3. It dothe strengthene all partes of ye breaste, and doth open ye pipes.

4. It is a singular good remedie for a stutteringe and stammeringe in ye speeche.

5. It is the best meanes to preserve a perfette pronunciation and to make a good orator.

6. It is the only waye to knowe where nature hath bestowed ye benefytte of a good voyce,—whiche gifte is soe rare yt there is not one amongste a thousand yt hath it, and in manie yt excellente gifte is lost because they want an arte to expresse nature.

7. There is not anie musicke of instruments whatsoever comparable to yt whiche is made of ye voyces of men where ye voyces are good and ye same well sorted and ordered.

8. The better ye voyce is, the meeter it is to honor and

serve God therewith; and ye voyce of man is chieflie to be employed toe yt end. *Omnis spiritus laudet Dominum.*

> 'Since singinge is soe good a thinge
> I with all men woulde learne to singe.'

It was to Emily that Elijah sent the bundle of broadsides for distribution. Emily lost no time in apprising Sophy of that fact. While Sophy vainly tried to conceal the deep hurt she felt from Elijah's having ignored her, the other girl, a glint of malice in her eyes, comforted:

"Take it not ill, Sophy. You may help to give them around. Be assured that Elijah would have sent some to you also but for your father's hostility. Ah, what a clever lad he is!"

Sophy managed a smile. "He is in truth. I doubt not you have already written him your thanks for these. Surely they will establish our singing-school in father's despite."

"Indeed the post already has my letter," Emily answered. "Oh, Sophy, can you guess what I wrote?" She giggled. "You know that couplet of verse at the end of the screed about 'I with all men would learn to sing?' Well, I did devise another version of it of my own. Would you hear it?"

"Aye." Sophy nodded rather coldly. She never had noticed before that her best friend simpered.

Emily coyly recited, simpering the while:

> "Since singing is so good a thing,
> I with *one man* would learn to sing."

She giggled again. "Will not Elijah think me monstrous clever?" she demanded.

"No," said Sophy shortly. "He will think you a forward, bold virgin."

The former friends flounced away from each other.

Singing-school—all Deacon Briggs' fulminations had failed to halt it—was vastly successful from the start. Pressure from within and without his own home had even forced the deacon to permit the attendance of his daughter Sophia. School would come to naught without her lovely soprano voice, the old man heard from all quarters, and so he had nodded a gruff assent, dissembling his pride.

Two evenings a week saw singing-school conducted in the school-house. Eagerly the pupils flocked to it, the young men escorting the maidens. They ranged themselves along the long benches behind the desks. Master Wadsworth had informed them that now, since they were under instruction, they need not sit separated by sex and part. Shyly at first the song-books were shared. Hands supporting them beneath touched—were hastily readjusted—somehow met again. Soft eyes, lustrous in the mellow light of the tallow candles, ventured to glance up briefly from notes into a kindling gaze awaiting them. Voices rose in full-throated song, and youthful spirits soared as joyously.

No lugubrious laments for Samuel Wadsworth. Hymns in which he rehearsed his scholars were the cheerful ones which William Billings favored—hymns where often the sacred words were adapted to lively old dance tunes like *Babbling Echo* or *Little Pickle*. Or anthems such as:

> O, praise the Lord with one consent,
>   And in this grand design,
> Let Britain and the Colonies
>   Unanimously join.

And what if you did have to sing that last word "jine" in order to comply with Billings' rhyme?

Yet though young hearts were attuned to harmony in the singing, there was an undercurrent of feud between the leading soprano and the leading alto. And it was expected to grow worse when Elijah Cushing came home on vacation. (Some wondered why Emily had been receiving letters from him and Sophy none.)

Meanwhile neither girl lacked beaux or partisans. They divided into opposing camps. Each was tagged with a name on that evening when a spirited exchange took place between the rival maidens.

Emily had been displaying a letter from Elijah during a recess in the singing. To the accompaniment of much giggling, she declared coyly:

"You may not see all he has written, but you may see this side of the sheet where Elijah has made both a picture and a poem for me."

She showed them a drawing of a fat cupid playing upon a lyre and holding a bunch of grapes in his mouth. Below were the lines:

> Perhaps a bosom may be found
> That ne'er was touched with dulcet sound,
> That wine had ne'er the power to warm,
> Nor love, resistless love, to charm;
> But who will not his heart resign,
> Assail'd by music, love, and wine?

"Wine!" sniffed a local swain. "Do they think of aught else at Harvard College?"

"Aye," Emily answered with a taunting toss of her head in the direction of Sophy. "Aye. Of love."

When there was a pause in the hum of laughing, teasing talk, Sophy was heard to remark in distinct tones to the swain beside her:

"William, have you remarked Emily's mouth when she sings. I can think of naught, as I watch her, but a trap door."

Emily flushed and bit her lip but her retort was soon ready. Addressing the man by her side, she observed loudly:

"Nathan, 'tis a pity about Sophy. She must soon leave the class, since she scarce can open her lips to sing. Poor maid, she is threatened with lockjaw."

Amid the laughter, Master Wadsworth rapped for the resumption of the class. Thereafter the class arrayed itself into two groups: the "Locks" and the "Traps."

It was the last session of singing-school. So tunefully did his scholars render an anthem, Master Wadsworth was beside himself with pride as the young voices blended and answered one another and came together again like chiming bells. His mobile hands gestured toward one part after another, following the melody.

"Now here! Now there!" he cried out above the singing. "Now here again. Oh ecstatic! Push on, ye daughters and ye sons of harmony!"

Sophy's glorious soprano swept up the scale—to halt in midcareer. Elijah Cushing stood in the doorway. The anthem ended in a babble of greeting.

"Good friends, salutations," the student called back. "I bring you good tidings. Once more are we become the choir, and we shall sing again at meeting, come next Sabbath."

He held up a hand to still the chorus of questions. "How was it wrought? Why, I out-deaconed the deacon. Aye, in his very den. I confronted him with the carrier of the post to whom I had paid many a shilling to deliver letters—letters unanswered." He bent a frown on Sophy. "The carrier swore he had put my missives in the deacon's own hands. 'But,' quoth I, 'they were not for the deacon but for his fair daughter. Who dared withhold what rightfully was hers?' "

Sophy's hands fluttered to her breast and clasped tightly. So he had been writing to her, and she had lacked the wit to guess why his letters went astray—and lacked any faith in him, too.

"Friends," Elijah continued, "I forebear to state how the deacon answered my question. Suffice it that he roared at me like a lion. He bellowed like a bull or even a behemoth. When he paused to breathe, I shook him by the hand, astounding him vastly. 'Sir,' quoth I, 'has any ever told you that you have a bass voice of most admirable power and profundity? Such a voice would be the making of any choir.' " Elijah grinned and finished, "The rest you will guess. Our choir revives— without the old counter-tenor but with a new bass."

When the tumult of mirth and talk had ended, Master Wadsworth led his class in a farewell song. Half way through it, Sophy slipped away. Why wait to make vain explanations and watch Emily's triumph? She slipped out into the starry night and hastened homeward.

Poignant strains of song followed her. Then there were quick steps following her, too. Hands, strong but gentle, grasped her arms and turned her around. Incredulous, she gazed up into Elijah Cushing's face.

"Your mouth, Sophy," he chided. " 'Tis gaping wide. And I had thought you were of the 'Locks,' not the 'Traps.' "

Hastily she closed her lips. Elijah, the scamp, bent down.

Strains of song drifted still from the school-house—such music as there was at Creation when the foundation of the earth was laid and the morning stars sang together and shouted for joy.

GERMANS OVER THE RIVER

An Artillery Sergeant Reports an Amphibious Operation

1776

Brought armies o'er by sudden pressings
Of Hanoverians, Swiss, and Hessians.
John Trumbull: *McFingal*

There they were on the other side of the river. Germans, and no doubt about it. Over there on the other side of an American river, holding the American town we'd retreated from and given up to them.

It couldn't happen here. Plenty of people would have told you that. But there they were: honest-to-goodness Heines, actual Krauts. I saw 'em with my own eyes. I even shot at 'em. A squad started to launch a boat to come over and take a look at our bank. My gun heaved some hardware at 'em and they decided it wasn't jolly boating weather.

How come there was a German Army on American soil? While you couldn't say we were particularly friendly, we hadn't declared war on each other. How did they get here? Where was our Navy when this G.E.F. was coming across?

Search me for the answers. How would I, just a sergeant of artillery, know when there hasn't been any real news for anybody since this ruckus started? The whole country is in the damndest confusion. Riots, sabotage, pitched battles with fifth columnists, everything disorganized. And in the midst of it here is a German Army on our home grounds—crack troops who have been polishing off European opposition since the time of Freddy the Great. In spite of the fact that they are invaders, they're far better supplied and equipped than we are. Our whole supply system has been broken down under

153

inefficiency, graft, dirty work at the political crossroads, and
what not. It's a disgrace, considering our national resources,
that an American Army should be in the shape we are: poorly
armed, hungry, ragged, and cold.

Just the same we're going to attack, and that's no latrine
rumor. We're going to have a go at those birds over there beyond the river. It's a wild risk. We've got only a slim chance.
But there isn't a file in this man's army who isn't rarin' to go.
It's dawned on a lot of us at last that this land of ours is worth
keeping and that to keep it we've got to fight for it now that
these German sons have come over to take it away from us.
If only we'd been readier and met 'em more than half way!
But it's too late for that now.

There are no bridges over this river, and we've got most
all the boats. Brother Boche is content to wait on the other
side till it freezes over, which will be any day now. Then he'll
walk across and smash us. He's as cocky as that about it, and
the hell of it is he probably can do it. He's in strong force
there in the town—infantry, artillery, and cavalry—with heavy
reinforcements up the line. A spy of ours says that for the
first few days they stood to arms in full equipment—infantry
sleeping that way and artillery horses harnessed and hitched
all night. After a bit they relaxed, but they've got plenty of
pickets out. The old Prooshian in command holds formal
guard mount every day, his band going full blast. The music
drifts to us across the river and sounds grand. We've got nothing but buglers, all terrible. But with all their guard mount-
ing, the Germans haven't fortified either the river bank or the
town. Our scouts report that their sentries aren't any too alert
at night because of their general feeling of contempt for Americans. We're no soldiers, they say, just a bunch of farmers.

Okay, we're farmers. As a matter of fact, a lot of us farmed
before we joined the Army, including, they say, the Commander-in-Chief who, though he was a gentleman farmer,
took it serious and made it pay. But farmers are fighters, and
don't let anybody tell you different. They'll fight to hold
ground, the land they've ploughed and sweated over to make

a living out of. So farmers and all of us who've seen some of the burning and looting the Germans have done are going to ferry over that river tonight and sock 'em.

Tonight's the night. Orders are out. It must be surprise and a quick knockout before help can reach them. If we fail tonight we may never get another chance.

We break camp in the dark. Marching order at night is bad enough, but now there's sleet and it's freezing cold. The snow is crusty underfoot, and a lot of the boys have no shoes but only sacking wrapped around their feet. Those infantry columns passing us will be leaving blood-stained tracks long before we get where we're going tonight.

"Sergeant!" That's my Battery Commander popping up beside me. Kind of runty but a game little guy and he knows his stuff. "Sergeant," he orders, "mount up and take your gun down to the river for embarkation."

I salute and we mount up and roll. Down by the river our broad-beamed artillery brigadier is bawling out the orders given him for transmission by the tall figure at his side. It's the Commander-in-Chief himself, they say. I get a good look at him when he's reading a dispatch by a sheltered light. Man, he's one cold looking general—pinched face, red nose, and all. It gives you a feeling of confidence to see him taking it with the rest of us, not inside hugging a fire.

A regiment of marines is manning the boats and barges for the ferrying. Seacoast men, fishermen and so on, this is their stuff and they're doing a job. If you doubt it, they, being typical marines, will tell you. But it's something to see—the way they're shoving off loaded to the guards with infantry on that black river, a stiff wind churning up waves and ice cakes grinding and banging away.

Back shoots a skiff with good news. Our vanguard is over and has established a bridgehead which they'll hold till the whole outfit gets across. And no alarm has been given! Where are those Krauts, letting us catch 'em asleep like this? Thought they were better soldiers. I up and ask the Captain.

"Sergeant, the enemy is engaged in festivities this evening," he says in the highfalutin' talk he likes. "In short, the foemen have abandoned themselves to revelry, not to say debauchery. At this moment vast quantities of the potent local brew are gurgling down Germanic gullets and they are becoming obfusticated."

"The Captain means they're throwing a party and getting cockeyed?" I interpret with a sigh of envy.

"Correct, Sergeant," says he. "And can you doubt that the General counted on that very circumstance? By now they are well liquored. When we arrive——"

"Will there be any left, sir?" I'm asking anxiously when our talk is broken off. It's our turn to embark.

My squad manhandles our gun aboard a barge and lashes it fast. Then it's time to lead on the team. Our big stallions don't like the idea of a voyage. They cut up and take considerable persuasion. First chance I get I'm going to trade 'em for a team of geldings off some other battery's picket line. Fire and spirit are all right in their place, but this isn't it. But at last we manage it and shove off, rowed through the black, icy river, gunwales nearly flush with the water and the blame barge like to sink any minute.

A light boat eases past us. Our brigadier is in it, I can tell by his foghorn voice talking to the C-in-C. I prick up my ears. Maybe the General will say something historic I can repeat to my kids when they ask what daddy did in the great war. Now what do you think he comes out with to our broad-bottomed brigadier? Our dignified General calls to him, "Shift your arse and trim the boat."

It got a laugh fit to wake the dead or the Germans. That General of ours is human, which is more than you can say of some of 'em. It's no brasshatted stuffed-shirt that's running this show tonight.

Now we land. The ground sure feels good. Hitch and limber up. Off we roll after the infantry through the night. It's bad footing for the horses, and the gun carriages slip and skid to hellandgone. But it's silence in the ranks now, and nobody even cusses out loud. You wouldn't think a long column could move so quiet. Miles are ticked off. Looks like we're going to circle around and hit the town from the other end where the Krauts least expect us. Walk 'em out, drivers. We've got to get into position before dawn.

Once the whole show is close to being given away. A dog dashes out of a farmhouse barking, but all of a sudden it's choked off: some doughboy has clouted the poor beast. Still it beats me why some fifth columnist hasn't spotted us and warned the enemy. As a matter of fact one of those babies tried to, we learned later. He saw us and double-timed into town, howling for the Commanding Officer. They wouldn't let him in the house, so he sent in a note. The head Heine, pretty well potted by that time, was shooting craps. The bones must have been hot for him, for all he does is say "Don't bother me" in Dutch and stuffs the note in his pocket, unread.

Well, we're about set to bother him plenty, shortly. We split into two columns, and my battery and two others move up to head off the column on the main road into town. There I catch another glimpse of our General. Some infantry officer is complaining to him that his outfit's ammunition has been lost. "Damn it!" snaps the Old Man. "You've got bayonets, haven't you? Use them!"

Snow muffles hoofs and wheels as we take the lead. Now it's the half-light before dawn. We can't go undiscovered much longer. We'll be in action any minute now. I get that dryness in the throat and the funny feeling in the pit of the stomach you do before a scrap. You know you're going to be scared as hell and hope to heaven you won't show it. Somebody's going to get killed in this ruckus, but you console yourself that it'll be the other fellow, poor guy.

Shots rattle up ahead. The party's on.

We top a rise, and there are the roofs of the town, white with snow. It looks clean and cosy and pretty—like my home town. There are women and kids in those houses—like I've got at home. I hope the townsfolks are down in the cellars by now. There'll be hell to pay down there soon. I get thinking what might happen to my town and my family. There's no telling whether they'll be out of the path of the invasion. God, we've got to stop these German bastards here and now!

Off to the flank I see an enemy outpost detail come boiling out of a farmhouse, catching up their stacked arms and opening fire on our doughboys. Big fellows, those Boches, looking like they deserve all of the tough rep as fighters that came ahead of 'em. We're just a citizen army tackling professionals, but we're so fighting-mad we forget that. We've caught 'em off guard and we rock 'em back on their heels. All their pickets are driven back in on the town, our sharpshooters picking off their officers and noncoms. We roll past a lieutenant, dying by the side of the road. Just a kid—can't be more than 18. I feel kind of sorry for him even if he is a Boche. All along the line we're pushing them in, giving them no chance to rally.

Our guns are in action now, dropping shells in among them. Suddenly two German guns come dashing forward. The sharp, black eyes of my little Battery Commander spots 'em. Quick orders, and we let 'em have it. We catch one of their gun teams at the dead gallop and fair ruin it. Horses, gun, and cannoneers pile up in a mass of wreckage. The other piece unlimbers and fires six rounds before we get the range and smash it. When the smoke clears away, only the platoon commander and the gunner are still on their feet. They leave in a hurry, abandoning the gun.

Our lads sweep into the town, and it's house-to-house fighting. You've got to hand it to these Heines, though. Surprised as they are, the steady, disciplined regiments form up and blaze away with volleys. The streets are so dense with powder smoke it looks like a heavy fog's come down. The smack of bullets against brick walls mingles with the rattle of hailstones on roofs to sound like a thousand rolling drums.

They say the German commander was still asleep when our assault on the town began, and his adjutant had to rout him out. In spite of a terrific hangover, the old boy pulls on his uniform, climbs on his horse, and starts to rally his men.

Four guns of another battery and two of mine get into position on a rise of ground where we command the full length of two streets jammed with Germans. Man, we bowl ironware down 'em like bowling balls, and there aren't many pins left to be set up in the other alley. Our infantry floods along in a charge. I see an American captain get shot through both hands. He keeps going just the same, leading his company. So does a lieutenant who's hit in the shoulder. The way the blood spurts it must be an artery, but he clamps it off with his fingers and never stops. You can't beat nerve like that.

Hand-to-hand fighting rages through the narrow streets. The Krauts give way before American bayonets. Our infantry swarms over their guns and silences them. German remnants are trying desperately now to break through our encirclement. Wherever they emerge, our artillery blasts them, and rifle fire rolls up their flanks. Down in yonder orchard the German commander is riding around trying to get his men to turn and counterattack with the bayonet. But they're dropping by the dozen and they haven't got what it takes anymore. Some of our sharpshooters crack down on the commander, and he topples out of his saddle with two bullets through the belly. He'll soon be under the American soil he's tried to take from us.

The Germans are in full retreat now, trying to break through and make a getaway. Everywhere they turn our boys are waiting for them. We've got the fords, the roads, the passes. A German officer tries to parley, but a general of ours snaps at him: "Tell your commanding officer that if you do not surrender immediately, I'll blow you to pieces!" That's the kind of language they understand. Guns are tossed away, and hands begin to go up. One outfit after another surrenders. We've got most of them. Very few escaped. We've captured 868 officers and men. The German casualties in killed and wounded are 106. And our loss is only four wounded.

As battles go, this isn't such a big one—this one we've won. There are a lot more Germans over here, and we'll have to be taking them on. But on this winter's day we've beaten them to a frazzle. They can be licked, and Americans can do it!

*   *   *   *   *

This story of a German invasion and a battle on American soil is not fiction. While told in modern language and as if it were happening today, it is an historically accurate account of the Battle of Trenton, December 26, 1776. The sergeant-narrator is the only fictitious character. The Commander-in-Chief is of course George Washington, and the broad-beamed artillery Brigadier is General Henry Knox. The Battery Commander—Alexander Hamilton. That officer who gallantly continued to lead a charge in spite of a bullet-severed artery in his shoulder is James Monroe, who survived to become President and establish a Doctrine to the effect that America is for Americans.

THEY CALL IT BUNDLING

*Lieutenant Marbry, of His Majesty's Foot, Notes a Quaint American Custom ***

1777

Nature's request is, give me rest.
　Our bodies seek repose.
Night is the time, and it's no crime
　To bundle in our clothes.

Since in a bed, a man, a maid
　May bundle and be chaste;
It doth no good to burn up wood;
　It is a needless waste.

Let coat and shift be turned adrift,
　And breeches take their flight.
And honest man and virgin can
　Lie quiet all the night.

　　　　　　　　　　　Anon.

*Based in part on the Remarkable chronicle of a young British officer: Thomas Anburey's *Travels Through the Interior Parts of America*.

It was still bewildering, still hardly credible that an army of his Brittanic Majesty, George III, had surrendered to a rabble of raw Americans. Yet Lieutenant Geoffrey Marbry had seen it happen with his own eyes after the disastrous battle at Saratoga—had seen his commander, Gentleman Johnny Burgoyne, yield his sword to the Rebel General Gates.

"We bowed with becoming dignity to a reverse of fortune," the Lieutenant kept reassuring himself. "Honor is safe. General Burgoyne is not to blame for our melancholy catastrophe. Mortal man cannot command success."

But it had been a humiliating scene, that day of the surrender, when regiment after regiment of British and Hessian troops had marched down to pile their arms before the ranks of their conquerors while American drums rolled and their fifes shrilled *Yankee Doodle*. The Yankees had adopted that tune, once contemptuously flung at them, as their favorite paean ever since the Bunker's Hill affair. They esteemed it as warlike as *The Grenadier's March*. Hearing it played at Saratoga was not a little mortifying. And yet, as Marbry wrote in his first letter to his wife after the surrender: "As we filed before the American Army, I did not observe the least disrespect or even taunting looks, but all was mute astonishment and pity. The antipathy long shown us was consigned to oblivion."

The war was over now for Lieutenant Marbry and the rest of the long column of prisoners, being marched eastward by their American guards. In crisp fall weather they crossed the Green Mountains. Crowds gathered along the route to watch the column pass, an ordeal not easy for the vanquished Britons. Once indeed the temper of Lieutenant M'Neil, of the Ninth Regiment, broke its tether at the sight of an old woman, who must have been nigh 100, goggling at him and the other prisoners of war as they marched by. He shouted at her:

"So, you old fool, you must come and see the lions."

"Lions? Lions?" the crone called back with great archness. "I declare now I think you look more like lambs!"

It was well to think twice before you bandied words with the Yankees. Their tongues were quick.

On another occasion a bevy of curious women approached Lord Napier and several other British officers. "We hear you have got a Lord among you," said one female. A captain laughed, pointing to Napier and reciting all his titles like a herald. A buxom dame scanned the nobleman from head to foot, lifted her eyes and hands toward Heaven and exclaimed: "Well, for my part, if that be a Lord, I never desire to see any Lord but the Lord Jehovah!"

These and many other anecdotes of America Lieutenant Marbry wrote home, and his letters were perused with interest by his wife. But it was a later long screed of his that so intrigued young Mistress Marbry that she called in her two dearest friends to hear it read. The letter dealt with a curious custom the lieutenant first had observed when he was quartered in a log cabin one night during the march.

Here in America (wrote Lieutenant Marbry) you must know that there are few inns. He who travels must depend for shelter upon farmhouses or cabins along his way, nor are their accommodations often ample. Houses are small, rooms few, beds preempted by the householder, his consort, and his progeny. Yet hospitality is seldom refused.

So I found when on our march we came to the village called Williamstown in the province of Massachusetts. The billet assigned me was a small log-hut of only two rooms, a bed in each. Now the Americans have remarkable good featherbeds, extremely neat and clean. Nonetheless I prefer my own hard camp mattress and would readily have spread it for the night in a corner of the hut, but owing to the badness of the roads and the weakness of my mare, my servant had not arrived with my baggage when it was time to retire. Plainly I must occupy one of the two beds, so I inquired which of the good wife.

"Mister Leftenant," said she, "Jonathan and I will sleep in this, our daughter Ruth and you shall sleep in that."

Thus (wrote Lieutenant Marbry) was I first apprised of a strange practice of the Americans. They call it bundling. Ruth, by the bye, was a very pretty, black-eyed girl, of about sixteen or seventeen.

"Oh, la!" exclaimed Mistress Marbry's best friend, Dolly.

" 'Very pretty . . . black-eyed . . . sixteen,' " repeated her other best friend, Lady Jane, eyebrows raised high.

" 'By the bye' indeed!" sniffed Dolly.

"Read on!" urged both Mistress Marbry's best friends.

I was moved (wrote Lieutenant Marbry) to inquire into this matter of bundling. It was, I learned, not peculiar to New England but also owned numerous and enthusiastic adherents in Pennsylvania and in New York * where the Dutch call it *queesting* which is to say, a quest for a wife. Some

---

Vide Washington's Irving's *Knickerbocker's History of New York.*
". . . A singular custom . . . known by the name of *bundling.*
. . . This ceremony was likewise, in those primitive times, considered as an indispensable preliminary to matrimony, their courtships commencing where ours usually finish, by which means they acquired that intimate acquaintance with each other's good qualities before marriage, which has been pronounced by philosophers the sure basis of a happy union. Thus early did this cunning and ingenious people display a shrewdness at making a bargain, which has ever since distinguished them, and a strict adherence to the good old vulgar maxim about 'buying a pig in a poke.' "

Yankees insist that the custom by no means originated in America but was imported from Holland—and from England. Albeit I encountered it as a rite of hospitality, it is essentially a form of courtship, chiefly employed during the cold season.

Be assured that the winters in the northern parts of this country are bitter. Icy blasts blow fiercely down the chimneys, held at bay only by a roaring log fire in the hearth. In the room where the fire burns—and in that room only—is warmth and comfort. Of an evening, the day's work done, comes a faithful swain to court a daughter of the house. Where may the young couple sit save before the hearth with her parents and others of the family? Nowhere else or they freeze. Some lovers resort to an instrument which is called a courting-stick: a hollow tube eight feet in length, fitted with ear- and mouth-pieces. Through this, young man and maid, seated on either side of the hearth, whisper their endearments, unheard by kith and kin. Yet you will acknowledge, my dear, that this device is not altogether adequate to courtship.

The old folk could, to be sure, retire to their own bed, leaving the fire to the lovers. Yet consider how much wood and how many candles must needs be burned. And all too soon the swain must leave to trudge ten or twelve weary miles back to his own dwelling through snow or storm. Both economy and humanity urge an alternative: that man and maiden bundle together.

With the approval and full consent of her parents, the young couple lie down together upon a featherbed and pull its warm coverlet over them. It matters not whether the bed be in the same room with that of her parents. Indeed her mother may oblige by tucking them in, bidding them a good night as she retires to her own apartment. Unheeded, lad and lass whisper the night through. No harm need come of it. They have lain down fully-clothed, save for their shoes and mayhap some of their outer garments. Sometimes, 'tis said, a special bundling dress is worn by the maid—a garment with legs, like breeches, drawn at the waist and neck with strings tied with a very strong knot, and over it ordinary apparel.

A maiden may bundle virtuously and innocently. A sofa in summer, say the Yankees, is more dangerous for young lovers than a bundling bed in winter. Bear in mind that a girl does not admit any passing gallant to her bed but only a favored suitor, and he only after long and continued urging. Where there are no bad intentions, there can be no evil consequences.

"Aye, Madge," Dolly interrupted Mistress Marbry's reading, "but what of the Leftenant and that black-eyed wench?"

"He returns to that later in the letter."

"Skip to that part," Lady Jane begged.

"Pray, do, my dear," Dolly seconded earnestly.

"In good time. Be patient," Mistress Marbry reproved her best friends.

Later in the course of our march south (wrote Lieutenant Marbry) I was presented to the Marquis de Chastellux, Major-General in the French Army. The French for reasons of their own came hither to aid the Americans and are our enemies. Yet I found pleasure in conversation with this nobleman, an officer of distinction and polished gentleman, after forced association for so long with boorish Americans. It chanced that the Marquis and I fell into a discussion of bundling. He declared that while the custom may be practiced innocently at the outset, oft it did not finish so. He asked, reciting a rhyme current here:

> "But where's the man that fire can
> Into his bosom take,
> Or go through coals on his foot soles
> And not a blister make?"

More than once, the Marquis told me, he has encountered here unwed women, big with child, living unreproached with their parents.

"May it not be just," he demanded, "that among a people so remote from us in every respect as these Americans, a girl who should resign herself too hastily to the man she is engaged to, with the consent even of her parents, should not be censured? Consider that the girl is without distrust, in a country where such an idea is never taught them, where morals are so far in their infancy. Shall such commerce between two free persons be deemed less blameworthy than the infidelities, the caprices, and even the coquetries which destroy the peace of so many European families?

"This freedom prevails among all ranks here, particularly so among the middling classes and the common people," affirmed the Marquis. "In Philadelphia I have seen a grave Quaker and his wife sitting on their bench at their door, as is the custom in that city in the summer evenings, and alongside them the 'prentice boy of 16 and the servant girl, or perhaps one of the daughters of the family, not only kissing and embracing but proceeding to such familiarities as would shock modesty and draw down the vengeance of the virtuous citizens of London. And all this not only without repression but even with marks of complacency on the part of the good old folk.

"Even the last slip is no essential blemish in the character of the frail fair one. Both sexes arrive early at puberty, their constitutions are warm, there are few restraints, and they lose no time in completing the great object, the populating of the country.

"Aye," finished De Chastellux, "the acquisition of a citizen in this country is so precious that a girl by bringing up her child seems to expiate the weakness which brought it into existence." *

"Is not that vastly interesting?" asked Mistress Marbry, laying down the letter.

"Madge, surely you are going to finish reading it!" Lady Jane cried.

"Even if you are content to leave your husband in that log-hut with that American hussy, we are not," Dolly spoke up.

Mistress Marbry smiled teasingly and read on.

*Chastellux. *Travels in North-America.* 2v. Dublin, 1786.

To return to my narrative (Lieutenant Marbry wrote), I was much astonished at the proposal of the parents of the fair Ruth that she and I should occupy the second bed. I offered to sit up all night. Whereupon her father immediately replied:

"Mister Leftenant, you won't be the first man our Ruth has bundled with, will it, Ruth?"

Ruth coyly answered: "No, father, not by many but it will be with the first Britainer."

In this dilemma what could I do? The smiling invitation of pretty Ruth—the eye, the lip, the—Lord ha' mercy, where am I going to? But wherever I may be going now, I did not go to bundle with her—in the same room with her father and mother, my kind host and hostess, too! I thought of that— I thought of more besides—to struggle with the passions of nature; to clasp Ruth in my arms—to do what? you'll ask, my dear? Why, to do nothing! For if amid all these temptations, the lovely Ruth had melted into kindness, she had been an outcast from the world, treated with contempt, abused by violence, left perhaps to perish! No, even if I had not been bound by bonds of matrimony to a fair young wife, I could not have allowed myself to be blessed by Ruth, only to have her become the victim of so vast a sacrifice.

Suppose how great the test of virtue must be, or how cold the American constitution, when this unaccountable custom is in hospitable repute, and perpetual practice.

Mistress Marbry ceased reading and expectantly eyed her two best friends, still all agog.

"But they contradict each other—your husband and the French general," Dolly bubbled. "Marbry says the American constitution is cold, and De Chastellux declares it so warm it melts all scruples."

"Well, one was a prisoner of war and the other an ally— and a Frenchman. That might make a difference," Lady Jane suggested helpfully.

"Anyway, my dear, 'tis good to know your husband is no longer exposed to the perils of war nor to any hardships save sleeping on the floor," said Dolly sweetly, rising to depart.

Mistress Marbry quizzically bade her best friends adieux. It had not seemed worthwhile to read them the letter's postscript.

It occurs to me (Lieutenant Marbry had written) that you might read this missive of mine to certain suspicious and feline friends of yours. Assuredly they will regard it as full of contradictions, omissions, and mendacities. Nothing will persuade them that I did not bundle with Ruth. However, you might ask them why, if I had aught on my conscience, would I write to you of the incident at all?

Your loving, loyal and unbundled husband,

Geoffrey

ADVICE TO A YOUNG MAN

Old Ben Franklin Imparts Some Worldly Wisdom *

1787

May I govern my passions with absolute sway,
Grow wiser and better as my strength wears away,
Without gout or stone, by a gentle decay.
Anon.: The Old Man's Wish.**

*Based on Franklin's writings.
**A favorite verse of Franklin's.

Old Ben Franklin sat writing at the desk in his apartment in Passy, suburban Paris. As he wrote, he sighed. A long exile, this latest one, serving his country in a foreign land. He was old now—past 80. Soon he must go home to die in his beloved America. His hair was snow-white against his coat of brown homespun and thin enough to make wearing his famous coonskin cap, even indoors, a wise precaution against drafts. But his eyes were bright and twinkling behind that handy device of his, the bifocal spectacles he was wearing, and his face, though wrinkled, was clean-shaven, thanks to his having turned his shaving-glass into a magnifying mirror. Just now, however, a sharp twinge darted through one foot. Ruefully Franklin wrote several more lines on a manuscript headed *Dialogue between Franklin and the Gout.*

Franklin. Oh! oh! for heaven's sake leave me! and I promise faithfully that from now on I shall play no more chess but shall take daily exercise and live temperately.

Gout. I know you too well. You promise beautifully: But after a few months of good health, you will go back to your old habits. Your fine promises will be forgotten like the forms of last year's clouds.

He laid down his quill and chuckled, glancing around his apartment. On the walls hung several choice prints: a Hogarth, a plate from James Stuart's *Antiquities of Athens,* and others. One corner was adorned by a marble statue of a woman, a voluptuous nude. Yonder stood his four-sided, pyramidal music stand and near it another of his inventions, the armonica, or musical glasses. By rubbing a finger on the rims of the glasses, filled to varying levels with water and revolved by a treadle, Franklin could play many a merry tune.

How often last night he had played that jolly catch, *Cama-*

rades, Lampons? At least two score times and drunk as many bottles of wine with the old friends, come to celebrate with him the anniversary of American Independence. Abbé André Morellet had bade him in advance to learn the tune. Then the Abbé had sung to it his specially-composed words: *A Drinking Song in Honor of Benjamin Franklin,** sung it to his host's accompaniment and with all hands joining in as soon as they caught its drift.

Glowing inwardly at the hearty tribute paid him, Franklin read over stanzas the Abbé had written down for him.

I

Though on bronze Franklin's
    name
Is engraven by fame,
More still his glory demands.
So with glasses in hands,
Voices, chime in.
Here's to our Benjamin.

II

Politics he can play.
As a toper he's gay,
The while an empire he founds.
See him call for more rounds,
Grave or agrin.
Some lad! our Benjamin.

III

Like an eagle bold, he
With his kite and his key
From heav'n its thunder he
    stole;
Of the lightning took toll
Mid fright'ning din.
Clever, our Benjamin.

IV

The American, untamed,
Liberty has reclaimed.
What two helped let freedom
    ring?
'Twas a sage and a king,
Efforts akin—
Louis and Benjamin.

V

Yankees fought not that fight
For a mere abstract right.
No, they formed firm battle line
To make free with our wine.
That idea pin
On good, old Benjamin.

VI

In the Congress they said
They would drink our wine red,
And 'twas for our good cham-
    pagne,
That they made a campaign,
Destined to win,
Long planned by Benjamin.

*The song appears in Morellet's *Mémoires sur le Dix-Huitième Siècle*. v. 1. Paris, 1821. This free translation of nine of its twelve stanzes is by Fairfax Downey.

VII

The inhuman English
Stated tea was the dish
To make the Rebels relax.
Then they slapped on a tax.
What vast chagrin
Was shown by Benjamin!

VIII

Oh, I would not persuade
That we England invade.
What use? We'd find no good
    cheer.
There they drink only beer.
Oh, grievous sin!
So says our Benjamin.

IX

If the tough British fleet
We could only defeat!
When we could victory boast,
We would teach them this toast:
Britons, chin-chin!
Here's health to Benjamin.

The old gentleman was smiling, as he finished, and moisture glistened in the corners of his eyes. There was none like the French—if they were fond of you—to do you honor. Had he reflected a while ago that he was in exile here? Not while good friends, Frenchmen and Frenchwomen, conspired to make him feel at home.

Someone was knocking rather diffidently at the door. *"Entrez, entrez,"* Franklin called, and when there was no response, said in English, "Well then, come in."

Entered then Jonathan Strange, a handsome young American who had called once previously. He was dressed in the mode but simply; his clubbed brown hair, tied back with a narrow black ribbon, was not powdered. The old ambassador greeted him cordially.

"Ah, my young friend Jonathan. *Entrez.* Come in. You are welcome in any language. Sit down. You have heard from my old friends, your parents?"

"I have, Dr. Franklin. By the latest packet from Philadelphia. They are well and charge me to present to you their affectionate compliments."

"Thank them in my behalf. Or better, I shall write them.

I doubt not they suffer some misgivings as to your welfare. And not without reason. Springtime and a young man alone in Paris. Hmmmmmm."

Young Jonathan's diffidence had increased to embarrassment. Perched on the edge of his chair, he admitted: "Aye, sir. Paris has its——"

"Hazards," Ben Franklin supplied. "Aye, so it has."

"Sir," the young fellow plunged ahead earnestly, "my parents bade me seek your advice in any perplexity—you are called the sage of our country."

Franklin bowed. "You have only to ask. I am at your disposal."

Young Jonathan's embarrassed gaze, roving around the room, fixed suddenly on the nude statue. He started and turned away, but his eyes, will-nilly, kept returning to it. Shifting in his chair, he blurted:

"Indeed, sir—in fact, sir,—in short, sir, it concerns——"

"A woman." Ben Franklin missed little.

"How did you guess?" the other exclaimed. "You have hit upon it!"

The philosopher smiled again. "Young Jonathan, I, too, was young once, if youth can credit it."

"Oh, to be sure, sir."

"I am mindful of the days when I was a young printer's apprentice in Boston. Do you know the pretext on which I escaped from my brother's shop and fled the town to Philadelphia?"

"Nay, sir. I do not."

"The rumor was spread that I must leave in haste because I had got a naughty girl with child."

"Why, Dr. Franklin!"

"I said 'rumor', young Jonathan."

"I crave pardon," Jonathan begged, but inwardly he doubted that he need apologize. It was bruited abroad that old Benjamin, even now, still loved the ladies. Some of the young man's thoughts must have shone transparently on his face, for Franklin, reading them, said with a chuckle:

"Young Jonahan, you fix me with an accusing stare. So, once, did our good John Adams. 'Franklin,' quoth he, 'at 70-odd has neither lost his love of beauty nor his taste for it.' And his prim wife Abigail declared of my dear friend, Madame Helvetius: 'She is bold with Franklin—and he likes it.' "

"You mistook me, Dr. Franklin. I would not presume——"

"Fret not, young Jonathan. Others also have mistaken the kindness of the French ladies to me. 'Tis only that the French are the civilest nation upon earth. Somebody, it seems, gave it out that I loved the ladies. And then everybody presented me their ladies (or the ladies presented themselves) to be embraced. That is, to have their necks kissed. Kissing lips or cheeks is not the mode here. The first is reckoned rude. The other may rub off the paint."

Young Strange did not return Franklin's broad grin but rushed out with: "Sir, I would not be reckoned rude, but—but I can no longer sleep. I——"

Franklin shook his head gravely. "I know of no medicine fit to diminish the violent natural inclinations you mention and if I did, I think I should not communicate it to you. Marriage is the proper remedy. It is the most natural state of man."

"Marriage! Sir, I cannot afford to marry."

"It is the man and woman united who make the complete being. Separately, she wants his force of body and strength of reason; he, her softness, sensibility, and acute discernment. Together they are most likely to succeed in the world. A single man——"

"But, Dr. Franklin——"

"A single man has not nearly the value he would have in the state of union. He is an incomplete animal. He resembles the odd half of a pair of scissors."

"Sir, you speak ripe wisdom. I am most deeply grateful. But——"

" ' 'Tis better to marry than to burn.' "

Jonathan: I cannot marry until later and even now I am burning.

Franklin: If you will not take this counsel and persist in thinking commerce with the sex inevitable——

Jonathan: Sir, I dread that it is.

Franklin: Then in all your amours, you should prefer older women to young ones.

Jonathan: Prefer older women to young ones! Why, Dr. Franklin!

Franklin: You imagine I speak a paradox. Let me give my reasons. Older women have more knowledge of the world, and their minds are better stored with observations, their conversation more improving, and more lastingly agreeable.

Jonathan: Minds, sir? Observations! Conversations! 'Tis other attributes haunt my dreams!

Franklin: When women cease to be handsome, they study to be good. To maintain their influence over men, they support the diminution of beauty with an augmentation of utility. They learn to do a thousand services, small and great, and are the most tender and useful of friends when you are sick. Thus, they continue amiable. And hence there is hardly such a thing to be found as an older woman who is not a good woman.

Jonathan (*desperately*): Sir, I want no nurse! I want no good woman!

Franklin: Another reason then. You should prefer an older woman because there is no hazard of children, which, irregularly produced, may be attended with much inconvenience.

Jonathan: Now there you have made a telling point, Doctor Franklin.

Franklin (*ruefully and wryly*): Aye, aye. That I have.* . . . Fifthly, older women are more experienced and more pru-

---

*Ben Franklin knew whereof he spoke. His son William, who became Governor of Pennsylvania, was illegitimate as was William's son, Temple, who in turn carried on the bar sinister tradition. Lawful Franklin lineage lay on the distaff side. Ben's legitimate daughter Sarah married Richard Bache, and their issue became prominent in Philadelphia affairs. A resultant quip, attributed by Dr. Rosenbach to his uncle, Moses Polock, declared that Philadelphia was run by the Baches and the sons of Baches.

dent and discreet, in conducting an intrigue, to prevent suspicion. Commerce with them is safer with regard to your reputation. And with regard to themselves, if the affair should
happen to be known, considerable people might be rather
inclined to excuse an older woman, who would take kindly
care of a young man, form his manners by her good counsels,
and prevent his ruining his health and fortune among mer-
cenary prostitutes.

Jonathan: You give me most excellent advice, sir, but—
forgive me—I fear you have forgotten the burning urgency
of your own youth. When youth calls to youth, an older
wom——

Franklin: Remember that with an older woman the sin is
less. The debauching of a virgin may be her ruin and make
her life unhappy.

Jonathan (*eloquently*): But think, sir, on a virgin—all rosy
and eager and yielding! Oh, Doctor, you can no longer understand! When the sturdy oak ages, when its limbs wither
and its sap no longer runs, then——

Rapid, imperious knocking rattled the door. Almost without waiting for an invitation, a Frenchwoman burst in. She
was, Jonathan observed, undoubtedly an older woman but
her Gallic vivacity and charm were just as undeniable.

"Papa Franklin!" she cried. "I am desolated! You have not
come to see me. *Voila!* I come to you, and it is not at all
comme il faut."

"My dear, I was only waiting until the nights are longer,"
instantly responded the gallant Franklin. "Let me present a
young friend from my native land. Master Jonathan Strange.
Madame Helvetius."

Jonathan bowed and kissed her hand. "Madame, I am honored."

"Done with the grace of a Frenchman, monsieur," the
sprightly dame complimented. "Ah. I knew there was a
visitor here. Could I otherwise have trusted myself in the
apartment of Papa Franklin. *Jamais!* My virtue it would not
have been safe for an instant."

Franklin, with a side glance at Jonathan, said: "Madame, you flatter an old oak, withering and sapless."

"Oh, la la!" trilled Madame. "The ladies of Paris know better. Old oak? It is to laugh. Young shoot!"

Franklin held up a deprecating hand, and Madame Helvetius turned a rapid flow of words on the shamefaced Jonathan. "Monsieur, all the ladies of France love him, your Franklin. All of us, truly, from *jeunes filles* to aging widows like myself. *Oui,* even the wedded wives. Have you heard what my rival, Madame Brillon, wrote him? Thus she wrote him: 'Papa Franklin, people have the audacity to criticize my pleasant habit of sitting on your knee, and yours of always asking me for what I always refuse.' Oh, la la!" Paying no attention to the embarrassed Jonathan, she chattered on. "And you rascal, Papa F., I have heard you lately stayed in the chamber of Madame Brillon till past midnight, playing chess with her while she sat in her covered bathtub. *C'est scandaleuse ca!* But I am not jealous."

"You need not be," Franklin said. He and Madame Helvetius seemed to forget Jonathan's presence while they indulged in a lively passage.

Franklin: 'Twas only last night, Madame, I dreamt I visited the other world, the Elysian Fields whither our loved spouses have passed on before us. And whom should I meet but Monsieur Helvetius!

Madame: My lamented husband. Of all people! How droll!

Franklin: Madame, I regret to inform you that in that other life he has taken another wife. Naturally I chided him. Said I to him, "Your old companion in the world of mortals is more faithful to you. Though offered several good matches, she has refused. I confess that I myself have loved her madly, but she has been adamant and rejected me because of her love for you.

Madame (*patting his cheek*): You dear Papa Franklin!

Franklin: Then entered the new Madame Helvetius. Lo and behold, I recognized my own late wife, Mistress Franklin!

Madame: So our late consorts are wedded to each other in the other world?

Franklin: So indeed they are. I would have spoken to my wife, but she first addressed me coldly. Said she to me, "I was your good wife forty-nine years and four months, almost half a century. Be content with that. Here have I formed a new bond which will last for eternity."

Madame (*in peals of laughter*): Oh, Papa F! You rogue!

Franklin (*with mock indignation*): The ungrateful shades! Angrily I left Paradise to come back to this good world, again to see the sun—and you. *J'y suis.*

Striding toward her with open arms, Franklin cried: "Come, Madame, let us be avenged on them!"

Although almost helpless with laughter, Madame Helvetius held him off and turned toward the door. "*Ma foi!* How can I resist you?" she demanded. "I must go while I still can."

Young Jonathan, having now succumbed to her charms, offered: "May I escort you to your carriage, Madame?" But Ben Franklin interposed:

"No, no. Allow *me*, Madame. Young man, do you tend to your own fires. The Franklin stove burns well enough."

Neither of you must derange yourself. I go alone," declared the Parisienne, sweeping out. "Farewell, Monsieur. Papa Franklin, *au revoir.*"

Jonathan turned impulsively toward his host and handsomely acknowledged: "A charming woman! And I had thought you superannuated. It is you, sir, not I, who are young. Pray proceed with your advice on the choice of a mistress. I listen with renewed interest and respect."

"I was speaking of the superiority of older women," Franklin resumed. "Now 'tis true that in every animal that walks upright, the deficiency of fluids that fill the muscles appears first in the highest part. The face first grows lank and wrinkled; then the neck; then the breast and arms. But ah? the rest continues as plump as ever. Furthermore, young Jonathan, is not night the time of love?"

"Aye, sir."

"Then remember this. In the dark all cats are gray."

"Most true, sir."

"Having made a young girl miserable may give you frequent, bitter reflections, none of which can attend making an older woman happy. And lastly, young Jonathan——"

"Aye, Dr. Franklin."

"Mark well this reason why you should choose older women——"

The sage paused, his eyes brightened with reminiscence and he sighed with infinite gusto:

"Ahhhh! They are so grateful!"

BEEFSTEAK FOR BREAKFAST

The Amazing American Appetite and How It Grew So Great

Now to the banquet we press;
Now for the eggs, the ham,
Now for the mustard and cress,
Now for the strawberry jam!
Now for the tea of our host,
Now for the rollicking bun,
Now for the muffin and toast,
Now for the gay Sally Lunn!

W. S. Gilbert: *The Sorcerer*

The traveler from Boston climbed stiffly out of the stagecoach. It had been a day-long journey and he was weary.

Entering the inn, he found his fellow-travelers already at table. All day they had sat without exercise in the coach. At noon they had stopped and baited at a wayside tavern. A light meal they called it: a dish of bacon and beef, venison and bear steaks, hot breads and pie, washed down with cider and rum flips. Now it was still early in the evening, but these wayfarers were attacking the victuals on the heavily-laden board with the voracity and velocity of men famished.

Every place was taken. The waiting Bostonian stood and utterly appalled, watched the violent exertions of the trencher-men. Certainly there was altogether too much truth in the saying: "A Frenchman dines, an Englishman eats and an American devours."

Were Americans, he wondered, still striving to make up for the early, lean years when some of the Massachusetts and Virginia settlements had been close to starvation? Nonsense! The incredible bounty of the new land had ended short commons soon enough. For a time the Pilgrims had rationed each

person to five kernels of corn a day, but there had always been a plenty of clams, oysters, lobsters, fish, and eels.

Salem lobsters often weighed 25 pounds. Huge lobsters, five-to-six-feet long, had been trapped in New York Bay until the cannonading of the Revolution drove them off.* Virginia crabs measured one foot long by 6 inches wide, with many succulent legs. Oysters ran to a length of one foot long; an English visitor, gulping one, avowed he felt as if he had swallowed a baby. Why, so strong was the craze for oysters nowadays that estates along the New York shore advertised for private oyster beds. New York City abounded in oyster bars, where the barbarous custom prevailed of dipping raw oysters, preliminary to downing them, in rawer whiskey. Such was the multitude of fish in the rivers and streams that you could scoop them out with frying-pans or pitchforks; your horse was likely to slip on them when you rode through a ford. Governor Dale of Virginia once had caught 5,000 sturgeon at one cast of the seine. The New England sea fisheries were so rich that certain uncultured and commerce-minded people were proposing that the emblem of Boston be the cod.

There were so many deer around the settlements that the Colonists came to call venison a "tiresome meat" and killed the animals chiefly for buckskin. Nowadays along the east coast, a man couldn't shoot a deer or a wild turkey in his backyard any longer, but hunters continued to bring considerable venison and numbers of the big birds, forty pounds and heavier, into the market, along with pheasant, partridge, woodcock, quail, plover, and snipe. Wild duck also; Chesapeake Bay was black with masses which covered expanses of water seven miles long by one wide. As for wild pigeons, they sold for a penny a dozen and no wonder, when men and boys with sticks could bag thousands a night simply by knocking them out of trees where they were roosting.

Even though game was being rushed westward along with the frontier, there had been such increase in herds and flocks that there was no lack of meat for any American who lived

*Earle, Alice Morse. *Home Life in Colonial Days.* New York, 1898. P. 118.

on the land, as most did, nor for any townsman of very moderate means. Americans must certainly be classified as among the greater carnivora. They could and did eat meat three times a day. Thirty meat dishes could be expected at a formal banquet. But wives warned husbands, apt to bring unexpected guests home to dinner, not to count on more than three kinds of meat.

Large tureens of soup having been gustily consumed, the meat course had been placed on the inn table. The traveler from Boston observed the gourmandizing with distaste and alarm. That withered old gentleman yonder, his face barely visible behind a huge turkey drumstick, had been complaining all day of a colicky stomach. The ruddy-faced man opposite, president of a temperance society, was already beginning on a second slice of corned beef, nearly as large as Boston Common. That dignified personage in black broadcloth, eating with silence and celerity, was a clergyman who last Sunday had preached a powerful sermon on the text: "He who eateth and drinketh unwisely eateth and drinketh damnation unto himself." Obviously none of the diners realized that in stuffing themselves to the limit they were as guilty of intemperance as if they drank themselves under the table. More men dug their graves with their teeth than with their tankards. The Bostonian made a note that he would unhesitatingly state in an article for the *Boston Morel Reformer* * that while alcoholism killed 50,000 Americans annually, downright gluttony destroyed around 100,000.

There was an old rhyme, eminently suitable. How did it go?

Many more men by gluttony are slain
Than in battle or in fight, or with other pain.

His countrymen not only ate three or four regular meals but ate between them, the Bostonian sadly reflected. They were addicted to snacks. Not only was the dinner table the

*Vol. I (1835).

scene of pitched battles, but guerilla warfare was carried on all day against the cupboard.

You'd see few New England larders without a pie or so on the shelf, a knife laid handy across the top for the convenience of those needing to cut a slice to stay their stomachs. "Nothing like a mince pie for breakfast to ward off a headache," Yankees had the folly to declare. A New Hampshire woman, lacking the usual ingredients, had made her Thanksgiving mince pies out of bear meat and dried pumpkins, sweetened with maple sugar and with a crust of corn meal; her husband—either a man with an iron stomach or a great liar—had vowed them the best he ever ate. Small wonder housewives baked such capacious pots of beans; not only were they served for supper but spoonfuls were scooped from them at odd hours all week by ravenous members of the family.

Going on a journey, Americans never risked getting hungry—not they! They'd take along some portable soup (leg of veal boiled down to jelly, poured into cups and set out in the sun to dry). Or a slab of the cornbread originally called journey-cake but now johnnycake. Or if they were doing some winter traveling, they'd just tie a chunk of frozen bean porridge to the sleigh and chip off a piece when wanted.

A land of plenty, this. Like the streets of Heaven it flowed with milk and honey, not to mention every kind of liquor that could be distilled or brewed. While most of the yield of the orchards went to the stills and cider presses, many a housewife nevertheless had all the peaches she could brandy and all the apples she could dry, and a surplus to feed the hogs. There was an astounding abundance and variety of wild fruits: mulberries, cherries, currants, plums, gooseberries, blackberries, raspberries, cranberries, and strawberries. People lay down in fields and gorged themselves on them. And wild nuts, too. Onions, peas, cucumbers, pumpkins, melons, squash, sweet potatoes, asparagus, carrots, turnips flourished in this fresh and fertile soil, as did grains: corn, barley, rye, wheat, buckwheat.

Why, in this very inn for breakfast tomorrow each guest

would be confronted by a towering stack of buckwheat cakes, doused in butter and maple syrup or wild honey, with sausage, fried ham and eggs, mush and milk, pie, doughnuts, hot biscuits, a variety of cold dishes, plus great pots of tea and coffee.

Yet every traveler was wolfing dinner as if he never expected to see another meal for days. The Bostonian shuddered. What this country needed was a Society for the Suppression of Eating.*

Americans devoured such vast quantities so rapidly—they ate as if they were too busy to spare time for meals—that they were seriously undermining their health. They ate meat morning, noon, and night; even gave it to children before they had their teeth. Manners? Such fol-de-rol got in the way of the business of engulfing food. English travelers were inclined to be hypocritical, but no great libel was the statement by a Britisher that Americans ate with their knives, picked their teeth with their forks and virtually tubbed in their finger-bowls. The Tremont House of Boston had introduced four-tine forks in 1829 in an effort to persuade the guests to use knives less as food-conveyers, but there was still plenty of "sword-swallowing."

Women didn't seem to mind cooking all day in a vain attempt to satisfy the tremendous American appetite. Housewives who did mind usually could afford to hire a cook, with twenty-five dollars a year considered good wages.

To be entirely fair, though, there *were* reasons why Americans ate so prodigiously. Many of them led strenuous, outdoor lives. Chores before breakfast made a man pretty sharp-set. In cold winters, people stoked themselves with food, just as they did with ardent spirits, to keep warm. Yet down South where it was hot, they seemed to eat just as hearty; apparently they lacked resolution to refuse the tempting dishes prepared by their Negro cooks.

Since only a limited number of foods could be preserved

*Proposed in the *New England Magazine*. Vol. 2 (1832).

by pickling, drying, or smoking, the motto was: Eat, drink and
be merry for tomorrow it will spoil. Only large estates like
George Washington's Mount Vernon rejoiced in such complete equipment as smoke-, salt-, spring-, milk-, and ice-houses.
In 1803 a Maryland farmer had invented an ice-box, insu-
lated with rabbit fur, but not many people had them. More
recently a plow-like ice cutter had been devised to harvest ice
from lakes and streams; stored in sawdust, the ice blocks kept
well. But still feasts after a harvest or slaughtering were
deemed the best way to keep good food from going to waste,
and nobody seemed to mind laying waste his digestive system.
The United States might be a democracy, but Regina Dispep-
sia reigned.

"We Americans," mused the Bostonian, "are under the
most extraordinary misapprehensions as to food. Far from re-
garding it for what it is—nourishment—we appoint it a symbol
of hospitality. Hosts are insulted unless you overeat. It's no
use crossing your knife and fork on your plate as a sign you
have had enough. Even in my own New England, a man has
difficulty escaping a lavish dinner. If he declines—perhaps because he has indigestion—the hostess will send several dishes
from the dinner, which she calls a "cold party," straight over
to his house and next day ask embarrassing questions as to
how he relished them."

Americans actually celebrated occasions by eating, just as
they did by discharging firearms and setting off fireworks. The
State of Maryland had signalized peace in 1783 with a mighty
feast. To honor a general or observe someone's birthday, a
banquet was the thing, and the more superfluous dishes the
greater the tribute. Sea captains, returning from a voyage to
the West Indies, always brought a huge sea turtle and a keg
of limes for punch to regale their friends at a "turtle frolic."
More than once the Bostonian had heard hearty old gentlemen declare that there was nothing they enjoyed more than a
fine, full-course dinner, unless it were a large, well-attended
funeral. Sometimes they could count on both together for the
custom of funeral dinners had not yet gone altogether out of
fashion.

Such inns as this were giving way in the cities to large establishments beginning to be called hotels where, under the so-called American plan, a guest for one dollar a day or less got a room and four whacking big meals, with brandy, whiskey, or a bottle of Madeira at each. European observers insisted that when the dinner gong rang and two hundred Americans rushed into a hotel dining room, sat down and began eating —sticking strictly to their muttons and indulging in no conversation—it sounded exactly like feeding time at the zoo.

Yes, it was high time a Society for the Suppression of Eating was organized. Fancying the idea, the Bostonian took a seat by the hearth to meditate on it. Such a Society might help end these abominable excesses, might save his countrymen's health. Its watchword might well be: Disease lurks behind the fat sirloin, and there is death in the tureen of turtle soup. Among its rules must surely be included:

Go without dinner at least once a week.
Eat meat no more than once a day.
Eat nothing after 8 o'clock at night.

The Bostonian enthusiastically told himself: "Should this Society of mine succeed, it would justify an inscription on my tombstone such as this—and I could ask none better:

" 'Here lies the man
Who was the means of lessening by one quarter
The food consumed in the U.S.' "

The gentleman from Boston was becoming a trifle impatient by now—not that he was hungry, but his fellow-travelers seemed to be striving to match the feat of diners who sat seven hours at table, eating and drinking steadily. Well, they would pay for their over-indulgence. The inn provender probably was as monotonous and ill-cooked as American food was as a rule.

There were, to be sure, exceptions to the rule. The Bostonian recalled a few from his travels. A well-baked Smithfield ham in Virginia. (William Byrd of Westover was said to have written his ham recipe on the fly-leaf of his Bible.) Golden-brown waffles with honey, as served in one of the old Dutch manors (on each the waffle-iron was stamped the family crest and the initials of the head of the house and his good wife, along with the date of their wedding, and those waffles deserved it). Diamond-back terrapin, shad roe, and canvasback ducks in Maryland. In Carolina, fish boned and rolled in corn-meal and fried in deep bacon fat, candied sweet potatoes, and spoonbread. Philadelphia pepper-pot and the steaming, rich fish chowder of his own city. Flap-jacks with cinnamon and maple sugar between each layer. Those crisp potato chips they served at the Saratoga spas. Tender young lobsters with drawn butter or with that delicious pink Newburg sauce made by the French cooks who had been coming over since the Revolution. New Orleans crab gumbo or crawfish bisque and a *jumballaya* of fricaseed chicken and rice (each light flake separate). Tipsy cake, fragrant with fine Spanish sherry. A heaping dish of ice cream, smothered in wild strawberries.

The traveler from Boston leaped to his feet with a half-suppressed cry. His mouth was watering. There was a sharp, gnawing sensation in the pit of his stomach. What if he had previously decided that this would be a good evening to follow his Society's rules and go without dinner? What if he had already eaten meat once today? What if it was after eight o'clock?

He rushed over to the dinner table, cleared at last of diners but also, alas, of food.

"Sorry, sir," the landlord apologized. "They've eaten me out of house and home. I didn't realize there was still someone who'd had no dinner."

"Do you mean to say you have nothing left for my dinner!" the Bostonian stormed.

"Oh, yes, sir. Happens I have one dish. Both food and drink it is. Made from a fine old Salem recipe of my grand-mother's."

From a brass kettle simmering over the fire, the landlord ladled out a strange-appearing concoction.

"Sour household beer, with crusts of brown bread—rye-and-Injun *—crumbled in and dulcified with molasses," he identified it.

"God have mercy on me!" besought the Bostonian. "What do you call that?"

"Whistle-belly-vengeance, sir."

*Bread made from rye flour and Indian cornmeal. The concoction, whistle-belly-vengeance or whip-belly-vengeance, took its name from an old English term.

IMMORTAL AMERICAN HORSE

Justin Morgan, Foaled 1789, and His Curious Colts

Once when the snow of the year was beginning to fall,
We stopped by a mountain pasture to say 'Whose colt'?
A little Morgan had one forefoot on the wall,
The other curled at his breast. He dipped his head
And snorted at us. And then he had to bolt.
We heard the miniature thunder where he fled,
And we saw him, or thought we saw him, dim and grey,
Like a shadow against the curtain of falling flakes.
I think the little fellow is afraid of the snow.
He isn't winter-beaten. It isn't playing.
With the little fellow at all. He's running away
I doubt if even his mother could tell him, "Sakes,
It's only weather." He'd think she didn't know.
Where is his mother? He can't be out alone,
And now he comes again with clatter of stone,
And mounts the wall again with whited eyes
And all his tail that isn't hanging straight
He shudders his coat as if to throw off flies
'Whoever it is that leaves him out so late,
When other creatures have gone to stall and bin,
Ought to be told to come and take him in.'

Robert Frost: *The Runaway.*

May, 1795. Green Mountain Vermonters, with mares to be bred, read with interest an advertisement of stud printed in the *Rutland Herald* and signed by one, Justin Morgan.

> *"Figure will cover this season at the stable of Samuel Allen. . . ."*

Figure? That must be the little bay with black legs Morgan took for a debt down in West Springfield, Mass., two or three years ago. Getting right well known, he was. People had started calling him "Justin Morgan" after his owner. Just a runt of a horse—not much over fourteen hands and less than a thousand pounds. But Morgan must know what he was about, putting him at stud. School teacher and singing master he might be, but he knew horses. He'd been standing his own and other folks' a long time.

> *"Figure will stand at Williston till the eighteenth of May; then to Hinesburgh, where he will stand one week; then back to Williston, to continue through the season, one week in each place. . . ."*

Humph. Morgan wasn't calculating to let that little stud horse of his do much resting, was he?

> *"With regard to said horse's beauty, strength and activity, the subscriber flatters himself the curious will be best satisfied to come and see. . . ."*

Well, granted those who had seen him, he wasn't a bad-looking nag. Heavy black mane and tail, small ears set wide apart, large dark eyes. Plenty of power there. Deep chest, legs short but sturdy, heavy-muscled hindquarters. Gentle—broken to ride or to harness. And fast for such a chunky piece of horseflesh. If you happened to be around when Morgan raced him, bet a gallon of rum on him. Likely you'd drink the other man's.

"Figure sprang from a curious horse owned by Col. De-Lancey of New York. . . ."

Readers of the advertisement chuckled over that line. Vermonters still liked to tell the story of what happened in the Revolution to Colonel DeLancey, King's man and wealthy, high-and-mighty New Yorker. Seems the Colonel went raiding patriots' cattle with his Tory cavalry and when he came back, tied his mount, a bay stallion called True Briton, outside a tavern and went in for a drink. Well, it turned out to be the costliest drink he ever downed. That horse, imported from England, had cost DeLancey two hundred pounds. Up sneaked a smart young fellow, name of Smith, and galloped off on the Colonel's charger. They chased him miles and never even saw his dust. Smith sold the animal in New England. That was how a horse named True Briton started siring Yankee colts, and a good one on the British, that was. With such a sire, there was no denying Morgan's little bay came of fine stock—and through his dam, too. In both flowed the "rich, high blood" of famous Arabians and thoroughbreds.

"But," finished the stud advertisement, *"the greatest recommend I can give him is, he is exceeding sure and gets curious colts."*

Curious colts they were. Mares served by the stallion Justin Morgan produced offspring which might take the color of their hide from their dams but bore them little other resemblance. All were the spit and image of their sire and not only in physical but in other characteristics: intelligence, willingness, endurance, gentleness.

The schoolmaster rode home after the stud season, naturally far from suspecting that his mount had founded the first great line of American horses. That this horse he still called Figure would take his own name of Justin Morgan and lend it renown. That the stock of this runt, grudgingly accepted for a twenty-five-dollar debt, would make fortunes. That he would be honored with memorial tablets, medallions, a joint-resolution of the Vermont Legislature, sesquicentennial celebrations, and a bronze statue. That he would inspire books, magazines, articles, stories, and poems. And that he and his line of curious colts—Morgan horses—would gallop through American history.

The teacher rode his namesake to district school and to the jolly, sociable singing classes he led. Everybody liked the tall, lanky schoolmaster. If any laughed at the spectacle he made mounted on his little horse—long legs almost trailing if he took his feet out of the stirrups—he laughed with them. You could depend on the two Justin Morgans, Green Mountain people said. Through drift-snow or sleet, over road, trail, or cross-country, they always arrived where you expected them.

Nobody ever saw the little bay stumble. Being so obedient and bridlewise, he was always in demand by borrowers. Girls begged him of his master to ride to dances—the Morgan horse never chucked a party-goer, all dressed up in her best frock, off in a mud puddle. On muster days the most dashing officer on the parade ground was the lucky man who'd been able to manage the loan of the schoolmaster's nag, for his mount would rise to the occasion by becoming a spirited charger, with prances and caracoles at the right moment.

The Morgan horse loved to be groomed and caressed. He was full of life and play when led out on a halter-rope. Somehow he was never at ease with children, gentle though he was. Dogs he disliked intensely; one must once have nipped his heels. If loose, the little stallion would chase any dog he sighted, snorting wrathfully.

Seldom was he idle. With school-teaching paying so poorly and a wife and five children to support, his master counted more and more on what the bay could earn. Justin Morgan the man had found all heavy farm work beyond his strength since he contracted the lung sickness at the age of twenty. Justin Morgan the horse, hired out, did it for him, and though the rate of hire, ran low, it still was a help.

Other times it was the stocky bay's utterly surprising speed that brought in money. Some folks up and vowed that Morgan oughtn't to have any part in such doings as horse-racing, and he a hymn-writer—author of *The Judgment Hymn*.

Didn't seem fitting considering all the betting and the rum-guzzling that went on at races. But Morgan, he allowed as how people really enjoyed themselves and forget their troubles, watching a good horse race.

There was that race at Woodstock that time, a great place for running or standing horses, account of its being central. Some New Yorkers had come up with a long-legged racer named Silvermine, figuring to take home all the sporting money in Vermont—if there was any such thing, said the New Yorkers, looking down their noses. They doubted, they let it be known, if they'd find any New Englanders, even such as fancied themselves judges of horseflesh, willing to take their hands out of their pockets, unclench their fists and put up hard money.

Money was right scarce in Vermont, but those New York macaronis made folks mad, even Mister Justin Morgan. He got so riled he wagered the big sum of fifty dollars on his little horse.—And that was about fifty times what the schoolmaster could afford to lose. Green Mountain men, who had seen the Morgan horse run, covered the rest of the New York money and there was enough rum bet—at $1 a gallon—to drown an ox.

River Street was picked as the race course—from Mister Myer's house up the river as far as the school-house—eighty rods. Myer took a stick and scratched a starting line in the dirt. With two light-weight young fellows up, the two horses were brought up to scratch: Silvermine, a tall roan with slender, racer's legs, and Justin Morgan. The New Yorkers eyed the chunky, short-legged Vermont work horse and started laughing fit to kill. One of them yelped, "Say, you forgot the plow!"

A lot of the people around the starting point began to think they'd been a mite rash, betting the way they had. But they felt better when they looked at the Morgan horse. Seemed like his eyes were a-flashing fire. Those well-shaped ears of his were pricked forward and fair twitching with excitement. He was grinding his bit. Every muscle was a-standing out and quivering. Those stocky hind legs of his were drawn up under him—kind of like the way a catamount does, getting ready to spring.

The starter dropped his hat. Both horses plunged over the scratch. Everybody yelled so loud and so sudden that a sharp echo came bouncing back off the hills.

That Silvermine horse was fast and he ran for all he was worth. But the little Morgan was simply amazing. He didn't have a sign of what racing people call form, but he was 950 pounds of power and rapid action. He shot out in front. . . . He stayed there. . . . He drew so far ahead that the other horse might have been pulling that plow his owner had yipped about. Over a long course it might have been different, but for a short distance Justin Morgan was just plain lightning. He finished going away.

While folks were getting back their breath from shouting —they were going to need it for long swigs from the rum jugs being passed around—Mister Morgan stepped up to the New Yorkers.

"Gentlemen," he offered in his best schoolteacher and singing-master voice, "Since your horse didn't seem to be in the running, I'll give you two more chances to win the stake— walking or trotting."

The New Yorkers didn't take him up. Seems it was a long ways back to York State, and they had to be getting on.

Well, sir, the little Morgan always won. It got to be so that no one from anywhere near around would race a nag against him. Even the foreigners caught on after a while. There was no more racing money to be won, with the bay such a sure thing over a short course, but now and then there would be a race, with drinks for the crowd wagered.

After all, each victory was as good as a stud advertisement. Farmers with horsing mares figured it did no harm to breed a little speed into their stock, providing they got plenty of bottom to boot. Besides, they had all the bargain anybody— even a Vermonter—could ask, considering the modest stud fee Morgan charged: one dollar the single leap and two dollars the season, if paid down. The one dollar payment was safe enough at that, for the little stallion was, as his master claimed, "exceeding sure."

Whether he ever equalled the record of his sire True Briton: a remarkable performance of sixteen colts sired in one day, chronicles do not state. But the Morgan horse stood all season year after year (he was still standing well on in his twenties). As in everything that was asked of him, he was always ready and willing. Sometimes a farmer came in with a tall mare to be served and took a look at the small horse and grumbled he hadn't come all this way for a stud no bigger than a pony. Morgan, he'd only smile pleasant. Just you lead your mare a ways up that slope yonder, he'd say. Then face her down hill, and the little stud horse, a mite higher up the slope, he'll do the rest. It's a true saying that you can't measure a man—nor a horse, either—by the length of his legs.

But all the Morgan horse could earn wasn't nearly enough. In 1798 the schoolteacher died in debt; creditors realized only eighteen cents on the dollar. The horse was sold to Sheriff William Rice of Woodstock in whose house his master had been cared for during his last illness.

The sheriff sold the horse to Robert Evans, and again Justin Morgan was working for a poor man with a large family. He was Evans' only team. After chores were done at home, man and horse hired out to neighbors.

It's one thing to pull something on wheels—Justin Morgan could trot with the best of them—but another to haul a heavy log or a stone-boat, piled high with those boulders the Lord saw fit to sow in the soil of Vermont. 'Round and about Randolph village, considerable land was cleared, stone fences built, and fields ploughed by Evans and his one-horse team. When there was a hard haul to be done and folks stood off and looked at the big load and the little horse, Evans would pick up the reins and remark with a proud and confident look at the Morgan:

"Don't often have to ask him but once. Whatever's he's hitched to gen'rally has to come first time trying."

It did, too. You could gamble on it, and Evans did.

There was that time at the Randolph saw-mill. A hefty pine log lay some ten rods from the mill. Nary a horse had been able to move it and some that weighed as high as 1200 pounds had tried—and lost a wager for their owners. Along about dusk Evans came by with his horse from a field where he'd been logging all day. Soon as he'd been told about the drawing match, he walked into the tavern and challenged the whole company to bet a gallon of rum against his horse's hauling that pine square onto the logway in three pulls.

The company accepted with a shout. Everybody took a glass, smacked lips and stepped out. Carrying lanterns—it was dark now—the line of men went weaving down to the log like a lot of fireflies that had got into cider pressings. Making fast his toggle-chains, Evans grinned and allowed he was ashamed to hitch his horse to a little stick like that. He wouldn't feel right winning the wager and drinking their rum, he said, unless three of 'em got on and rode. So three of the company, who were a touch unsteady on their feet and glad of a chance to sit down somewhere, climbed on the log, whooping and hollering.

Men forget kindness when they get bragging about their animals. Justin Morgan had been hard at work all day and long before now he ought to have been fed and stabled. But he was willing as always. At Evans' command he put his weight into the collar. Those mighty breast and thigh muscles of his flexed and stood out with the strain of his effort.

"Watch your feet," Evans yelled to the log riders. "When this colt gets a-pulling, something's got to come!"

The Morgan horse plunged ahead, bent so far forward that he appeared almost to be crawling on his knees. He drew the heavy log and its riders half the agreed distance before he halted. On the next pull, he made it to the logway, with one pull to spare.

He won all the drawing bees as he had won all the races. He worked early and he worked late, day in and day out, with that iron endurance he bequeathed to his progeny. But Evans failed to make ends meet and, for the third time Justin Morgan went to settle a debt. Members of the Goss family owned him for some years. All manner of hard work was still his lot, but he was well cared for and now he was valued at one hundred dollars. Those curious colts of his, begotten in his image, were winning wider appreciation, particularly three foaled during these years: Sherman, Woodbury, and Bullrush Morgan. (The next generation had bred taller and heavier.) These colts were destined to be the three chief channels of the Morgan blood.

Autumn, 1811. Justin Morgan was twenty-two, well on toward old age for a horse. He changed owners rather often now—seemed as though nobody wanted him dying on their hands, not while there was still a sale or a swap to be had. Yankee horse-trading, you say? For certain it was, but a horse needs feed and keep, and sentiment, like it says in the book, is a luxury for them as can afford it. You'd not find many luxuries in Vermont or New Hampshire, either, in those days.

But while there were plenty of people who worked their cattle hard but treated them decently, there were some, too, like the freighter named Langmaid who bought Justin Morgan and put him the lead pair of a six-horse team. Cruel hard he used the old horse, hauling freight from Windsor to Chelsea. Yet in any and all weather the little bay in the lead always pulled his best. In icy, blinding sleet or snow storm, he never looked back. He always faced the blast.

Thin and worn, the Morgan horse was bought by his next owner for a pittance. He was a bargain, for there were still years of usefulness ahead of him both as a work horse and a stud. He was still sound, spirited and vigorous in 1821 when at the ripe old age of thirty-two he died from an infection, the result of another horse's kick.

And yet he seems to be alive today, so faithfully is his image reproduced in his descendants. If the schoolmaster of Randolph, Vermont, came back to earth, he might easily take some living Morgan horse for his old nag. Not only the appearance of the horse Justin Morgan but his other characteristics, both physical and temperamental, have been transmitted through generation after generation. Even after crosses with other well-established breeds the Morgan traits survive. It is probably the most extraordinary case of prepotency recorded.

Thus the story of Justin Morgan remains unfinished. It is a saga, a serial. It is one of those serials of family chronicles in which the founder keeps cropping up.

If you swiftly flipped the pages of such a history, illustrated, you would catch glimpses of pictures of horses—Morgans all—such pictures as these:

A trotting race being won by the beautiful Black Hawk, grandson of Justin—he never was beaten. . . . A Morgan pulling the doctor's buggy through a snowstorm, never looking back but always facing the blast. . . . A Civil War charge by that fine regiment the 1st Vermont Cavalry, its mounts all Morgans . . . Rienzi, a Morgan horse, carrying General Phil Sheridan to save the day "from Winchester twenty miles away" . . . Morgans hauling Concord wagons in the westward march of empire. . . . Morgans as cow ponies, as mounted police horses. . . . Acting in the movies with Tom Mix. . . . Imported by foreign countries to improve native stock. . . . Winning blue ribbons in county fairs and horse-shows and firsts in endurance rides. . . . Morgans, as always, doing the hard work of the farm when you couldn't get gasoline and tractor parts—or when you could.

Yet though Morgans had made their mark as one of the great breeds of American horses, toward the turn of the century the line was in danger of being lost. Justin Morgan and his "curious colts" were close to becoming a tradition and a legend, for the Morgan blood had been considerably diluted or scattered. Then, in 1894, Col. Joseph Battell established an American Morgan Horse register and in 1907 gave a 400-acre farm at Weybridge, Vt., to the U.S. Department of Agriculture. There the best Morgan blood in the country was assembled for conservation and perpetuation. The farm continues today in successful operation, with many calls for registered stallions and numerous visitors and inquiries.

And there stands a bronze, life-size statue of Justin Morgan, the gift in 1921 of the Morgan Horse Club. Song and story increasingly celebrate him and his line. Plaques and markers have sprouted in the New England towns which knew the sire of all the Morgans during his earthly career. West Springfield, Mass., proclaims: "Here lived Justin Morgan (the man). Born in West Springfield, 1747—died in Randolph, Vt., 1798. From this farm came the stallion Justin Morgan, progenitor of that famous breed known as Morgan horses." The same town boasts itself "the birthplace of the biggest little horse in the world." Woodstock, Vt., announces: "On this site Justin Morgan, the Progenitor of the famous Morgan breed of horses, was kept in 1800-01 by Sheriff William Rice, his second owner." Chelsea, Vt., declares: "Near this spot lies the famous stallion Justin Morgan. Foaled 1789—Died 1821." Still more such tributes may be expected. "Seven Cities warred for Homer being dead". . . .

In 1939 the General Assembly of the Vermont Legislature passed a joint resolution in special observance of the 150th anniversary of the birth of the horse Justin Morgan. The State of Iowa, demonstrating that the occasion could not be confined to New England, commemorated it with a horse-show. But it remained for the Vermont Senate to signalize it most memorably by printing in its *Journal* a history of Justin Morgan with this proud and sprightly conclusion:

Vermont is famous for men, women, maple sugar, and Morgan horses.
>*The first are strong, the latter fleet,*
>*The second and third are exceedingly sweet,*
>*And all are uncommonly hard to beat.*

Fame in full measure has come at last to Justin Morgan, "the greatest little horse in the world." Yet print and plaudits are as nothing to the unique immortality which is his. What other mortal creature has ever had, after a century and a half, so many living images?

LAST BUT NOT-SO-SAD RITES

A Funeral Dinner in Boston, 1797

Rejoice for our brother deceased,
Our Loss is his infinite gain;
A soul out of prison released,
And free from its bodily chain;
With songs let us follow his flight
And mount with his spirit above,
Escaped to the mansions of light,
And lodged in the Eden of love.

Charles Wesley: *Burial Hymn*

"Rum," muttered the housekeeper, ticking off an item on her list. "Rum and plenty of it. What remains in the house will not suffice, and 'tis as necessary a part of a funeral as the corpse."

Death had taken Caleb Dawes,* of the town of Boston in the young state of Massachusetts on the 6th day of July, 1797. Preparations were being hastened for his funeral dinner, and a large and elaborate function it must be, for the deceased had been a prominent citizen, well endowed with worldly goods. Successful careers as a grocer, merchant, ship owner, and sugar refiner had been his. As a Son of Liberty he assisted at the birth of the Republic, and through the Revolution his ships had helped keep her flag flying at sea. He long had been a friend of the renowned John Hancock, though the two had fallen out toward the end of the Governor's life. Member of the Boston Court and church deacon, Caleb Dawes had crowded much into his span of fifty-nine years, including two wives who had passed on before and a third, his present relict.

"Rum," the housekeeper repeated. "The good Lord knows Master Dawes sold enough of it as a grocer, and 'tis no more than fitting that his friends drink to the departed in his own goods."

*Based on the funeral dinner of Caleb Davis, an account of which will be found in the *Proceedings* of the Massachusetts Historical Society, v. 54.

She also augmented the liquor already in the Dawes cellar by ordering quantities of beer, gin, and brandy and 122 bottles of wine, consisting of eight varieties, mostly strong, fortified vintages. Lemons, oranges, and sugar for punch went down on the list. Selected as the funeral baked meats were beef, ham, bacon, and fowls. They were supplemented by fish, oysters, 150 eggs, peas, onions, and potatoes. Dessert would be cheese, fruit, and sweetmeats.

The provident housekeeper then arranged for extra linen and crockery, six dozen chairs, and the hiring of ten waiters. It could hardly be expected that the regular resources of the household would serve for this occasion. There were to be no less than one hundred guests, all men. Women were not invited to funeral dinners.

Frequently there were other funereal expenses than for food and drink. A pair of gloves customarily was presented to each mourner by the family of the deceased. A Boston minister, who had accumulated 3,000 pairs, sold them in 1742 for $640. While his act was criticized by some as disrespect to the dead, others condoned it on the ground that the parson needed the money since he had eleven children to support. The New York Dutch, in addition to gloves, sent each funeral guest a scarf and a bottle of Madeira. Often given were gold funeral rings, enameled in black and engraved with some such appropriate emblem as a skull or a skeleton in a coffin and a motto such as:

Prepared be
To follow me.

Indeed this mortuary custom was so lavishly indulged that not a few families, particularly in South Carolina, were impoverished by the cost of gifts and liquor.

Because of the late Mr. Dawes' commercial and political connections, a number of the guests from other States had been bidden to his funeral dinner. One, a Virginian, was obliged to decline, being incapacitated from having recently attended another funeral. Sending his regrets, he wrote:

"We long have maintained here the rite of firing three volleys over the grave, not confining it to military funerals by any means. Since the firing party has always taken a glass or two after the service, furious fusilades sometimes result.

"In view of the accidents that have taken place, the county court has forbidden the volleys unless an officer of the militia is present to command and control them. While lately acting in that capacity, I was winged in the left shoulder by a member of the firing party, a young kinsman of mine, somewhat in his cups. Happily he was using only a fowling piece, yet my physician advises that I had best not make the trip north for the obsequies of the esteemed Mr. Dawes."

Other out-of-town guests attended, however, including a friend from New York and a cousin from New Hampshire. As soon as the wine and rum began to flow, it became evident that the funeral dinner would be a very convivial occasion. The solemn aspect worn by all on arrival rapidly began to disappear. Conversation grew animated. One gentleman, whose head was not as strong as the ordinary, was with difficulty prevented from rising and proposing the health of the late lamented, a toast which was obviously a trifle tardy.

The New York guest observed that it had long been the practice in his State to look forward to and provide well in advance for such sad events as the present. On Long Island far-sighted young men quite generally began early to lay aside funds and a stock of good wine for their funerals. An acquaintance of his residing in Albany had taken commendable though unusual action at his own wedding; when not all of a cask of excellent Madeira, broached for that festivity, was consumed, the bridegroom had ordered the remainder set aside for his funeral. However, the New Yorker was moved to confess that of late years there had been no such splendid funerals as those of the old Dutch days when tenants of the vast Hudson River manors came by hundreds to pay their respects and drink heartily when a member of one of the great *patroon* families, like the Van Renssalaers, passed on to his or her reward.

A touch tartly, a Bostonian remarked that the "good old

days" always seemed clothed in glamor. Personally he believed that obsequies today were observed in a far more
refined and suitable manner than of yore. He would always
remember his grandfather's description of the informality of
a New England funeral of the past century.

"Everyone as he entered," the old gentleman had related,
"took off his hat with his left hand, smoothed down his hair
with his right, walked up to the coffin, gazed upon the corpse,
passed on to the table, took a glass of his favorite liquor, went
out in front of the house and there talked politics or swapped
horses till it was time to lift."

The new hearses, the company agreed, were decidedly a
forward step in funerals. When pall-bearers were compelled to
carry all the way to the burying ground, there was likely to
be trouble. Some or all of the bearers, imbibing to lighten
the gloom, might have become perilously unsteady even
before it was time to "lift." The coffin on a black bier, covered with a pall, was no inconsiderable load. Relays spelled
each other during the journey to the grave, often several
miles. Though the off-shift refreshed themselves freely from
a bottle, kept in steady circulation, and the course of the
cortege was erratic, the destination was ultimately reached.

The cousin from New Hampshire declared that he, too,
preferred more ceremoniousness at funerals to such informal
rites as he often had attended in the country where a de-
canter and glasses were placed right on the head of the coffin.
Give him a sideboard to hold the liquor, said he.

And what did the company think of women and children
taking an active part in funerals? he asked, introducing a
new topic. He had recently, he said, witnessed a funeral of a
child where six little playmates, the oldest not thirteen, had
served as honorary pall-bearers. They had walked all the
way to the burying ground by the side of the funeral chaise.
Later they had, as a matter of course, been refreshed with a
tumbler of gin and water and sugar, mixed for each. But
funerals, he felt, were primarily men's affairs.

" 'Tis hard to change custom," another guest interjected.
"I recall that when Mrs. John Morgan, the sister of Francis

Hopkinson, died in Philadelphia, her funeral was held on an icy winter's day. The pall was borne by the first ladies of the town, and how those good dames kept their footing on the slippery street is more than I shall ever know. I had looked for at least a few sudden contacts of the ice and some of Philadelphia's best and buxomest buttocks."

It was agreed by all that while girl pall-bearers, dressed in white and wearing long white veils, made a pretty picture, certainly woman's place was not at a funeral dinner.

Now the waiters, worthy of their hire, filled glasses again. The minister rose and delivered a eulogy on the deceased, concluding with some appropriate remarks on the democracy of death.

"We here are enjoying a delectable dinner in honor of our departed brother," he declaimed. "Yet we do not forget the humblest when he shuffles off this mortal coil. When the veriest pauper dies, our Massachusetts towns provide at least a gallon of wine and another of cider to be drunk at his funeral." *

By this time the moment was reached where a number of those present had drunk enough to be moved to lift their voices in song. Naturally only hymns would be appropriate to the occasion. One guest remarked that he rather liked the old Cornish custom of singing all the way from the church to the grave.

"That," coldly remarked a local gentleman, "would never do in Boston."

A rather heated argument developed on the choice of the hymn to be sung. Some urged the old favorite beginning—

*"Why do ye mourn departed friends,
   Or shake at death's alarms?"*

Others insisted on the hymn entitled *Who'll Be Next?* The

*Town accounts carried such items as "incidentals." The custom was continued well into the Nineteenth Century when observance of the funeral of President Lincoln cost Chicago more than $800, charged to drinks for "mourners."

minister smoothed away the dispute by telling his story about the chorister's epitaph.

"There was once a choir leader familiarly known as 'Stephen,' who always beat time at an arm's length," he narrated. "So much emphasis did he seem to give the music that many supposed that good church singing was altogether dependent on the motions of those long arms."

Here the reverend gentleman stopped and smiled broadly in anticipation of the coming point as he always did.

"In the midst of Stephen's usefulness," he continued, "death succeeded at length in stopping this musical pendulum from swinging. On a plain marble slab at the head of his grave were inscribed these lines:

" *'Stephen and Time at length are even,*
Stephen beat Time and Time beat Stephen.' "

Everybody laughed immoderately, including those who had heard the story not a few times before. All then joined the minister in singing Wesley's *Rejoice for Our Brother Deceased*. Guests rose from the table replete, agreeing that it had been a most delightful funeral dinner, marred only by the unavoidable absence of Brother Caleb who would have enjoyed it vastly himself.

It was indeed a pity he could not have been present. The minister was reminded of one more epitaph which he quoted from the gravestone of a Virginia planter:

"Here lies Dick Cole, a grievous Sinner,
That died a Little before Dinner,
Yet hopes in Heaven to find a place
To Satiate his soul with Grace."

Indeed the worthy Master Dawes would have enjoyed the banquet—except perhaps paying for it. A reckoning up showed the cost came to 420 hard dollars, an outlay which other funeral expenses raised to $844. In terms of modern purchasing power that sum would amount to between five and ten thousand dollars.

But an end to such overflowing obsequies was approaching. Already a number of citizens were following the example of the testator who in his will strictly forbade the serving of drinks at his funeral, "having observed in the daies of my pilgrimage the debauches used at burialls."

Early in the Nineteenth Century, a worthy old gentleman, residing in New York, was heard bitterly complaining that temperance had taken all the fun out of funerals.

FERVOR ON THE FRONTIER

Reverend Lyle Keeps a Revival Diary
1801

Here blue-eyed Jenny plays her part.
Inured to every saint-like art,
She works and heaves from head to heel
With pangs of puritanic zeal.
Now in a fit of deep distress,
The holy maid turns prophetess,
And to our light and knowledge brings
A multitude of secret things;
And as enthusiasm advances,
Falls into ecstacies and trances;
Herself with decency resigns
To these impulses and inclines
On Jimmy Trim, a favorite youth,
A chosen vessel of the Truth,
Who, as she sinks into his arms,
Feels thro' his veins her powerful charms.
Grown warm with throbs of strong devotion,
He finds his blood in high commotion,
And, fired with love of this dear sister,
Is now unable to resist her.

Jacob Bailey: Poems

A red glare seemed to light up the fair white pages of Reverend John Lyle's diary, when with half-closed eyes he tried to remember more vividly the events he was recording. Characters his quill set down in sober black ink took human form and leaped and writhed against a lurid background. Small wonder it should be so. Enough to inflame the imagination of anyone who beheld them had been those fantastic, almost incredible scenes at the great Cane Ridge Camp-Meeting. . . .

Hundreds of camp-fires blazing high, and torches glowing crimson against the night. The trees of the forest, festooned with lanterns and candles, burning bright as the bush whence Jehovah spake in awful accents to Moses. A dark multitude, thousands upon thousands, flowing through clearing and glade, shouting and singing hosannahs in the hope of Heaven, wailing and shrieking in dread of Hell—Hell whose bottomless pit appeared to yawn at their very feet—Hell into whose eternal fires they, miserable sinners, saw their shrinking souls descend.

Preacher Lyle shuddered a little as he wrote; then sighed with satisfaction. True, there had been wild excesses, but many a brand had been snatched from the burning.

When John Lyle and other ministers planned a meeting

to be held at Cane Ridge, Kentucky, in August of 1801, their hopes were high. Signs and portents were plain of a mighty resurgence of the Spirit, another Great Awakening. It was sixty years now since that epochal revival when stern Jonathan Edwards had roused the slumbering conscience of New England, and the eloquent Englishman Whitefield had traversed the Colonies from Boston to Savannah holding huge open-air meetings to set the feet of transgressors upon the path of salvation. But the balance of the Century had witnessed a woeful relapse. Americans had won their Independence, yet risked the loss of their immortal souls. In the wake of the Revolution had followed the looseness and licentiousness which are the sequel of wars. Religion had grown cold and comatose. Now once more it was quickening. The zealous labors of the missionaries had borne fruit.

Reverend Lyle was still a little amazed that the seed had fallen on fertile ground here on the frontier, here in the rough new State of Kentucky where it might so easily have been choked by tares. One Kentucky county was nicknamed "Rogues' Harbour" because a majority of its inhabitants was declared to be murderers, horse thieves, and highwaymen. In another county which, it so happened, was the site of the projected Cane Ridge meeting, the accidental discovery had been made that sour mash whiskey could be marvelously mellowed in charred kegs. The resultant smooth potion was called Bourbon after the county of its origin and it was guzzled by gallons along with every other kind of liquor frontiersmen could lay hands on. Gambling, brawling, and all manner of coarse amusements were as common as heavy drinking. Nevertheless camp-meetings organized during the year 1800 had been excellently and enthusiastically attended. Undeniably the frontier held God-fearing folk who bowed knee neither to Mammon nor to Thomas Paine.*

---

*Thomas Paine, it was sometimes recalled, had wielded a powerful pen in the cause of Liberty but as a deist he was anathema to the clergy.

But that there were so many of them John Lyle and his
colleagues never had dared believe—not until their own eyes
beheld the people flocking to Cane Ridge by scores, by hundreds and then by thousands. Watching them congregate,
Preacher Lyle was aware that by no means were these all
earnest seekers after the Light. Some came out of curiosity,
some for entertainment, many because they were desperately
lonely in their isolated cabins. Some came to scoff or with
nefarious intent. No matter, John Lyle assured himself. They
would all hear the Word.

They came from all parts of Kentucky, Tennessee, and
north and south of the Ohio River, making journeys of
more than a hundred miles as willingly as ten. They arrived
on foot, on horseback, and in wagons, wagons more often on
sledge runners than on wheels. They came prepared to stay
days, to camp out under the trees or in tents or their wagons.
Provisions they carried could be easily supplemented by
game abundant in the vicinity.

And still they came until incredulous clerics had counted
five hundred wagons and at least ten thousand people—some
said thrice that number—a mighty concourse, men, women,
and children.

Biting the end of his quill as he looked up from his diary,
Reverend Lyle recalled certain misgivings. At revivals in
Virginia only men had remained in the meeting-ground over-
night; women had returned to their homes. At Cane Ridge
women had stayed, and meetings had carried on through the
day far into night. Aye, there had been incidents. . . . It
could not be denied, the diarist conceded, that the revival had
occasioned undue excitement of animal feeling and too free
communications of the sexes.

A charming spot, finely shaded and well watered, the Cane
Ridge meeting-ground was ready for the first arrivals on
August sixth. A central area had been cleared and leveled,
and a spacious preacher's stand erected, other stands sprang

up like mushrooms through the forest as it was seen how inadequate were preparations for so unexpectedly vast a throng. Ministers were far too few. Though planned as a union meeting by Presbyterian and Methodist clergy, bars had to be let down. Baptists stepped into the breach. So, to the dismay of John Lyle and his colleagues, did scores of voluntary exhorters, hedge-priests, the laity.

The first services were decorously opened with prayer. Solemnly the swelling congregations chanted a favorite revival hymn, *Mercy of God.*

> Thy mercy is more than a match for my heart,
> Which wonders to feel its own hardness depart.
> Dissolved by Thy Goodness, I fall to the ground.
> And weep to the praise of the mercy I've found.
> The mercy in Jesus exempts me from hell;
> Its glories I'll sing and its wonders I'll tell . . .

Preachers launched on their sermons. Vehemently, unsparing, they spoke out, direfully threatening sinners with a hereafter of hellfire, thundering at the unregenerate as had Jonathan Edwards in the Great Awakening.

"What abominable lasciviousness have you been guilty of! * How have you indulged yourselves in all manner of unclean imaginations! With what unclean acts and practices have you defiled yourselves! What lewd company have you kept, wherein were things not fit to be spoken, and in which you have taken great delight!"

Tears of shame and repentance were flowing freely now. The upturned countenances of listeners were flushed or blanching. But unrelenting, accusing voices thundered on.

"How have you corrupted others as well as yourselves by the abominations you have committed in company, and in the dark! You have reason to tremble every moment, and to be afraid that eternal burnings will be your portion. But

---

*Jonathan Edwards, *The Justice of God in the Damnation of Sinners, explained, illustrated* and *proved in a Sermon upon Romans III:19*. Boston, 1788.

let your fears be ever so great, let damnation be ever so dreadful——"

A scream, shrill and piercing, cut through the harange from one of the stands. Some pious female had been unable to repress the violence of emotions aroused. Spurred on, the exhortations of the preachers became more impassioned still. Cries for mercy mingled with shouts of ecstacy. "Glory! Glory to God!" In a crescendo of clamor that rose to such heights it was heard five miles away, "probably the wildest and most ferocious religious meeting ever held in the United States" * got under way.

On the first day it was two o'clock in the morning before the services ceased. Thereafter it was as late as four—or not at all. For seven days and six nights the vast encampment never was still. Cooking, eating, sleeping, all the human functions were carried out simultaneously and in chaotic melange with divine services.

Day and night Reverend Lyle and his brethren, always close to the point of exhaustion, ministered to their charges. At once overjoyed and appalled, they witnessed the revival surpass their most sanguine expectations. They saw people assailed by consciousness of sin, so profound, so despairing, that repentant ones could not rest without unmistakable assurance that, washed in the Blood of the Lamb, they could be saved. They saw religious fervor rise to such an intense and overwhelming pitch that it raced from group to group, like an ignited powder train, to fire the massed multitude.

Vainly the more responsible clergymen sought to stem and restrain the growing hysteria. John Lyle pleaded with the people: "Guard against this enthusiasm, which like a worm, destroys the beauty of this revival and will ere long discredit the work of God." He persuaded one tumultuous congregation to end the Babel of singing six different hymns at once and unite on one. But volunteer exhorters fed fanatic flames.

For many, the feverish emotions stirred up within them

*Herbert Asbury. *A Methodist Saint. The Life of Bishop Asbury.* New York, 1927.

became intolerable, too powerful to be contained. Weeping and crying out gave little surcease. Minds in anguish demanded relief of the body. Extravagant manifestations, termed by the ministers "bodily exercises", seized on the people and the meeting took on the semblance of Bedlam, a battlefield, and a pagan rout combined.

Wrought-up worshippers began to fall to the ground. Shaken by tremors, shrieking and groaning, men, women, and children keeled over. Singly or by scores or by hundreds they dropped as if struck by lightning or mown down by a volley of musketry. They lay twitching convulsively or stiff and still in deep trances lasting from quarter-hours to days.

The slightest suggestion was enough to start the Falling Exercise. Let a group but sing a line from the hymn:

Dissolved by Thy goodness, I fall to the ground . . .

and in a trice "the slain of the Lord" were scattered all over the field.

A man vowed he would not fall for a thousand dollars—and fell with the words in his mouth. Another toppled while defying God and His angels to throw him down. Women riding to the meeting fell from their horses and lay by the roadside unconscious or flinging themselves about and kicking their heels against the ground. "My blood tingled as I fell," one girl declared. "A sweet feeling darted through my body. I felt great weakness during and after the falling."

John Lyle recalling a number of deplorable cases where weakness persisted, wrote a rueful sentence in his diary, strongly underlining a word: "Several who have fallen in religious ecstacy have since *fallen* still more woefully."

None was immune. A fashionable couple, attending the meeting out of curiosity, joked as they watched people roll in the mud, screaming and crying for mercy. Sportively they agreed that if either one of them should fall, the other would stand by and help. To the man's consternation, his companion suddenly collapsed. Forgetting his promise to her he fled at full speed but had not gone 200 yards before he, too, dropped as if he were shot. Crowds gathered around and prayed over the prostrate pair. A father, concerned as to what might happen to his daughters during their frequent swoons, threatened to beat them if they ever came to such a place again; in the midst of his tirade he crashed to the ground. On one occasion at least 500 people fell in swathes, uttering shrieks that rent the very heavens. So many fell on the third night of the meeting that Lyle and others toiled for hours picking up inert bodies, lest they be trampled on, and laying them in rows on the floor of the big meeting-tent like so many disaster victims. All told, 3000 were computed to have fallen at Cane Ridge.

And sweeping through the meeting like an irresistible pestilence spread "The Jerks." People excited by the praying and preaching suddenly were seized by involuntary spasms. Arms began to jerk from the elbows downward; then the convulsive motions spread until every member was spasmodically twitching. Women presented particularly pitiable spectacles. They gasped like fish on land. Eyes rolled in distorted faces, and bosoms heaved. Heads jerked back and forth with such frightful celerity that necks seemed about to snap, while long tresses cracked like whip-lashes. Some, on recovering from one spell of the jerks, had their hair shorn. Those afflicted were utterly unable to control themselves except at times by prayer or dancing. It was difficult or dangerous to try to hold them. Four strong women were barely able to restrain one young girl's violent jerking. Attempts at restraint were sometimes prevented by zealots who cried out that it was impious to thwart the will of God.

Few dared mock or scoff. If they did, some seizure might fasten its grip on them—they had seen it happen. In the ears of doubters rang the menaces of the Watts hymn:

> Laugh, ye profane, and swell and burst
> With bold impiety,
> Yet shall ye live forever cursed
> And seek in vain to die.

Ye stand upon a dreadful steep,
    And all beneath is hell.
Your weighty guilt will sink you deep
    Where the old serpent fell.

Half-longing for a moment of meditation and quiet con-
templation, John Lyle dizzily watched the hurly-burly. Past
him darted folk taken with the Running Exercise. They
dashed about at top speed, leaping over every obstacle in the
way with preternatural agility, or crashing into trees, seemingly without feeling any pain. Some rolled over and over
like a wheel or sidewise like a log. Women raced through
the woods, hair streaming and shrieking like veritable Furies.
Yonder a girl spun like a top. She must, Lyle estimated,
growing dizzier than ever, be making at least fifty revolutions
a minute.

Reverend Lyle and the other clergy did their best to ease
the throes of poor creatures, tortured by convictions of mortal sin. Hour after hour they passed from one group to another, praying with the afflicted and inquiring of them if
they had received comfort, whether they had found Christ.
Some gave assurance like the youngster of seven who was
heard proclaiming to playmates: "Oh, the sweetness of redeeming love! Oh, if sinners knew it, they would all come
to the overflowing fountain!" Yet there were others who had
found no relief. Such was the small boy who wailed in terror:
"Oh, I am lost forever! I am going right down to Hell! Oh,
I see Hell and the breath of the Lord like a stream of brimstone kindling it!"

Loud as the roar of Niagara was the crowd noise, and
punctuating and swelling it was a constant barking, baying,
and yelping. Not all the hounds brought to the camp-meeting, giving tongue in concert, could have raised such a
racket. The barking was human, the result of another sort of
seizure as compelling as the jerks. Sinners of all ages and
stations went down on all-fours to snap, growl and bark so

realistically that newcomers believed the noise was being made by actual dogs. One child was regarded as blessed because he produced a deep bark like a mastiff's while the best his small friends could manage was shrill yips like a spaniel's.* Many found this barking manifestation extremely mortifying but could not escape it—not even some of the revivalist preachers while in the very act of delivering a Scriptural text. One cleric was heard to declaim:

"Every knee shall bow—*bow-wow-wow!*—and every tongue shall confess." **

No, the preachers had not all been able to hold aloof from the waves of excessive emotionalism sweeping through the revival, Reverend Lyle admitted to himself. The Presbyterians, of course, had maintained a measure of decorum. But as for other denominations and the volunteer and lay exhorters. . . .

Preachers shouted at the top of their lungs during their sermons or gave vent to the "Holy Laugh," a whoop of mirth delivered with a grave and solemn expression of the features. Crowds drifted to stands where services were "more lively." On all sides sprang up the volunteer soul-savers. A boy of twelve, supported by two men as he neared exhaustion, threatened his auditors with hellfire for two solid hours.

Girls forgetting their reserve and modesty, besought sinners to repent in a most passionate manner. Reverend Lyle was distressed to see the serenity proper to the sex vanish and in its stead appear boldness and forwardness. Carried away by the transports of their feeling, females from fourteen to forty began hugging and embracing everyone in their

*Previous instances of similar religious hysteria had been recorded in Europe. When a nun was moved to mew like a cat, others followed suit until the whole convent rang with miaouws. An epidemic of barking like dogs raged through a monastery, with an even more unfortunate sequel: the brothers began to growl and then to bite each other.

**Rev. Robert Davidson. *History of the Presbyterian Church in the State of Kentucky.* New York, 1848. P. 152.

vicinity, and men—especially clergymen—came in for a liberal share of these caresses. They bestowed the Kiss of Charity, cited in Holy Writ, but bestowed it so fervently that it seemed to the discomfitted minister to depart from the sacred and verge on the profane.

"Women in their frantic agitations," John Lyle wrote, shaking his head over his diary, "often unconsciously exposed their persons in a manner shocking to common decency. Not only did they tear open their bosoms, but they at times had to be held by main strength to keep them from the most indelicate attitudes."

Hubbub rose to a peak of pandemonium. Animals fled the forest. Bacchanalian revels vied in uproariousness with religious rites, as liquor was brought in by men of ill will and sold freely. Reverend Lyle perceived that the blackleg, the cut-purse, and the prostitute had filtered in among the godly, and it was impossible to separate the sheep from the goats. Through the meeting-ground swaggered wild young fellows from adjoining towns with bold-eyed, free-mannered young hussies tripping by their sides, come for no good. The confusion and excitement of a revival afforded such opportunities as no masquerade, no barn-raising or corn-husking ever offered. Well aware of what was toward, disturbed ministers laid plans to segregate the sexes during hours allotted for sleep and to organize night watches to patrol and recconnoitre the camp. But the men of God were too few, too occupied, too weary. In their despite, the very preaching-stand in the clearing was made the scene of nocturnal assignations by wretches.

Verily the wicked shall have their reward, and the wages of sin is death. Yet the just-minded could not but concede that not a few transgressed in all innocence, acting not of their own volition, knowing not what they did—that some were more sinned against than sinning.

Alas, the aspirations of the spirit and the lusts of the flesh are contained in one weak vessel. Emotions roused to fever heat by fierce and fervent exhortations too often burst the thin barrier. August nights were warm, and the deep, sheltering shadows of the forest were only a few steps beyond the circles of illumination.

Mustering such philosophy as ne could, John Lyle mused on the fact that the rate of illegitimate births inevitably rose after revivals.

Aye, there had been wild excesses at the Cane Ridge Camp-Meeting, but many a brand had been snatched from the burning. There was strong testimony to that effect from a young Virginia parson, George Baxter, who traveled through Kentucky the following October and wrote in a letter:

"On my way to Kentucky, I was informed by settlers on the road that the character of Kentucky travelers was entirely changed; that they were now remarkable for sobriety as they had formerly been for dissoluteness and immorality. And indeed I found Kentucky, to appearance, the *most moral place* I had ever seen. A profane expression was hardly ever heard. A religious awe seemed to pervade the country . . . and a friendly temper among the people."

There may have been some moved to wonder whether Parson Baxter would still have found Kentucky the most moral place he had ever seen had he visited it not three months after Cane Ridge but nine.

John Lyle wrote finis on his diary, corded up and put away its sheets. Never published, forgotten, it was not found until after his death. Then it was close to being thrown into the fire as wastepaper and blazing up like those flaming scenes of 1801 depicted in its pages. Some chronicler with a sense of values fortunately rescued it. It was such stuff as history is made of.

WHERE BEAVERS BECKONED

Tales of Two Trappers and of
Uncle Sam's Hat

1810 and 1832

I reside at Table Mountain, and my name is Truthful James;
I am not up to small deceit or any sinful games . . .

Francis Bret Harte: *The Society upon the Stanislaus*

The canoe glided in to the wooded river bank. John Coulter swung himself ashore from the bow and knelt to make fast. Then he looked up and saw the bushes come alive with Indians in war paint.

Coulter's partner in the stern reached for his rifle. Scarcely had his hand touched it before he was dead with a score of arrows through his body.

Coulter, helpless, waited for death, penalty of carelessness in the unexplored West, in Indian country. But the expected flight of arrows never was loosed. Red hands seized him, stripped every bit of clothing from him. The white man braced himself for the torture stake.

But that day the tribe was in the mood for a sporting event. Coulter found himself suddenly freed, with his grinning captors motioning him to run. For an instant he stood dazed; then sprang through the bushes and ran for his life, whooping Indians hot after him.

The sprinting naked figure drew rapidly away from the pursuers. Angry shouts grew fainter. It had been a mistake to give a chance for life to a prisoner who proved to be so extraordinarily fleet of foot. John Coulter, taking hope, glanced back over his shoulder. To his dismay, one warrior, with an expression of horrid purpose on his face, was gaining on him fast.

The fugitive spurted desperately. The red man matched

his spurt and the gap between them narrowed steadily. Now Coulter could hear the thud of flying feet—could almost feel the final leap—knees in his back—a knife between his shoulder blades.

No frontiersman was willing to be cut down like a hunted animal. Coulter slackened his pace, halted suddenly, whirled and met the Indian head on. They crashed together and grappled, rolling over and over on the ground, Coulter gripping the wrist of the savage's knife hand. A sudden wrench. A thrust. A groan. John Coulter flung off a limp red body and staggered up.

The rest of the tribe were pounding up now with fierce war whoops. The white man took to his heels again, his breath coming in gasps, his bare feet torn and bleeding from stones. He was near exhaustion, yet he held his slight lead.

And then the runner burst from the forest to find his escape barred by a broad stream. If he turned and ran along its bank, he was lost. In the second or so of his approach, his practiced trapper's eyes caught sight of a half-completed beaver dam toward the farther bank. John Coulter plunged in and the waters closed over him.

In vain the Indians, arrows notched and bowstrings taut, watched for him to come to the surface. They dove in after him, scoured both banks of the stream. At last they gave him up as drowned.

Coulter had swum to the underwater entrance of one of the beaver mounds, forced his way through and emerged into the air space beneath the dome of the refuge which the clever little animals construct. Overhead he heard the thread of his enemies. Waiting for some time to be sure they had gone, he swam out and, naked and unarmed, somehow found his way out of the wilderness to a trading post. Thus in that year of 1810 the first white man visited the region which today is Yellowstone National Park.

It was primarily the beaver that drew Coulter and others before and after him westward. Trappers hunting down the beaver for its rich fur opened the West. Back from the ever-advancing frontier to St. Louis flowed beaver pelts by the hundred thousand, bought at a thousand dollars a pack, and shipped so that dandies of the eastern cities and the gay bloods of London might have fine bell-crowned beaver hats to doff proudly to the ladies. The sombrero would become the typical hat of the West, but the beaver hat—which, by the way, is the headgear Uncle Sam is always pictured in—must stand forever as a symbol of the impulse of our nation's westward course.

Beaver pelts also were the magnet which drew Jim Bridger into the Yellowstone country, and the manner of his going there was no less dramatic and as nearly disastrous as that of John Coulter.

In the year 1832 a party of trappers rode west into Blackfoot territory. At their head was Jim Bridger who was then only twenty-eight but already had laid the foundations of his fame as one of the greatest frontiersmen the West has ever known. In the column rode a young Mexican trapper named Loretto and at his side his squaw, carrying their papoose. The squaw was a pretty young Blackfoot girl who had been a captive of the Crows when Loretto ransomed and married her. The two were much in love and devoted to their baby. Grizzled older mountain men grinned sentimentally at the tender family scene.

Alertly Bridger halted the column. The trappers slid off their horses with rifles ready. A band of Blackfeet had appeared across a forest clearing.

Loretto's squaw uttered a cry, thrust the papoose into her husband's arms and ran across to the Indians. They were her own tribe and she recognized her brother whom she had not seen since she was caught in the Crow raid. While both sides watched this touching reunion, the chief made friendly signs and rode forward.

Jim Bridger rode out to him, but, always mistrustful of Indians, he carried his cocked rifle across his saddle bow. Face to face in the center of the clearing, they talked. Then the trappers saw the chief push the barrel of Bridger's gun toward the ground and heard its sharp report. The two leaders wrestled for the possession of the weapon. The white man was swung around. Among the Blackfeet, bowstrings twanged and Jim Bridger dropped. Off galloped the chief, and the leader of the trappers limped back to his men with two arrows sticking in his back.

Whining bullets and whistling arrows filled the air. Through them the trapper Loretto rushed over to the Indians and restored to his wife the child who would have starved without her. The Blackfeet melted away into the forest, taking the girl and her papoose but leaving the brave Loretto unharmed. Months later the Mexican was able to rejoin his wife among her people.

Soon after that encounter the American party broke up. Jim Bridger with Tom Fitzpatrick, another famous mountain man, pushed on into the unexplored Yellowstone, the former with two arrowheads still embedded in his back, remarking that "good meat won't spile in mountains."

Bridger, who already had discovered Great Salt Lake, was to achieve many other feats as a pioneer, scout, guide, and Indian fighter. His was a most adventurous career, yet in it there was nothing stranger than the effect on the man himself of his early exploration of the Yellowstone. It made him one of America's grandest tellers of tall tales, an unrivalled inventor of whoppers.

This is the way it happened. Jim Bridger's astounded eyes looked upon the marvels of Nature in the Yellowstone. He beheld the spouting geysers of that dying volcanic region, the steaming pools, the petrified forest, a cliff of glassy obsidian, and other phenomena that can be seen there today. But when he came back and described what he actually had witnessed, not a soul would believe him. Again and again he told his story, protesting it was true, only to meet the same scoffing incredulity. At last he decided that since he was going to be set down as a liar anyway, he might as well make an artistic job of it and really deserve the reputation. So—and here was the clever part of it—he took the actual facts and enlarged on them until he had some really bang-up yarns.

A group around a western campfire would lead Jim Bridger

on to talk about the Yellowstone and he, after a little persuasion, would hold forth.

One day (he would drawl) I was hunting in the Yellowstone and caught sight of the biggest elk ever. Drew a bead on him and fired. Missed, by gravy. Blame' elk never even looked up. Acted like he never heard the shot. I aimed more careful. Missed again, and I'm a good shot, too. Fired twice more and that elk paid me no mind. Then I got mad. I clubbed my gun and rushed at that haughty animule. Danged if I didn't run smack into a glass cliff. The elk was way on the other side of it. What's more, I looked again and found that cliff was made out of the kind of glass they have in telescopes. Yes, siree. That elk had looked like he was only a hundred yards off to me. Matter of fact, he was way to hellan-gone twenty miles away.

If hunting in the Yellowstone held such hazards, how was the fishing? Listeners would ask.

Convenient-like, was Bridger's answer. You find pools there that are boiling-hot on top and cold underneath. All you have to do is drop in your line, hook a trout and before you've pulled him out, he's cooked to a turn.

One of the most remarkable things of all in the Yellowstone was the echo, Bridger would declare. Funny thing about it was it took the echo just so long to echo. Once I found that out, said Jim, I used to holler out "Time to git up" when I turned in at night. Six hours later on the dot that echo roused me up by shouting back, "Time to git up."

Sure, there were other queer things, he admitted when pressed. For instance, a place where dead trees had turned right into rock. Petrified forest was the book-name for it. Some Indian medicine man must have put a spell on the place, for not only the trees were turned to rock but the sagebrush, the grass, the antelope, the bears, and even the birds flying. You could sort of hear music and smell sweet perfume around there all the time, so the music and the perfume, Jim reckoned, must be petrified, too.

Queerest thing of all, Jim would remark unblushingly,

was the time I made to jump my horse over a chasm which was too wide for him. It was a mighty lucky thing for me that the—you know—the reason why you fall—yep, the force of gravity—well, that was petrified, too.

Jim repeated all those stories of his while acting as guide for Sir George Gore when that Irish nobleman was on a western hunting trip in 1854. The delighted Irishman used to try to match Bridger by reading to him selections from the adventures of "Baron Munchhausen," especially the tale which tells how the Baron's horse was cut in two in a battle and the Baron, nothing daunted, rode off on the front half. Jim's innocent comment was: "I'll be doggoned ef I kin swaller anything that air baron sez. Derned ef I don't believe he's a liar!"

LOG CABIN AND HARD CIDER

Electioneering Takes a Tip from Tippecanoe

1840

What has caused this great commotion-motion-motion
    Our country through?
It is the ball a-rolling on
For Tippecanoe and Tyler, too,
For Tippecanoe and Tyler, too!
And with them we'll beat little Van!
Van, Van, Van is a used-up man.
And with them we'll beat little Van.
    Campaign Song

A double team of grunting oxen dragged the 50-foot ridge-pole for the log cabin into the clearing soon after daylight. Willing volunteers, hard at work with ax, adze, and saw, cheered its arrival and plunged back into strenuous action. There was no time to lose. The cabin must be raised and ready for its dedication and the speechifying that very evening.

Pennsylvania hadn't been frontier country for many a year, but there were still plenty of men around who knew how to put up a log cabin. This one would be as stout and weather-tight, chinks closed with clay, as the General's own cabin 'way out West in North Bend, Ohio—the one he built with his own hands after he'd whipped ten thousand Injuns in the Battle of Tippecanoe. The man raising this cabin wouldn't be ashamed to show it to the General—to William Henry Harrison himself—if he came by this way in the course of his election campaigning.

"Gee, Tip. Gee thar, Ty." That was the driver who had brought the ridge log, bawling to his oxen. Builders howled with glee. There was an-up-and-coming fellow for you. Had a team named for the next President and Vice-President of the U-nited States already. Hooray for Tippecanoe and Tyler, Too! Everybody burst into a campaign song, set to the tune of *The Old Oaken Bucket*. While they worked, they roared the refrain:

The iron-armed soldier, the true-hearted soldier,
The gallant old soldier, Old Tippecanoe.

On the road from town shone a flash of colored calicoes.
Yonder came the womenfolks, to be given a boisterous welcome. The way they set to work building campfires showed
there were still pioneer women in the State of Pennsylvania,
even if 'twas 1840. They boiled coffee and served apples and
doughnuts to the cabin builders for a nine o'clock snack; then
busied themselves preparing a noon meal that would really
stay a man.

There hadn't been such fun in the Lord knows when for
plain people all over the nation as this Presidential campaign.
Hard times—that's all they'd had—hard times since '37. But
things certainly were brightening with the prospect of victory
for the Whigs and defeat for the Democrats. A great day it
would be when Old Tip tossed that New Yorker, Martin Van
Buren, right out of the White House on his aristocratic Dutch
bottom. All the misery nowadays was mostly Van's fault.
Didn't the song say so?

Van Buren cannot be the working man's friend.
He has left him nothing to do
But starve or to beg, his country defend
And to work for Old Tippecanoe.
So I'll shoulder my flail, pack up for North Bend,
Where I'll thresh for Old Tippecanoe.

For Tippecanoe and Tyler, too.
For Tippecanoe and Tyler, too.
And with them we'll beat little Van, Van, Van.
Van is a used up man. . . .

How rapidly the cabin was rising—corner-posts, rooftree,
rafters! It would be ready, all right. Sharp at noon builders, knocking off, laid into the victuals the womenfolks had

cooked. Hot soup, barbecued beef and pork, regular mountains of boiled potatoes and mashed squash, slabs of pie, pots of steaming coffee. Everybody was most too busy eating to say much excepting Judge Parkins who could and would manage to talk even with his mouth full.

The Judge assured all that the election was as good as won; that the Whigs had 'em on the run. He'd lay a bet that Matty Van Buren and the Democrats wouldn't carry seven States. And it had been a Democratic editor down in Baltimore that really started the ball a-rolling for Harrison by writing an editorial against the General. In spite of a large mouthful of mashed squash, the Judge with drama and gusto recited the editorial's telling passage: " 'Give him'—that's the General—'a barrel of cider and pension of two thousand a year, and, our word for it, he will sit content for the remainder of his days in a log cabin by the side of a sea coal fire and study moral philosophy.' " Maybe that hadn't backfired on the Democrats! Now log cabins, like this here one, were going up all over the country, and barrels of hard cider were——

A roar from the thirsty interrupted him. "Where's that cider? Tap a barrel." Protests that it ought to be saved for the ceremonies were drowned by yells that there was plenty. A barrel was broached, and gourds dipped in, frontier style, just the way the General drank it out in North Bend. (Some folks said the General never touched a drop of anything, but they were probably Democrats, and who believed them? If you wanted facts, you read in good big print in a Whig campaign biography that "General Harrison's table, instead of being covered with exciting wines, is well supplied with the best cider.")

Soon everybody was singing loudly to the tune of *Auld Lange Syne:*

> *Should good old cider be despised*
> *And ne'er regarded more?*
> *Should plain log cabins be despised,*
> *Our fathers built of yore? . . .*

The answer must be an emphatic "No!" judging from the fervor with which the last lines were chanted——

> *We'll take a mug of cider yet*
> *For Tippe-ca-an-oo.*

Taking several mugs for good measure, all hands went enthusiastically back to work, the menfolk on the cabin, the women to cook a dinner which would make the noon-day meal look a mere morsel. At this rate the cabin would be up in good time. There'd be a fire on the hearth, and smoke curling up from the chimney. On the door a raccoon pelt would be nailed to dry just like in the old days. Come to think of it, this campaign was right hard on 'coons. There had to be a coonskin for every cabin door, and a whole lot of Whigs were taking to wearing coonskin caps, tails hanging down behind 'em. (Looked like a whole passel of Dan'l Boones, they did.) And the cabin's latchstring always would be out the way it was at the Harrison cabin out West. (Some folks, likely Locofoco liars, swore up and down that the General's dwelling was no log cabin at all but a good-sized two-story frame house, with two one-story wings. Well anyway, one of those wings had been a log cabin once.)

Like the Judge said, log cabins were being raised everywhere for the campaign. At the Baltimore ratifying convention, attended by 30,000 good Whigs, every State had brought its own log cabin on wheels and pulled it in the parade. New York City had one the size of a convention hall. Iron matchsafes, were being turned out in the shape of log cabins. Log cabins were printed on Harrison silk campaign badges, along with the legend: "The Poor Man's Friend." Souvenir silk kerchiefs—a lot too pretty to blow your nose on—with a decorative border of hard cider barrels and mugs, displayed a graphic scene in which William Henry Harrison was portrayed standing in front of his North Bend log cabin "which the old General has been able of late years to construct by many hard knocks and industry." He was welcoming two comrades-in-arms from the glorious field of Tippecanoe. Usually at least one of the veterans, shown being greeted by the General, had stumped up on a peg-leg, having lost a limb in his country's service. And always a mug of hard cider was being promptly tendered. Calicoes were printed, all over portraits of Harrison and log cabins. Log cabins adorned Harrison letter paper, cups, plates, and Sandwich glass; pins, soap, medals, fans, whiskey bottles, flags, and almanacs which pictured the General successively giving away his only blanket to a chilly soldier, saving the life of a Negro, and presenting a horse to a Methodist minister. (Just catch Thurlow Weed and the other smart Whig politicians, running the General's campaign, missing any kind of a vote!) All such souvenir articles, selling in vast quantities, spread the gospel for Old Tip.

That New York editor, Horace Greeley, was bringing out a campaign weekly newspaper called *The Log-Cabin*. It sold like hot-cakes, its circulation upwards of 80,000 a week, especially when it printed campaign songs. Desperately the Democrats published an illustrated broadside, purporting to expose all the reprehensible doings in a New York City log cabin. It stated that it represented an "authentic view of the Bar Room in the Log Cabin, Broadway, New York, Headquarters of the 14th Ward Tippecanoe Club." Signs over the bar offered Irish whiskey, Harrison juleps, North Bend sherry cobblers, Tyler punch, hard cider. And the dive's motto, according to the broadside, was:

> *In all the States no door stands wider,*
> *Hurrah, hurrah, hurrah,*
> *To ask us in to drink hard cider,*
> *Hurrah, hurrah, hurrah.*

On the barroom-cabin floor lay a crockery crate containing two bald eagles, "once the free denizens of the boundless air but now *cabin*-ed, cribbed, and confined, with ruffled plumage, drooping wings, and faded eye in a den of abominations, breathing the fumes of alcohol and the odor of cigars, instead of the clear atmosphere of Heaven." An unhappy raccoon was chained on rafters. Here indeed, the Democratic scribe snorted, were being formed *Tip*-ling habits which had caused any amount of backsliding from the ranks of the sober and temperate.

But all such fuss and fulmination was futile. As a Whig wit retorted: "What do the Locofocos expect by villifying the Log Cabin? Don't they know that a Log Cabin is all the better for being daubed with mud?" That one turned the laugh right back on the Locos.

"Should plain log cabins be despised?" Never! Log cabins, hard cider and song would put General Harrison in the White House. As Judge Parkins pointed out: "Daniel Webster, he'd like to have had us Whigs make him President, and Henry Clay would likewise. But Dan'l, he wasn't born in a log cabin. He's publicly apologized * for it and allowed as how his elder brother and sisters was all born in a log cabin, but that don't help much. Too bad his ma moved out of a cabin and into a house before she had Dan'l."

Finishing touches were being put on the cabin. It was close to sunset, and whale-oil torches and pine-knots were in readiness when dusk fell. A tantalizing, appetizing aroma drifted from the campfires where the women and girls bent over their pots and kettles.

Gramp Caulkins, rejoicing in the largest audience he had in years, was sitting handy to the cider barrel and holding forth on the brave days when he had soldiered with Mad Anthony Wayne and William Henry Harrison.

"Yesiree," declaimed the old veteran, " 'twarn't fur from here me and Gen'ral Wayne and Lootenant Harrison fit and whupped the Injuns at the Battle of Fallen Timbers. I ever tell ye 'bout the time Lootenant Harrison he says to me, says he, 'Sergeant, take twenty men and——' "

"Yes, Gramp, you told us that one. Tell us about the Battle of Tippecanoe."

"Well, me and Gen'ral Harrison and 'bout a thousand

*Webster's apology is cited in *The Pageant of America*, v. VIII. *Builders of the Republic* by Frederic Austin Ogg. New Haven, 1927.

Reg'lars and milishy went a-scoutin' for Chief Tecumshy. We was camped comfortable on Tippecanoe Creek when the hull Shawnee nation jumped us in the middle of the night——"

"And a complete surprise it was," the schoolmaster remarked under his breath.

"The Gen'ral he says to me, says he, 'Sergeant, that thar one's Tecumshy. You draw a bead on him and drill him, but save me his scalp.' So I done so, and we run off the rest of 'em and won the great and glorious vict'ry of Tippecanoe."

The schoolmaster muttered: "You old liar! Tecumseh wasn't even there. Harrison lost 188 killed and wounded. If Tippecanoe was a great and glorious victory, I'm a hoot owl."

Gramp, going on to relate at some length his own and Old Tip's in the War of 1812, finally finished:

"So here we set all safe and peaceful-like. Twarn't so many years back I set in front of a cabin like this here one right here in Pennsylvany—set with a long rifle across me knees, watching woods like them yonder—woods full of Injuns——"

At that moment blood-curdling warwhoops rent the air. A party of mounted warriors, flourishing tomahawks and scalping knives, burst out of the woods and rode down on the cabin. Women and children screamed in terror. Men snatched up axes and clubs. Quickly the "Indians" were recognized as masquerading Van Buren men from Harbor Creek. The Whigs, equally ready to fight Indians or Democrats, prepared to defend their cabin. However, the assailants promptly dismounted, surrendered themselves as prisoners of war and announced they had come to enroll themselves under the Harrison banner.*

To cheering and hand-shaking, the hatchet was buried with ceremony. Two more barrels of hard cider had been emptied, and dinner was ready when the guest of honor arrived. He was Congressman Ogle of Pennsylvania whose ringing speech in the House of Representatives on April 14, 1840, was still

*This episode, which occurred at Erie, Pa. was described in an early issue of Greeley's Log-Cabin under the headline: "Thrilling Log Cabin Incident."

reverberating throughout the land and vying with cabins, cider, and song in carrying the campaign for Tippecanoe and Tyler, Too.

Torches were flaring brightly when Judge Parkins rose to introduce the speaker of the evening. First, sighing with repletion from the mighty barbecue, he paid a glowing and well-deserved tribute.

"Fellow Whigs, Fellow Pennsylvanians, Fellow Americans: Whence came all those wholesome viands, prepared for our refreshment? Whence but from the fair white hands of our womenfolks. Does it not prove that the wicked charlatanry and mad ambitions and self-schemings of the leading members of the present Democratic Administration has struck in vain at the very sanctum sanctorum of domestic life? Does it not demonstrate beyond peradventure that the blood of their Revolutionary grandmothers still courses in the veins of our wives and daughters? Gentlemen, a toast in good old cider: Tippecanoe and Tyler, Too, and the ladies, God bless 'em!"

Drunk with a will, the toast was followed by the spontaneous outburst of another campaign song.

> *The beautiful girls, God bless their souls, souls, souls,*
> *The country through,*
> *Will all, to a man, do all they can*
> *For Tippecanoe and Tyler, Too, . . .*

"Ma," whispered a buxom, blushing miss, "What's it mean about us doing all we can to a man for Tippecanoe and Tyler, too?"

"It don't mean what you think, Minnie," came the stern answer, "and you keep out of them bushes tonight or your pa'll take a strap to you."

Loud plaudits greeted Congressman Ogle as he rose and launched on the famous speech * which had done such irrep-

---

Cf. the ringing oration: "Change the Name of Arkansas? Hell, No!" which while never delivered on the floor of Congress, may have been given in a committee or cloak room of the House. A bowdlerized version appears in *A Treasury of American Folklore.* B. A. Botkin, Ed. New York, 1944.

arable damage to President Van Buren's chances of re-election. Requiring several hours at its original delivery, it was slightly curtailed for this evening.

How long, Ogle demanded, would the nation continue to support a Chief Executive who drove haughtily through the streets of Washington in a plush-lined maroon barouche, with flunky outriders—who sat sipping costly soup from a silver tureen with a golden spoon in the Presidential Mansion—in that gilded palace called the White House?

"Let us survey its spacious courts, its gorgeous banqueting halls, its sumptuous drawing-rooms, its glittering and dazzling salons," Congressman Ogle invited. "All their magnificent array of gold and silver, crimson and orange, blue and violet. Screens of Ionic columns, marble mantles, gilt eagle cornices. Rich cut-glass and gilt chandeliers. French bronze gilt lamps, gilt framed mirrors of prodigious size, mahogany gilt bronze mounted secretaries."

Yells of derision interrupted. Somebody shouted: "Van even has his seckertaries ridin' around on hosses."

"Let us," Mr. Ogle again bid his auditors, "survey its damask, satin and double-silk window curtains. Its Royal Wilton and Imperial Brussels and Saxon carpets. Its gilt and satin settees——"

The last reference touched off another campaign song, the assemblage roaring out:

> *Let Van from his coolers of silver wine drink,*
> *And lounge on his cushioned settee.*
> *Our man on his buckeye bench can recline.*
> *Content with hard cider is he.*
> *Then a shout for each freeman, a shout for each State,*
> *For the plain, honest husbandman true.*
> *And this be our motto, the motto of fate,*
> *Hurrah for Old Tippecanoe.*

Now Congressman Ogle thundered out the final damning items of his incriminating catalogue.

"Sofas, bergeras, divans, tabourets, and French comfortables. Elegant, mahogany-gilt-eagle-mounted French bedsteads. Gilt plateaus, gaudy artificial flowers, rich blue-and-gold bombons, tambours, compotiers, ice cream vases. Olive boats, octagonal bowls, silver tureens, golden goblets, table spoons, knives, and forks.

"How do you relish the notion," he roared, "of paying out your hard-earned cash for silk tassels, galloons, and gimp and satin medallions to beautify the Blue Elliptical Saloon? Let Mr. Van Buren, if he chooses, lay out hundreds of dollars—of his own money perhaps—on perfumes for his toilet, on Double Extract of Queen Victoria, Corinthian Oil and Cream, and Concentrated Essence of Eglantine. But, my friends, should the working people pay for hemming his dish-rags and filling his foreign wine coolers? Should the taxpayer's money go to buy brooms, tart pans, and chamber buckets for Little Van?" *

Thunderous shouts of "No!" were joined in on even by girls who hankered to try those alluring-sounding extracts and essences. The log cabin duly dedicated, everyone marched home full of high spirits and hard cider and singing:

> *We know that Van Buren can ride in his coach*
> *With servants forbidding the Vulgar's approach—*
> *We know that his fortune such things will allow,*
> *And we know that our candidate follows the plow!*

(Some folks maintained that if General Harrison, son of a Virginia planter and himself a well-to-do land-owner, ever followed the plow, it was a good ten feet behind the hired hand who had a-holt of the handles. But anything Democrats said could be discounted as so much campaign flimflam.)

Yes sir, what with Matty's Panic of '37, plain people hadn't had so much fun in a long time as this campaign. When they weren't building log cabins and having barbecues

---

*Cost of items mentioned were quoted from White House accounts in a speech in Congress: 2 doz. brooms—$3.75; 2 doz. tart pans—$2.50; 1 chamber bucket—$2.00.

and picnics and drinking cider and listening to ripsnorting speeches, they were keeping the ball a-rolling.

"Keep the ball a-rolling for Tippecanoe and Tyler, Too." Some Whig had said that in a speech. It was just oratory, but behanged if people didn't take him literal! They made big balls, six to eight feet high, and covered them with hide. All over them they painted slogans like: "Tip and Ty" and "Hero of the Thames" and "Hurrah for Harrison and Tyler. Beat the Dutch or Bust Your B'iler." Through the middle of them they ran a rod, like an axel, sticking out far enough on each side of the ball so as seven men or so could push on each side.

The Whigs of Muskingum County, Ohio, paraded with a cowhide-covered ball 15 feet in diameter, drawn by twenty-four milk-white oxen. But most ball-rollers liked to foot it and push with their own power for Old Tip. They not only marched in all the parades but rolled balls many miles; one team shoved from Cleveland, Ohio, to Lexington, Kentucky, and that's no Sunday stroll. And as they rolled they sang to the tune of *Hail to the Chief:*

> *Hail to the ball which in grandeur advances,*
> *Long life to yeomen who urge it along;*
> *The abuse of our hero his worth but enhances.*
> *Then welcome his triumphs with shout and with song.*

Those balls sure rolled up Harrison sentiment, and only once did the Democrats get some mean satisfaction. That was when, smack in the middle of a parade, a big ball ignominiously collapsed. It may have been an accident but could very well be laid to the machinations of Matty's men. Nobody would have put it past 'em—not after that time at a Whig rally when some low-down Locofoco, lower'n a snake's belly, sneaked up to the hard cider barrel and poured in a bottle of ipecac.

Parades! Whole towns, counties, turning out to march in them. (Life was dull for Democrats; all they could do was stay indoors and bite their nails.) Parades that often were five miles long and stretched from one State into another. Log cabins on wheels, trappers carrying canoes, veterans bearing transparencies picturing the General's battles in vivid hues— Tippecanoe, Fort Meigs, the Thames. Brass bands blaring and marchers singing. Song leaders, quartets, and glee clubs touring the whole country, teaching people Harrison campaign songs. There were all of one hundred and twelve of 'em—not counting quick-steps and polkas—words usually set to familiar tunes. (Some folks—Democrats, of course—said it was a desecration to use the music of *The Star-Spangled Banner* that way.)

Monster rallies! Twenty-five thousand foregathered at Fort Meigs; 60,000 on the battlefield of Tippecanoe. Such vast numbers began to stream into flag-decked Dayton, Ohio, for the big rally one month before the election that campaign managers realized it would be impossible to try and tally 'em by the head. They up and hired civil engineers who *surveyed* the people massed for the rally and measured ten acres of humanity. Figuring four persons to the square yard, that ran to better than 80,000—maybe, close-clustered the way they were, to 100,000. Hooray for Tippecanoe and Tyler, Too!

Democrats kept on trying to make trouble but nobody paid them any mind. They kept demanding Harrison take a stand on the issues of the day and asking whether he had any platform at all.

Bah! What did the General need with a platform? Wasn't he a hero?

What were his views on Slavery? Hadn't he once joined an Abolitionist organization?

Nonsense! That was just a humane society.

Wasn't Van Buren Andy Jackson's chosen successor? Were the Whigs trying to push Old Hickory off his pedestal with Old Tippecanoe? All this talk about Van Buren being a lily-handed aristocrat was campaign hokum.

Well, if memory served, the Democrats had used that same line to lick John Quincy Adams. Sauce for the gander, eh?

Many of the campaign log cabins, the Locofocos charged, were rum holes, and every rally was a bender, with Whigs weaving around, drunk as coots. If it wasn't illegal, it was immoral.

Stuff and guff! Let the Locos read their history. George Washington himself when he was standing for the Virginia legislature had treated voters to rum, wine, beer, and cider Royal in spite of a statute against it—and won by a landslide. And Tom Jefferson, too, set up the drinks for his Virginia constituency and followed the custom of standing right by the polls to thank those who voted for him.

There was no getting around it. William Henry Harrison was the best man to represent the whole country, speakers orated, "because he was born in the South, lived in the West and had married the daughter of a man who had spent his life on Long Island, New York, and in New Jersey." Who could accuse him of sectionalism after that?

Sure as shooting, the General was going to be sung and drunk into the White House, but it was best not to take chances by missing any tricks.

None was missed. New York Whigs called a mass meeting with the following proclamation: "Meet—meet—meet, friends, of the honest old hero of Tippecanoe, and declare that you are not implicated, nor will defend the horrible morals of the Wall Street cliques. Come forth—come forth." In Connecticut, a broadside urged: "Vote for Harrison and divide the surplus of $50,000,000. Nearly $5 to every man, women, and child in the State." Commodity wholesalers ran such signed advertisements in the press as these: "The subscriber will pay $6 a barrel for flour if Harrison is elected and $3 if Van Buren is." "Five dollars a hundred for pork if Harrison wins; two-and-a-half if Van Buren does." Energetic Whig political heelers polled their precincts and on election day hitched up horses, loaded voters into buggies, carryalls, and wagons and drove them right to the polls.

When the shouting and the voting were over, seven States were all Little Van had carried. His 60 electoral votes were swamped by Old Tip's 234. The Democrats wailed that they had been talked down, sung down and drunk down. They sure enough had!

The General caught a chill being inaugurated President of the United States. Ailed for about a month, he did—all the office-seekers pestering him didn't rest him any—and then he passed on. There was one more big parade: the General's funeral procession. Tippecanoe was gone. There was just Tyler, Too. Folks felt sort of a let-down for a while.

But in that rousing campaign a wonderful time had been had by all excepting, of course, the Democrats, and it turned out there weren't so many of them. And the politicians had picked up a number of smart methods for future use in determining the will of a free electorate and the people's choice.

CLASH OF BROADSWORDS

An Affair of Honor in New Orleans

1840

That bruises and wounds a man's spirit should touch
With danger so little, with honour so much!

The Spectator

Be well assured, monsieur, the broadsword is an especially deadly weapon. We of New Orleans should know. For many years as a Spanish, French and then an American city we have heard the ring and rasp of steel on steel in a succession of *affaires d'honneur*. Many men have met under the Oaks or elsewhere to settle certain differences by resort to arms. And no sword can end the argument with such complete and bloody finality as the broadsword.

I have witnessed many a duel fought with the rapier, or *épée de combat,* strongly favored by our Creole gentlemen, or with the smallsword, called *colichemard.* For other encounters of my experience the sabre was the chosen weapon, wielded by duelists most often on foot but sometimes mounted. Even the foil have I seen employed button removed and sharpened to a needle-point, though the foil is properly used only for fencing in the *salle d'armes.* From all of these have I beheld men take wounds or death. Yet most stirring of all is the clash of broadswords.

The broadsword, monsieur, may be said to be legitimately descended from the swords with which knights hewed a foe in twain, but it has become smaller and much lighter. Its blade is long, straight; its edge razor-keen, for it is primarily a cutting, not a thrusting weapon. The Scottish Highlanders call it a claymore.

Now in the time of which I relate—the 1830's and '40's—
New Orleans was devoted to swordplay. It mattered not at all
that it was an age of firearms. True, duels were fought with
pistols, rifles and even—*quelle barbarie!*—with double-barreled
shotguns, loaded with one-ounce balls. But for diversion or
disputes gentlemen as a rule selected swords. You will comprehend readily why that should be so. Our people were still
chiefly of French or Spanish descent and *émigrés* from other
European nations: Germans, Italians, and so on—men born to
the tradition of the sword, not to that of the long rifle like the
native Americans. There dwelt among us numerous veterans
of the Napoleonic wars where musketry and artillery had not
altogether drowned the clash of sabres. Our young Creole
gentlemen, sent to Paris for their education, studied fencing
more closely than duller subjects and returned eager to display their adroitness and their knowledge of punctilio. So jeal-
ously did they guard their honor, so quick were they to take
offense that opportunity to cross blades seldom failed them.
If an occasion was lacking, they made one. For example, six
young bloods, strolling together through the streets in high
spirits on a fine evening, were suddenly inspired to fight *à la
impromptu* by the light of the great lantern over the entrance
to the Orleans Theatre. They paired off. Rapiers whipped
out, engaged. The music of steel was not stilled until two of
their number were stretched dead on the pavement.

Gentlemen fought over the relative merits of sopranos'
voices. A foreign visitor was challenged for having made remarks defaming our incomparable Mississippi River. There
were, on the average, three or four duels a day. For lesser or
greater reasons we had recourse to the field of honor, and some
came to old age with a proud record of participation in fifty
duels. But do not consider, monsieur, that New Orleans was
inhabited by swashbucklers, by bloodthirsty rufflers, and cut-
throats. Law or order prevailed in general, but you will comprehend that there are personal and private matters one does
not care to place before the courts. There the law, despite its
prohibition of duelling, must yield to the Code of Honor.
Few questioned it in those days when matters which would

be regarded today as clever or expedient were promptly and strictly rated dishonorable. With a gentleman's honor, as with a lady's virtue, there is no compromise—or so we then believed, monsieur.

Elsewhere in the United States, and notably in the North, disputes touching one's honor might be taken before a judge or settled by vulgar fisticuffs. Not so in New Orleans where good fighting ground was available on the Fortin plantation and later beneath the celebrated oak trees of Monsieur Allard, and none presumed to interfere.

You ask if the fair sex usually was the cause of a duel? By no means always, yet not infrequently. Rivalry for a lady's favor—*c'est inévitable*—and they were supremely lovely, our belles of New Orleans. Ah, their large, lustrous eyes, their curved red lips. Tresses, glistening under the candlelight, caught back in a *chignon* at the nape of a slender neck. White arms outstretched to pluck the strings of a gilded harp. Gowns *décolleté* to reveal snowy bosoms. The graceful swaying of crinolines down the aisle at the opera or over the ballroom floor. Ah, monsieur, forgive the ravings of an old man, remembering his youth.

I remember a girl at a ball one evening. Her education but newly completed at the Convent of the Ursulines, this was her first ball. How ravishing she was, light as gossamer in a man's arms—warm as flame. As the music paused, a gentleman approached us and bowed to the enchanting creature who was my partner.

"Honor me with half this dance," he begged her.

She did not, of course, curtly refuse but glancing toward me politely responded: "Ask monsieur. It belongs to him."

My answer? *"Jamais!* Never!" What else?

As the orchestra struck up, I whirled her off in a waltz. Yet I caught the remark softly addressed to me by my rival as we passed:

"Oh, monsieur, vous êtes bien mal élevé."

He had accused me of being ill-bred. What remained but to challenge and meet under the Oaks?

There were duels also over women of another sort.

Be it confessed that balls of elegance, such as that of which I have just spoken, were not always successful functions. As the evening passed, a marked diminution in the number of gentlemen present could not but be observed. By twos, threes, and fours they had quietly departed. Ultimately there were so many more ladies than gentlemen that the former were obliged to "form tapestry," which is to say they became wall-flowers. Everyone, including the ladies *en bredouille*—left in the lurch—knew well enough where the recreant gentlemen had gone. To the Quadroon Ball. There, declared the gentlemen, one was vastly more amused and decidedly more at ease.

Quadroons, as you may well know, were the daughters of white fathers and women of color. From their mulatto mothers they derived a strain of Negro blood, one-quarter or less, yet they themselves were nearly white. Raven hair and black eyes might betray the origin of some, but others (and especially so the octoroons) were almost as fair of complexion as any Creole lady—and might have passed as such if one did not observe the high cheek-bones and a faint violet tinge of the skin. The balls at which they appeared were subscription affairs, given at the Theatre Français, with admission strictly supervised so that only gentlemen could attend. White gentlemen, be it added. No quadroon men and certainly no Negro men were allowed to be present except as musicians or servants.

What an entrance they made, those quadroon girls! Each was announced with the greatest ceremony. The major domo would call, for example, "Mademoiselle Victorien de Sansejour," using the family name of the girl's white father. In they swept, gowned in the latest Paris fashions and fully conscious of their charms. They danced with grace, a credit to their French dancing masters. The balls were always gay, yet models of propriety, for mothers chaperoned their quadroon daughters with the strictest vigilance. Although the girls never failed to comport themselves in the most modest and decorous manner, they could coquette with an air at once subtle and infinitely tempting. Theirs was an exotic beauty. The result, monsieur, could be foreseen.

Yet all was most regularly arranged. The white gentleman

captivated by a quadroon signed an agreement with her mother to become the girl's "friend." A comfortable cottage on the Ramparts was obtained for the *ménage,* and the girl assumed her friend's name. At the same time the gentleman might and often did maintain a home for a legitimate wife and family; if the lawful wife learned of the separate establishment, she could do little but accept a prevailing custom. In several instances quadroon mistresses were bequeathed handsome fortunes. Daughters born of these alliances might be sent by their fathers to be educated in France where, well dowered, they made good marriages without difficulty.

While some of these women of color in their *ménages à deux* on Rampart Street were as faithful as ladies espoused at the altar, others could not prevent their fancies straying. Their protectors, discovering it, objected. But naturally! Then seconds paid a call on the interloper, cartels were exchanged, and there was another meeting on the well-frequented dueling grounds. Most certainly hundreds of duels resulted from rivalries arising at the Quadroon Balls and from subsequent jealousies. If you would learn the outcome of those encounters, monsieur, visit the Cemetery of Saint Louis and observe the numerous marble slabs inscribed: "Killed on the field of honour."

One's life, obviously, could depend upon one's skill with weapons. It is not to be wondered then that celebrated fencing masters flocked to New Orleans and that their *Salles d'armes* were crowded. At least fifty *maîtres d'armes* conducted establishments situated on narrow Exchange Alley, and there were more elsewhere.

No city, excepting only Paris, ever has seen the like. Day and night Exchange Alley resounded with the beat and click of blade on blade—the sharp exclamations of the fencers—the clatter of weapons to the floor as swordsmen disarmed one another. Spectators, seated along the fencing strips, sipped coffee and liqueurs and applauded a dexterous coup or parry. Often the masters gave stag suppers for their pupils, and there was drinking, singing, guitar playing, and gay roistering till all hours.

Formidable fellows, the *maîtres d'armes,* many of them having served in the armies of Europe. It may be pardoned that I, of French descent, esteemed the French masters highest, yet I shall not deny the merits of the Spaniards or the Italians nor even those of the Germans, somewhat slow and heavy but hard to defeat on fencing strip or in combat. I once saw one of them fight a broadsword duel in which his French opponent laid open his chest as one would carve the breast of a turkey. The German, bleeding copiously, wished to continue but his seconds would not permit it. Three days later the wounded man was marching in a military parade. They are like that, the Germans.

It was perhaps extraordinary that in New Orleans, a city where most black men were slaves, three of our fencing instructors were men of color: two mulattos and one free Negro. One of the former, Bastile Croquière, a handsome fellow, was one of our most notable masters of the *arme blanche.* It was a pleasure to cross blades with him. His fencing school always was thronged with eager pupils.

Not even the white *maîtres d'armes* were regarded as gentlemen and received socially. Some of them, nevertheless, may be said to have entered society through the bedroom window, as it were—by way of affairs of the heart with ladies. Husbands, learning of such a *liaison,* often decided that complacency was wiser than calling out so deadly a swordsman.

These experts in swordplay were not content simply with teaching. On the slightest provocation they would doff mask and plastron, lay aside foil with button and face in combat any man with any weapon. Nor were they ever reluctant to meet each other on the duelling grounds in a fight to the finish. One *maître d'armes,* running another through the heart, would take over the dead man's pupils.

Sometimes a swaggering fencing master would prove quarrelsome once too often. The skill of Marcel Dauphin with the rapier was never of any further use to him when he challenged a man who chose shotguns and fired first. The celebrated L'Alouette, splendid both with swords and firearms, committed the error of challenging an Acadian farmer who had horsewhipped him because of an insult. When the farmer named double-bitted axes as the weapons, L'Alouette declined to fight. It was not a master, I believe, but Monsieur Bernard de Marigny,* a gentleman of much belligerence, who called out a blacksmith over a quarrel in the legislature, where they were fellow-members. The smith, accepting, declared he would fight with sledge hammers, standing in Lake Pontchartrain in six feet of water. Since the challenged one was nearly seven feet tall, and De Marigny scarcely five foot nine, they passed off the affair for the excellent joke it was.

Greatest of them all was Pepe—José—Lulla, a suave and slender Spaniard who came to New Orleans in his youth, having shipped as a cabin boy from the Balearic Isles. Probably he had no superior with the broadsword or sabre. With the rapier or smallsword he was invulnerable. He was a crackshot with the rifle. With a pistol he could shoot coins from between friends' fingers or eggs from his son's head at thirty paces. The most notable duelist in the city, he would fight anyone under any conditions. He would duel with Bowie knives, the adversaries holding opposite corners of a handkerchief and never relinquishing it until one or the other was down (the best technique was to let your enemy plunge his blade into your left shoulder—then disembowel him.) Being a Spaniard and congenitally clever with knives, Pepe would fight with daggers in a dark room, or standing in the same sugar hogshead with his foe. Once he announced that he would kill his opponent by running him through a specified button of his waistcoat. Pepe did so and on the first thrust. Naturally those he called out often displayed the discretion of promptly offering him whatever apology he required, but still the list of his victims was reputed long. Some of them are said to be buried in the Louisa Street Cemetery which he himself owned. Most bereaved persons seeking a site there for a departed one did not recognize the

*M. de Marigny is credited with introducing from France to America a dice game which we forthwith named craps.

quiet, polite man showing them about as the formidable Pepe Lulla.*

Pepe Lulla did not take part in the notable series of broadsword bouts between the *maîtres d'armes* of New Orleans in the spring of 1840. Only those masters possessing a diploma were qualified to enter, and Pepe somehow lacked one. Consequently he was barred—which proved unfortunate on the dueling field for the official who had refused him.

This grand *assaut d'armes* took place in the Salle St. Philippe. Before crowds of devotees of the sword—their own pupils and others—the masters exerted themselves to the utmost to demonstrate their art.

One may imagine, monsieur, the intense interest with which we amateurs of the sword viewed those trials of skill between the professionals. Most of us had a favorite contestant, because we were his pupils or for some other reason, and our partisanship was no less zealous than the heated rivalries of the masters. Every bout's outcome was greeted by fervent applause or cries of bitter disappointment. As always in fencing matches, the decisions of the judges were hotly questioned. A glance at the flushed faces of the spectators revealed how close many tempers were to flaring.

For myself I sat enjoying the fine points of cuts and parries in the good companionship of a friend newly arrived from Paris. Between bouts we engaged in an animated conversation on the subject of duels. My friend related why duelists of older days were required to doff their cocked hats in salutation in the preliminary *révérence*. It was, he said, the survival of an old custom, designed less as a courteous gesture than as a means of thwarting low fellows with the deplorable habit of

*Lulla, or Llulla, Lafcadio Hearn states, was usually satisfied with disabling opponents and never killed enough to fill a single vault, nor were any of the fallen buried in his own cemetery. He would not fight against the Union in the Civil War, refusing to violate his oath of allegiance. His son graduated with honor at West Point. Lulla died in 1888 at the age of 73; long and complimentary obituary notices were printed.

carrying small pistols in the cocks of their hats; with these they planned to correct Fortune if she did not smile upon their efforts with the sword.

In turn I informed him of the deplorable state of dueling in the North. So far as I knew there had been no duel there of any consequence since the Hamilton-Burr encounter of some years ago, and even that was more of an ambuscade than an affair of honor if there were truth in the rhyme I had heard recited:

> O, Aaron Burr, what have you done?
> You've shot great General Hamilton!
> You hid behind a bunch of thistles
> And shot him dead with two horse-pistols!

But what else could be expected of Northerners?

My friend told of an unique rapier duel between two Parisian actresses. Unaware that women ever had met on the field of honor (though often the cause of meetings), I inquired if any blood had been shed.

"But certainly," my guest replied, "They inflicted several wounds on each other's faces and bosoms, two points at which both professional and female jealousy would instinctively aim. After several more furious passages, I regret to say they dropped their weapons, and the encounter degenerated into hand-to-hand combat. They kicked, clawed and pulled out one another's hair. Finally the lustier virago managed to gain a grip on certain of her rival's anatomical features I have already mentioned. She was prevented from tearing them from her squealing adversary only by the timely arrival of the police."

But now all our attention returned to the stage. We had watched an Italian *maître d'armes* named Poulaga, a giant of a man, win several bouts handily. None, so it appeared, could match him with the broadsword until a Captain Thimécourt, a former French cavalry officer, crossed blades with him. Ah, it was fine play! When the bout was over, the

Frenchman clearly had proved himself the other's equal if not his superior.

The big Italian was furious. He glared at his younger opponent and sneered.

"You are tolerably good for a beginner," he taunted. "But after all you are only a *tireur de salle*—a club-room fencer."

The hall was tensely silent, as Thimécourt replied:

"So? Well, I'll try you out on the field."

There was a rush for carriages and mounts to convey us to the Oaks. Nor was this the only such adjournment. No less than twenty duels between participants and spectators as well resulted from that *assaut d'armes*.

Withdrawn a proper distance, we spectators watched from among the trunks of the great trees on that familiar ground— many of us had fought there.

Seconds at their side, the duelists faced each other on the level sward—the huge Poulaga and Thimécourt. The former towered a head and more higher. His was the advantage in reach of sword arm and a strength that would make his broadsword cuts difficult in the extreme to parry. Though the captain, lighter and lither, had displayed a wrist of iron back there in the Salle St. Philippe, it seemed that the better weapon for him here would be the rapier or the smallsword.

A second proffered naked broadswords, not now the dulled weapons employed for fencing but with edges whetted keen. The principals drew them, tested their balance. Poulaga made his whistle through the air.

I had taken sides, monsieur. I liked not the great Italian's arrogance and the ill-grace with which he had taken defeat in the contest. On the contrary, I admired the spirit of the captain of cavalry and his ready resentment of the other's insulting aspersion.

Seconds stepped back. The duelists rendered the prescribed salute.

"*En garde,*" the referee called. Their broadswords crossed over his. Lowering his blade and retreating at once, he ordered, "*Jouez!*" The duel commenced.

Well-tempered steel, striking its like, gives forth a gallant, ringing tone. The glade rang with the martial music it had so often echoed.

Poulaga, smarting from his humiliation, pressed the attack with venomous fury. Warily Thimécourt gave way. Poulaga leaped forward to deliver a slash at the head so terrific it must have split his opponent to the navel. It was such a blow as scarcely could have been parried. The Frenchman did not attempt to do so but stepped aside. The blade whirred past his right ear and shoulder. His own sword flashed back with a riposte *en carte* that narrowly missed slitting the big man's throat.

Poulaga raged. But he was too veteran a swordsman to permit his wrath to betray him into rash, bull-like rushes. He rained furious blows on his enemy but did not forget his guard. Cut and parry—riposte and counter-riposte. The eye could barely follow the swift play of the blades.

A red stain spread across Poulaga's chest. Few of us had seen him hit, so lightning-fast had been Thimécourt's slash. Soon the Italian had another wound—a gash in his left flank. When the referee made as if to interpose, Poulaga bellowed at him. This, it had been agreed, was combat *à l'outrance*.

There was a moment's pause. It chanced that I glanced at the faces of my fellow-spectators. They were flushed and rigid with blood-lust. So must have appeared the faces of spectators in the Roman Colosseum two thousand years ago when two noted gladiators, short swords dripping crimson, closed in for the kill.

The duelists circled. Again and again the giant Italian lunged to the attack. The captain, contenting himself with defense, retreated, parried, flashed back a rapid riposte. Visibly Poulaga was tiring. It is the legs that age first. When they weaken, a fencer has only a sword arm. That does not suffice. It can deliver a cut only against an adversary who remains within its reach.

Now Thimécourt took the offensive. He feinted, struck and slashed open the other's left cheek just below the eye. He beat up the Italian master's blade and scored with a *coup de pointe* in the belly. A gasp ran around the encircling audience but the giant seemed not to be badly hurt. His riposte slashed away half the rolled up sleeve from the Frenchman's sword arm. A quarter of an inch closer, and Thimécourt would have been finished except for what defense he could have offered with a recovered blade in his left hand. He had not even been scratched, however. He returned to the attack vigorously, relentlessly.

We who watched now witnessed a man being slowly cut to pieces. When no vital spot is hit, it takes long to kill a large, strong man who cannot conceive either of defeat, or of surrender, or of death. This might have seemed simple butchery, if Poulaga had not continued to fight with undiminished fury —if he had not still been dangerous—if Thimécourt's cuts were not delivered with such admirable skill and finesse.

Of a sudden the end came. The cavalryman lunged and cut deep into the left side of the giant's neck, severing his jugular vein. As if one of the oaks about us had been felled, Poulaga toppled and crashed to the ground dead.

Monsieur, as I observed when I began my story, the broadsword can end an argument with complete and bloody finality. Clearly Captain Thimécourt had proved his superiority both in the *salle d'armes* and on the dueling ground.

We glanced at our watches. It was early still. Coachmen and grooms were called and we hastened back to the Salle St. Philippe to watch the remainder of the fencing.

FIRST WILD WEST SHOWMAN

Catlin's Indian Portraits Come Alive in England, 1844-45

Mr. Cooper says these red men
All were daring, brave and noble,
Frank, and honest, open-hearted,
Gentlemanly, proud, and stylish;
All were tall, and straight, and handsome,
Handsome, marriageable warriors;
So that all romantic maidens,
Who read Mr. Cooper's novels,
And the song of Hiawatha,
Think how nice 'twould be to marry
With some noble Indian Chieftain—
Live with him upon the prairies,
Live with him within the forest,
Sleep, at night, beside his camp-fire,
And have little Indian babies.
      Q. K. Philander Doesticks: * *Plu-ri-bus-tah.*

*Pseud. of Mortimer M. Thompson.

Daniel Kavanagh was harassed. He had hardly been more harassed when the two grizzly bears in his charge broke out of their cages on the ship coming across from the United States, with a fierce storm raging. The grizzlies did plenty of roaring and rampaging, but Daniel could manage bears as well as the original of his name did lions. Now these English here in Manchester really wore a man down with their questions, their countless, foolish questions. It was almost more than an American of Irish birth could stand, although it was part of Daniel's job as curator of the Catlin Collection to answer questions.

On the same ship with the bears, George Catlin had brought over his paintings of Indians,* along with the costumes, weapons, and other relics he had been gathering for eight years from forty-eight tribes. The Collection was drawing crowds at every showing. Europe's fascinated interest in the American Indian had waxed steadily since Columbus brought back his first specimens. It gripped kings and commoners equally. Good Queen Vic had bestowed her patronage on the Catlin Collection. So had the Tsar of all the Russias, wily old Leopold of Belgium, and Louis Philippe of France, who as Duke of Orleans had traveled through the United States and beheld the red men in their native haunts. Even more gratifying to George Catlin, whose portraits were as accurate in every detail as they were vivid, were the tributes of such scientists as Alexander von Humboldt.

All those questions from visitors to the exhibit were trib-

*The truly remarkable Catlin Collection is displayed in the National Museum, Smithsonian Institute, Washington. Catlin, losing all his money in speculations, gave the Collection as security to Joseph Harrison of Philadelphia whose widow presented it to the museum.

utes, too, yet they came so thick and fast all day and every day
that both Catlin and his curator were on the point of exhaustion. After closing time one evening, Daniel sat down,
stroked his chin whiskers and began to draw up for printing
and distribution a list of answers to typical questions that
would save his employer's and his voices if not their sanity.
His quill scratched busily and irascibly:

"The Americans are white, exactly the same color as the
English, and they speak the same language only they speak
it a good deal better in general." (That ought to fix the
Limeys who kept asking *that*. Now for another.)

"Mr. Catlin was among the Indians eight years and was
never once killed during that time."

An Irish bull that might be, yet it was a happy fact, em-
phasized in Daniel's mind by the artist-explorer's many narrow escapes from hostile savages, charging buffaloes, and
prairie fires. How curious it was that Catlin bore only one
scar, and that from a tomahawk thrown at him by a boyhood
companion while they were playing Indian. Daniel went on
adding items to his list.

"Don't Indians get drunk?" That was a favorite.

"Indians," Daniel penned on with truth and justice, "do
get drunk, but whites sell them the rum."

Next Daniel, snorting with virtuous indignation, set down
a series of answers to quizzings which, he declared, showed
where the minds of a good many visitors were running.

"Are Indians virtuous? Yes. I should say quite as much
as the whites if the whites would keep away from them and
let them alone.

"Ah, as amorous? No. Mr. Catlin says they have not the
spices of life and the imagination to set them on, or I'll ven-
ture they would be quite as bad as the whites.

"It is true that all Indian women stay away from their
husbands the seven days of their illness, and I think they are
the decentest people of the two doing it.

"Do Indians marry? Yes. They may have several wives at
the same time.

"Horns on a chief's head-dress have no bad meaning.*

"The Indians do lend their wives sometimes to white men, but it is only their old superannuated ones, who are put aside to hard labor, so it is a sort of kindness all around, and I don't see there is much harm in it."

Much as Catlin relished Daniel's efforts on answers, he felt compelled to rule them out as official information. To his curator, sighing that now it would have to be "done by hand," the artist explained that the trend of the questions was undoubtedly due to the influence of the American novelist, James Fenimore Cooper, and the French writer, Chateaubriand. Their books, widely read in Europe, had invested the red man with false and romantic glamor. Women readers especially reveled in it. Oh, for a wild free life in the forest, far from dirty, crowded city or dull village, as the consort of some noble savage! Striding forth from glowing pages into receptive female imaginations, the Indian warrior, splendidly barbaric, overwhelming virile, appeared the answer to the maiden's, not to mention the matron's prayer. While the American Indian had no stronger advocate and admirer than George Catlin, his rugged honesty scrupulously portrayed the red man as he was.

"Humph!" Daniel grunted when his employer had finished his explanations. "'Tis a foine thorough job thin this Misther Cooper did. He's made the English women wild about wild Indians. 'Tis bad enough they are over your pictures, as their questions make plain. Now if they were to set eyes on real——"

A tremendous racket in the street outside their lodging house interrupted him. A crowd had gathered. People were shouting words that sounded like "Indians! Real Indians!" The porter, barely stopping to knock, burst in to confirm it.

"Please, sir," he gasped. "There's a h'omnibus at the door quite full of 'orrible-looking folks, and h'I really believe they're h'Indians!"

---

*As the nail to his hole, the cuckold to his horn.—Shakespeare: *All's Well That Ends Well.*

Catlin had received a letter from a showman named Rankin that he was bringing over a small group of Ojibway Indians. Much as Catlin opposed taking Indians abroad on such speculative tours, he felt he could do no less than befriend them when they arrived. Accordingly he welcomed the party * consisting of an aged chieftain, a war chief, two warriors and their squaws, a young girl, and an interpreter, a tall and handsome halfbreed—his father was a Frenchman —named Strong Wind or Cadotte. Catlin told Rankin he would allow his exhibition to serve as the setting for the Indians' performance; that he would lecture on their dances and customs and would divide expenses and receipts.

Few more dramatic moments from a showman's viewpoint —and none more flattering to an artist—are recorded than the entrance of the Ojibways into Catlin's exhibition hall. Wrapped in buffalo robes, wearing head-dresses of eagle and wild turkey feathers, their faces painted with streaks of vermilion, black and green, they seemed to be the very figures in the portraits, come to life and stepping out of their frames.** To the Indians themselves the pictures were alive— or almost. They dashed around the hall, uttering ferocious war-whoops. They brandished tomahawks and scalping knives and aimed arrows at portraits of enemy tribesmen. They offered to shake hands with portraits of their friends, calling out "How! How!"

Promptly Catlin, knowing Indians, swore the band to ab-

*Subsequently Catlin managed the English and Continental tours of two other parties of Indians: 14 Ioways and 12 Ojibways. The former band arrived complete with papoose; the latter had one born in Paris. Shown the Foundling Hospital in Paris and told that of the 26,000 babies born in the city that year 9,000 were illegitimate, the Ioways groaned in sympathy for them. A chieftain asked Catlin why some of the thousands of French women he saw leading little dogs on strings did not get rid of the beasts and each instead take a little child and be its mother.

Indians who had toured both England and France far preferred the former. One Ioway explained it: "In London, ladies kiss 'em Indians heap. In France, ladies no kiss 'em, no like 'em—no good."

**It is interesting to speculate that Gilbert and Sullivan, using this idea effectively in *Ruddigore* forty-three years later, may have heard of the striking scene at the Catlin exhibition in Manchester.

stinence from firewater, an oath faithfully kept except when
he himself occasionally relaxed it to allow champagne or ale,
downed by his protegés with gusto. The show was planned
and duly staged. In full warpaint and costume the Ojibways
in single file leaped on to the platform. While spectators still
were shivering from their blood-curdling war cries, the Indians seated themselves in a council circle and smoked while
Catlin lectured on them. They danced to the throb of drums
and chanted their war songs, while the audience gaped, gog-
gled and applauded thunderously.

On the conclusion of one dance, a man spectator, who obviously had been prompted and sharply nudged, pointed
toward the dashing warrior Samah and called:

"Let that handsome little fellow come here. Here is a lady
who wants to kiss him."

No sooner had this request been interpreted to him than
Samah dove into the crowd as into a river. In a second he
had encircled the yearning lady's neck with coppery arm and
kissed her roundly. The hall rang with feminine screams and
excited gigglings. Every woman young or old, who touched
Samah's arm or bare shoulder as he made his way back to the
platform—and there were not a few—got a kiss, gave a scream
and presented him a ring, brooch, or other token. And there
was not one who did not carry home on face or dress a streak
of Samah's warpaint.

Back on the platform with his trophies, the kisser was
reprimanded by Catlin. "That was rude. It is not the fashion
in such crowds to kiss the ladies."

Samah grinned and replied in his own tongue. "I know
what I am about. The white ladies are very pretty and very
sweet, and I gave my kisses only where they were asked for."

Sensing that Samah was being scolded, members of the
audience instantly spoke up for him. "He did right." "No
harm done," came shouts from all over the hall.

The latter declaration was warmly seconded by the woman
who began it all. "No harm, indeed," she agreed in a shrill
and satisfied soprano. "I'll kiss him again if he will come
down, the charming little fellow!"

Samah understood that one without interpretation. He had to be restrained from making a second and even more headlong dive.

After that performance the show, already a success, was, in the parlance of a later day, a smash hit, packing 'em in. The police were called out to control crowds. There was standing room only and little of that when Catlin and the Ojibways moved on and toured other English cities. Audiences emerged, entertained and solidly informed on Indian lore by the lecturer and with many a woman or girl, thrilled and tittering, wearing a transposed streak of Indian warpaint like a campaign ribbon.

George Catlin, though he kept matters within the bounds of decorum, was worried. Several of the kissing warriors were married and, furthermore, the squaws of two of them were present during these carryings-on. However, a remark by the wife of the debonair Samah relieved him. When the other Indians began teasing her in their lodgings, that practical and confident young person replied coolly:

"The more kisses he gets from pretty woman, the more presents I get, for he loves me enough to give them to me."

In London they opened in Egyptian Hall, repeating the successes of their triumphant tour. Gifts continued to be heaped on the Indians—jewelry, medals, money, clothing, prints of English scenes to show their tribesmen at home, hundreds of religious tracts, scores of Bibles. Everyone was delighted with them except two clergymen who visited the red men with the object of converting them. After listening respectfully to arguments, the venerable chief replied.

"My friend, we love you and give you our hands, but we wish to follow the religion of our fathers.

"A few years ago a *black coat* came among us in the town where I live and told us the same word you have spoken this morning. After awhile a great many believed him. We lifted hard on logs to put up a house for him. Many sent their children to him to learn to read. Some girls got so as to read the 'good book', and their fathers were very proud of it.

"At last one of these girls had a baby. Not long after it another had a baby. The *black coat* ran away, and we have never seen him since. My friends, we don't think this is right."

The disconcerted dominies departed, admitting that under so unfortunate a handicap nothing could be accomplished at present. While politely accepting all proffered tracts and Bibles, the Ojibways continued heathen.

Their every performance was enthusiastically acclaimed. But a white Eve was about to end this showman's Eden.

Catlin and Daniel had noticed the constant presence at the shows of a certain woman whom they promptly christened the "jolly fat dame." She was, she avowed to them, passionately interested in Indians and she showered all the troupe with gifts. Before long it became clear that she was interested in one Indian in particular—the fine-looking interpreter Cadotte. The jolly fat dame's pursuit was assiduous and ardent. Daniel described it frankly. "Sure and she's mad after him," said Daniel.

Soon Cadotte fell ill and appeared no more in the war dances at Egyptian Hall. Every day the jolly fat dame, plainly pining, inquired anxiously for him. Catlin, worried also, sent his own physician to attend the interpreter.

But Cadotte's sickness was of another sort. He had fallen in love with a seventeen-year-old English girl who lived in the house next door to the Indians' lodgings, a sweet-mouthed, black-eyed maiden. Combining the spell of the romantic savage with the élan and impetuosity in his French blood, Cadotte's courtship was irresistible. The girl's mother and sisters encouraged the Indian's suit, though her father opposed it, and Catlin supported him with grave words of warning. Cadotte's caste and color would always be against him in London, the artist declared. Should the girl follow him into the wilderness of America, she would be totally lost to her family and lead a life of semi-barbarism. Excitement and novelty for a time there would be, but in the end—distress and misery.

They would not listen, the handsome Indian and the dark-eyed English maiden. And Rankin, the manager who had brought the Ojibways over and controlled them, hastened to give his consent to the marriage. Here was a chance for marvelous publicity. Breaking his agreement with Catlin, Rankin took over the entire management of the Indians. He announced that he had hired coaches-and-fours to carry the bridal party to the church and a band to play. Blatantly he advertised:

"Hereafter the beautiful and interesting bride of 'Strong Wind,' the interpreter, will make her appearance on the platform with the Indians, and preside at the piano."

The press condemned the scheme. Cadotte himself refused to participate in it and he and the English girl were married quietly. Whereupon Rankin discharged him, telling him to get home with his wife as best he could.

The sequel is to be found in the newspapers where so many stories are concluded in one way or another. The *New York Herald,* copied by the *London Times* of November 20, 1850, printed the story mailed in by a correspondent with an eye to human interest.

On a large island off the Canadian shore of Lake Superior a great concourse of Indians had camped, pitching several thousand wigwams. One of them sheltered an English girl, wife of an Ojibway halfbreed. Broken-hearted and desperately homesick she seemed, but she was making the best of her lot and conducting a school for children of her tribe.

Perhaps a few comforts sent her from home by her father had helped. Astonishingly the wigwam was floored with a Brussels carpet and upon it, there deep in the wilds, stood a piano at which the bride of Strong Wind could still "preside."

"CALIFORNIA OR BUST"

The Epic of the Donner
Party—1846

They rise to mastery of wind and snow;
They go like soldiers grimly into strife
To colonize the plain. They plough and sow,
And fertilize the sod with their own life,
As did the Indian and the buffalo.

Hamlin Garland: *Pioneers*

Grandma Keyes was seventy-five and bedridden, but just let them try to go without her! She waved aside their tales of Indians and other mortal perils of the long journey to California in that year of 1846 and refused to be parted from her daughter and grandchildren. Yielding, her son-in-law, James F. Reed, gently placed her on a feather-bed in his double-decker covered wagon, and the pioneer family joining friends, the Donners, rolled westward from their Illinois homes. Soon the indomitable old lady would lie in a grave in the Kansas prairie. Yet the flaming spirit which had filled her would carry on the Donner Party in the face of death by knife and bullet, thirst, starvation and bitter cold.

Unscathed they traversed the lands of the savage Sioux while spring waxed into summer. Campfires glowed on picnic gayety at hearty meals of buffalo and antelope steaks, followed by songs and reels to lively fiddling. No dark presentiments foreshadowed the cruel destiny which would forever engrave the story of these emigrants on the annals of the settling of the West.

By Little Sandy Creek, southwest Wyoming, they encamped with other wagon trains, and in the shade of canvas tops lettered "California or Bust" and "In God We Trust" the emigrants argued routes. All must eventually scale the Sierra Nevadas by the same pass. How they should reach it was the burning question.

Thousands before them had gone over the well-worn Oregon Trail to the Northwest. But these were among the earliest settlers California-bound. They were lured by John C. Frémont's reports of a paradise west of the Rockies, recently penetrated by the soldier-explorer. And they were encouraged by President Polk's announcement in 1845 that he intended to annex the vast territory, then feebly held by 500 Mexican soldiers and populated with a mere sprinkling of Mexican ranchers, Mission monks and Yankee fur traders. So now had started a stream of migration, presently to become a roaring flood.

There was a book, too, which had fired the imagination of these Middle Westerners—*The Emigrants' Guide to Oregon and California,* by Lansford W. Hastings. None suspected that the hypocritical Hastings was scheming to recruit a following from settlers to raise himself in still-Mexican California to the pinnacle Sam Houston had achieved in Texas. They only knew Hastings had taken several parties through successfully. And his cut-off—southwest through Wyoming to Fort Bridger and thence south instead of north of Great Salt Lake—would save at least 200 weary miles. Hastings had left word he would wait at the Fort and lead the way.

But veteran frontiersmen had gravely warned against the new route, and when the camp on Little Sandy Creek was broken July 20 only twenty wagons veered away on Hastings' route, while a far larger train stuck to the older trail.

Onward under the captaincy of good-natured George Donner rolled the smaller, more adventurous party—87 souls with their goods and cattle—typical builders of the West. Hope beat as steadily as that "litany of patience," the slow tread of the oxen. Together, sharing a dream, marched Americans, Irish, Germans; the learned and the unlettered; elderly folk past their prime and infants at breast; one family whose scant belongings did not fill one wagon and another with a string of wagons and a rumored $10,000 sewn in a quilt. Among the populous clans certain individuals stood out. James Reed, impetuous and able. Diminutive Tamsen Donner, an ex-school mistress, George's wife. Will McCutcheon, six-foot-six, who swore round oaths straight out of Shakespeare. Charles Stanton, with the clear gaze of the idealist. Brave William Eddy, a dead-shot. A tall, bearded, sinister figure, the German, Lewis Keseberg, who spoke four languages.

Reaching Fort Bridger, the Donner Party found Hastings had gone on with another train. Jim Bridger, Indian fighter and trapper, welcomed them heartily; he would have missed their trade had they taken the northern route. Sure, he told them, the Hastings cut-off was shorter and mostly good going. They'd strike one dry drive, maybe 40 miles, but could carry water and grass. He lied to them, and for that sin ghosts should have risen from the Sierra snows to haunt Jim Bridger the rest of his life.

On rolled the covered wagons over rough and rocky ground. At Weber River they found a note from Hastings, fastened to a twig, which told of trouble met by a better-manned train ahead in Weber Canyon and urged that they avoid the canyon and cross the Wahsatch Mountains. Wearily, double-teaming the oxen for steep climbs, they tackled it. Every mile had to be hewn through the wilderness. At last they got through, but it had taken them 21 days to go 36 miles. Summer was almost gone, provisions were dwindling. Snow soon would bar the Sierras.

South of Great Salt Lake, near the site of the present city, they loaded grass and water and plunged into the desert march. "Only 40 miles," Jim Bridger had said. It was nearer 80: Day after day they toiled on under glaring haze, the distant mountains seeming always to recede before them. Mirages mocked them. Once the entire train beheld itself reflected as if in a gigantic mirror. One of the emigrants stared at a flanking file of twenty replicas of himself, aping his motions. Water was almost gone, and men and beasts suffered agonies of thirst. The train stretched out, disintegrated. Wagons were abandoned, and oxen unyoked to be driven more quickly. Once loose, some of the crazed animals stampeded and vanished into the desert. For five torrid days they marched. For five frigid nights the children, wailing from the cold, huddled against the dogs for warmth. When at length they reached a spring, they had lost a fourth of their oxen.

The Donner Party was now dangerously behind schedule. Crippled by loss of cattle and wagons, they could never complete the journey without more provisions. In desperation, they sent Stanton, the idealist, and towering Will McCutcheon ahead to press over the pass to Sutter's Fort in the Sacramento Valley and bring back food by pack train. Meanwhile the diminished train creaked onward; and now they were in Indian country again. The furtive Digger Indians dared make no direct attack, but by theft and whistling arrows they whittled down the surviving cattle.

The tempers of the harassed pioneers were worn raw. On a steep hill, two wagons became entangled. Teamster Snyder furiously beat his oxen. When Reed protested, Snyder crashed the heavy butt of his whip down on the other's head. Reed's hunting knife flashed and was buried in the teamster's chest. Though more whip blows thudded on Reed and on his delicate wife, who thrust herself between the fighters, Snyder soon tottered and fell dead.

Rough-and-ready pioneer law tried the killer. Plainly he could plead self-defense. But Reed, considered an "aristocrat", was not popular, while Snyder had been a jolly fellow around the campfire. Keseberg, bearing a grudge, propped up the tongue of his wagon for a gallows tree and demanded death. The sentence, however, was banishment, and Reed strode off, on foot and unarmed, into the wilderness. His family managed secretly to provide him with a horse, rifle, and food, so the exile did not go forth to perish. The Donner Party, fortunately for them, would see him again.

Death marched often with the emigrants from now on, as desert sands again clutched the wheels and Indians raided by night. Old Hardkoop, a Belgian, put out of Keseberg's wagon to lighten the load, fell behind and disappeared. Some urged going back for him, but those with saddle horses refused to lend them. It was close to being every family for itself now. The desert also swallowed Wolfinger, a German reputed to carry a large sum of money. Accompanied by two young compatriots, he had dropped behind, and when the other two returned without him, they evasively declared that Indians had killed him. The kind Donners took in Wolfinger's widow, and dully the train pushed on, plagued by thirst and hunger.

Hope revived at the Truckee River where Stanton, back from the Sacramento Valley, met them with two Indian vaqueros driving seven pack-mules laden with provisions.

They rested, recruiting their strength. Between them and the Promised Land of California lay a climb over the lofty Sierra Nevadas. Already it was dangerously late in October, yet normally the pass would be open until mid-November. Alas, they were no mountaineers, these Middle-westerners, and they could not read the signs of an early and severe winter. Still, the dark gloom of the skies slowly crept into every heart, and there was near-panic in the dash the straggling train finally made for the last lap.

Past the present site of Reno they rolled and into the frowning outworks of the Sierras. Hurry, for God's sake, hurry! They streamed by an abandoned cabin on the shores of Truckee Lake. Wagons discarded, goods packed on bucking oxen, little children caught up, they flung themselves at the snow-capped pass. Mules breaking trail sank into deep drifts. Stanton and an Indian forged ahead to the summit but returned to help the others. Then dusk balked them and they encamped to wait and try again the next day.

That night the snow swept down, piling up 10-foot drifts. The emigrants retreated to the lakeshore cabin and hastily erected other shelters against the raging storm. Around them, the snow built vast, soft prison walls.

Shelter of a sort, clothing, firewood, they had. But food was scant and went fast. To attempt the snow-blocked pass again was futile. Days passed. Their few remaining cattle were slaughtered and eaten, and the dogs were next. Fishing proved useless. One day William Eddy, the marksman, tracked down an 800-pound grizzly bear, wounded it with his last bullet and then clubbed it to death. The bear meat did not feed hungry mouths long.

Urged by starvation ten men and five women left on December sixteenth for a despairing attack on the pass. They had a few provisions and snowshoes made by Uncle Billy Graves from memories of his Vermont youth. Guided by Stanton, and the vaqueros, they struggled on day after day. One morning Stanton told them to go on; that he would follow. Snow-blind and exhausted, he knew he never could. Once he had been safe in the Sacramento Valley but had returned to save his friends. Now, gallantly, he died alone in the snow.

Food gave out entirely. Finally, after two days of complete starvation, Pat Nolan uttered the dreadful thought that lay behind the wild, desperate eyes of them all. They still had something to eat—food of the last resort—human flesh.

Who? They asked the terrible question. Let lots be drawn. But what then? Should they butcher the loser in cold blood? Let two men fight it out with six-shooters to determine the victim. But they could not bring themselves even to that.

In the end, starvation, cold, and exhaustion chose for them. One by one, the men began to drop and die. Most of the wretched survivors succumbed to the fierce craving they could no longer resist. They cut flesh from the corpses, roasted it over the fire and ate it, "averting their faces from each other and weeping." One thing only they avoided. None would eat the flesh of his kin.

Now they were able to reel forward on bleeding, cloth-swathed feet, but soon they were starving again. Deer signs in the snow, seeming a token from Heaven, drew the indomitable huntsman, William Eddy, in pursuit, accompanied by Mary Graves, once the prettiest girl in the train but now a thin, wan hag. At last they sighted a big buck only 80 yards away. Then came a heart-breaking moment. Eddy was too feeble to lift his gun and aim. With all his will and strength, he painfully hitched the gun, inch by inch till the butt rested on his shoulder, let the barrel swing down until sights covered the deer and fired. The animal leaped, sprang away.

"Oh, merciful God," cried Mary, "you missed it!"

But he had not. The deer fell, and they rushed on it, cut its throat and gulped its blood.

The deer meat was soon devoured, and the pangs of starvation returned. This time the desperate, covert glances fastened on the two Indian *vaqueros*. Eddy, forbidding the sacrifice of men who had come to their rescue, warned them and they escaped. Too weak to flee far, for they, like Eddy, had refused human flesh, the Indians were overtaken, prone in the snow, still clinging to a spark of life. William Foster shot them. Once more there was sustenance.

Almost a month from the time they left camp, Eddy and Foster, out of 10 men, with all five of the women, tottered out of the mountains into an Indian camp and were helped on to a valley ranch.

California now rallied to bring out the rest of the Donner emigrants. A party starting February 1 got through to the camp back by Truckee Lake after valiant effort. Out from the huts flocked the starving remnants of the party, past dead bodies which had been dragged out on the snow. Cattle, dogs, and all other food had been eaten, and they had kept life in themselves with the gluey boilings of oxen and buffalo hides.

Distributing the scant supplies they had been able to pack, the first relief party started back to the California valleys with all the Donner party survivors who were strong enough to travel: three men, four women, and seventeen children, some so small they had to be carried. Seventeen of this group were still alive when met by another band of rescuers, a band led by James Reed, the man they had exiled for murder. He had fought his solitary way over the mountains to safety, after his banishment, and had made several heroic attempts to return through the snows with succor for his family.

His supplies on this final attempt came in the nick of time. His daughter Virginia tottered into his arms and led him to his wife who had collapsed in the snow. But joy was tempered by news that his two youngest still were starving in the snowbound cabins. Reed sent the rescued on and led a few hardy men back through the perilous pass.

Down by the cabins, they saw a figure move. They were in time. But horrible signs declared the price at which life had been bought. There were bodies in the snow from which flesh had been slashed. Once more it had been cannibalism or death.

But Reed's two children still lived. Carrying them and other little ones, mustering all those with strength to walk, this second relief expedition plunged back into the pass. Although almost overwhelmed by disaster when the food caches they had left on the trail were found to have been devoured by animals, Reed won through with his children and a few others.

Now Eddy and Foster, spurred by word that their little sons were still alive in the camp, dared the march back to the lake with two comrades. There dreadful tidings met the two fathers. Their boys were dead and eaten. Survivors accused Keseberg, the German, of this cannibalism, and he, "in a sort of perverted bravado," confessed. Somehow the fathers kept themselves from killing him, feeble, crippled, and defenseless as he was. It could not be proved he actually killed the children, who might have died of starvation. So he was merely left behind when the four men of this third relief party, each carrying a child, started back.

Left behind also, by her own choice, was Tamsen Donner. The mother bade her two young children farewell, as she had their two older sisters who had escaped earlier. She was strong enough to have gone with them, but nothing, not even his own pleadings, could move her from the side of her dying husband.

Tamsen Donner's two young children, and the two other little last survivors, crossed the Sierras safely in the arms of their four rescuers. Then, in mid-April, one year after the Donner Party left Illinois, a fourth and last relief marched to the lake. Humanity had prompted earlier expeditions, and heroism led them. This one was bent on salvaging the property of the emigrants, none of whom was expected to be found alive. They found the booty there—and one survivor, Keseberg. He told a story of the last grim days. Tamsen Donner had stumbled into his cabin, half-crazed, weeping that her husband was dead. That night, Keseberg said, she, too, succumbed.

The men did not believe him. Their suspicion that he had murdered and devoured the little ex-schoolmistress was strengthened when they found Donner jewelry in his possession. But Keseberg declared the valuables had been given him by Tamsen for safekeeping. All the rest of his life he maintained his innocence.

The salvagers took Keseberg back with them—the last man out. At a camping place of one of the earlier parties, Keseberg idly grasped a piece of calico showing above the snow. The softening snows loosened to reveal a dress and in it the frozen corpse of his daughter Ada.

So ended this most amazing saga of our westward march. A tale of death, sudden or torturingly slow, which claimed forty of these pioneers. A tale of epic endurance which brought forty-seven through to the Promised Land they sought. With varying vicissitudes, the survivors lived out their lives, some to a ripe old age. The last survivor of the Donner Party died in 1935. Their evil genius, Hastings, died in 1870 in Brazil where he was seeking to found a colony of ex-Confederates. Keseberg, after a brief period of Gold Rush prosperity, dragged out a long, miserable existence.

At their place of tribulation in the Sierras, re-christened Donner Lake and now a resort, there long stood the stumps of trees, 20 feet high, marking the height of the snow surface above which the emigrants hacked down firewood. Where one of their cabins rose is a rock with a bronze tablet. Upon it, today's summer tourist, or the winter sports enthusiast pausing on his skis, may read the eighty-seven names of the Donner Party.

BREAD AND MR. GRAHAM

How a Reformer Defied the Butcher, the Baker and the Ladies' Staymaker

1830-40

For pottage, and puddings, and custards, and pies,
Our pumpkins and parsnips are common supplies.
We have pumpkins at morning and pumpkins at noon.
If it were not for pumpkins we should be undoon.

Anon.

$\mathbf{B}$oarders—some called them inmates—at a well-regulated Graham boarding-house rose at
four o'clock, though as late as five o'clock in the winter
months. Rising with less reluctance from the fact that their
couches were never featherbeds but pallets with mattresses of
hair, moss, or straw (and the harder the better), they shut
their windows which had been wide open for plenty of fresh
air and began on their regimen.

First, a cold sponge bath. Rules also insisted that everyone
must bathe his whole body at least once a week in winter
and thrice weekly summers despite the prevailing opinion of
the 1830's and '40's that such abandoned ablutions were both
decadent and dangerous. Next for the sake of beneficial fric-
tion, Grahamites applied a flesh brush from head to foot.

Now it was time for exercise. A good, brisk walk. For the
vigorous, perhaps some boxing and wrestling. Horseback riding was thought very good, especially for the bowels. Hearty
laughter was also recommended. (It was echoed by outsiders,
highly amused by the goings-on in Graham boarding-houses).
An hour of rest, gratefully taken, was scheduled for ten.

Breakfast had been at seven, dinner was at one, and supper
at an hour agreed upon. No fourth meal, not ever, and no
snacks. No meat; animal food was sternly ruled out as unnec-
essary. No pastry. No condiments. No tobacco.* No coffee,

---

*Certain wily reformers were not above playing off one urge against
another, as indicated by a verse from *Godey's Lady's Book:*

> May never lady press his lips,
>   His proffered love returning
> Who makes a furnace of his mouth
>   And keeps his chimney burning.
> May each true woman shun his sight
>   For fear his fumes would choke her
> And none but those who smoke themselves
>   Have kisses for a smoker.

tea, nor chocolate, and certainly no liquor. The faithful drank only pure soft water. They ate sparingly of vegetables, "boiled fruits of the earth," and bread, made of the whole of the wheat, unbolted and coarsely ground, and at least twelve hours old—the bread which took its name and fame from Mr. Graham himself.

Sylvester Graham was the seventeenth and youngest child of a minister of the gospel who was seventy-two when his last son was born. Reared by a succession of relatives, the boy's health and education suffered. That, sniffed unregenerate Americans, was why he became a reformer when he grew up. But numerous other countrymen of his hailed Mr. Graham as a benefactor of the health of mankind, and thousands so affirmed in written testimonials.

The Demon Rum was Mr. Graham's first-chosen adversary. He was well launched on a career as a lecturer for the Pennsylvania Temperance Society when it forcefully struck him that moderation in matters other than drinking might well be advocated. Indeed, various other appetites and passions were being indulged in a large way. Mr. Graham heard a call to save the American people from their physiological follies.

He was appalled by their prodigious meals of meats and starches. Frontiersmen might manage ten pounds of buffalo meat a day or a pot pie whose one-inch crust covered a thick layer of ground ham and onions, beneath which lurked one turkey, two chickens, two partridges, two pigeons, and two rabbits (cooked, to be sure), decked with slices of bacon. But such fare was not for sedentary townsmen who took no exercise. Nevertheless they ate it, disregarding dyspepsia, gout, death and destruction. They gorged themselves on meat four times a day and on flap-jacks, doughnuts, and all sorts of hot breads. They topped off with rich desserts: ice cream, pies, pastries, jellies, syllabubs. The national sweet tooth was a menace. Mr. Graham shuddered to find the young so ominously fond of confectionaries, a fondness which seemed so insurmountable at female seminaries that it filled him with gloomy anticipations. There was no telling but that this craving might lead its victims along a downward path until they arrived at the lowest point of the scale of intemperance, gluttony, and debauchery.

And what help, pray, were the doctors? Mr. Graham found some enlightened members of the medical profession on his side, but others he made rather angry when he declared in one of his eloquent lectures that right living was a more certain means to health than resorting to drugs and doctors. Medicos, who ought to know better, ranked among the worst gourmandizers. Few of the gargantuan banquets of the day surpassed the feast—they called it a "supper"—tendered by the New York Society for the Relief of Widows and Orphans of Medical Men. One glance at its menu, and any Grahamite shrank back aghast.

Oysters in the raw opened the orgy (they reappeared several courses later escalloped, fried and baked in the shell). Filet of striped bass followed. Trifling with nothing so unsubstantial as soup, the dining doctors addressed themselves to *relevés* consisting of:

Roast Beef
 " Turkey, Giblet Sauce
 " Ham, Champagne Sauce
 " Capons, Mushroom Sauce
 " Goose, Apple Sauce
Boiled Ham
 " Tongue
 " Pressed Corned Beef
 " Capon and Pork
Stuffed Leg of Veal, Tomato Sauce

Having become somewhat heated, the company gratefully next partook of cold dishes: partridge pie and boned turkey with jelly and an array of cold side dishes:

Noix of Veal, decorated en Belle-vue
Paté de Foie Gras, with Jelly
Mayonnaise of Chicken, Parisian style
Aspic of Fillets of Chicken

Salad of Vegetables, with Jelly
Lobster Salad
Galantine of Quails
Form of Eels, Cottage style.

A gesture toward a balanced diet was made with an offering of vegetables: baked sweet potatoes, mashed and boiled potatoes, cauliflower, turnips, onions, celery, and spinach. But meat returned in full force with the game course when a saddle of venison and a veritable flock of wild fowl settled on the festive board and were "bagged" by the banqueters.

Roast	Canvas Back Ducks	Roast	Teal
"	Red Head Ducks	"	Mallard Ducks
"	Broad Bills	"	Partridges
"	Brandt	"	Grouse

Borne in with ceremony, the ornamental pastry elicited applause justifying the chef's artistic endeavors. Pieces included a group entitled "The Doctor's Visit," a medical pyramid, and a statue of Esculapius, with a Gothic temple and a pavilion thrown in for good measure. However, admiration for the exuberant decoration and vivid hues of the pastries soon gave way to more intimate appreciation. Medicos munched on Esculapius, eating him and the other offerings right down to the platter. They were bothered not at all by the fact that the green coloring of these sweet desserts smacked strongly of spinach and the red of beet extract.

The ornamental had only whetted appetites for real pastry, next served: Charlotte Russe, French cream cakes, blanc manger (as the printer put it), Swiss meringues, champagne jelly, claret jelly. Remaining nooks and crannies of stomachs were filled by confectionery in the form of almond macaroons, Lafayette cake, kisses, ladies' fingers, almond cakes, jelly tarts, fruit, ice cream, and coffee. Receipts to the amount of $2,278.98 were added to the society's relief fund, which sum, opined the Grahamites, probably would fail to go very far when one considered that effects of the "supper" were likely to make not a few additions to the ranks of widows and orphans of medical men.*

Banquets with a score or more meat courses surpassed only in scale regular family meals where from three to eight meat dishes were entirely usual. No wonder diners staggered away from the table whether or not they had washed down an avalanche of food with a flood of liquor. No wonder that after hearty repasts the sharp crack of waistband buttons and breaking stay laces rang out in many a household.

Mr. Graham took up gluttony's gauntlet. He launched a series of lectures in New York and New England, attended by audiences that ran as high as 2000. Listeners "trembled under the torrent of truth poured upon them." Converts and disciples, flocking to his standard, began giving up everything from third helpings at dinner to steak for breakfast. They foreswore beverages ranging from fish-house punch to tea. One coffee-drinker, after a bitter struggle during which he feared his rash resolve would cost him his life, wrote he had redeemed himself from the curse of caffein.

Reform was in the ascendant. Graham boarding-houses sprang up in the larger cities. Resort dining-rooms were forced to install Grahamite tables. The demand drove millers, willy-nilly, into producing Graham flour. A special bookstore opened in Boston to purvey Mr. Graham's and other works on bread, health and kindred reforms. The *Graham Journal* and other weeklies proclaimed that now was the time for all good men to come to the aid of their physiology.

Not only right but luck was on Mr. Graham's side. He made an important convert from the viewpoint of publicity: Horace Greeley, editor of the *New York Tribune*. Scoffers sniffed that Greeley could hardly speak with authority on food when he never knew whether he had lunched or not until he had asked a member of his staff. Since the editor suffered from

---

*Historians who are wont to list the quantity of wine imbibed by sundry fathers of this country, might in addition remind us of their capacity for roasts and barbecues.—Richard H. Shryock. "Sylvester Graham and the Popular Health Movement, 1830-1870." In *Mississippi Valley Historical Review*, v. 18.

dyspepsia (his mother had been a poor cook), he enthusiastically went to board at a Graham house. After a while he tired of vegetables and Graham bread and would have backslid had it not been for his wife, a born reformer. All the rest of his life she held him to the diet, allowing him no meat, condiments, tea nor coffee—"never even a pickle," the unhappy Horace moaned. However, his promotion of reform, though it distressingly rebounded personally, greatly furthered the cause.

Once roused, the zeal for reform could not be confined to urging temperance in food and drink. It plunged into the controversial question of bathing where there was an excess of temperance, amounting almost to total abstinence in some quarters. Dr. Daniel Drake declared that in the Mississippi valley people seldom or never bathed. One was apt to catch one's death of cold bathing in winter with the water heated before an open fire, and stoves made it only a little less hazardous. Plumbing was still in its infancy. Harriet Beecher Stowe, partisan of hygiene though she was, granted that the cold contents of the old oaken bucket that hung in the well could not be expected to be dear to the heart of childhood when flung over its shivering form. Undoubtedly a chore was the process of warming kettle after kettle of water on the stove, filling the wooden or tin tub for a bath, bailing it out afterward and mopping up the floor if the scuppers had been awash. Bathers living near a shore preferred to follow the custom of President John Quincy Adams whose daily habit it was to take a plunge in the Potomac at the foot of the White House garden. Weather permitting, he took his dip daily between daybreak and sunrise, but even so, untoward incidents occurred. Once some miscreant swiped the presidential pants lying on the bank, and Mr. Adams was forced to hail a passing lad and despatch him for more attire. On another occasion, a woman reporter, a pioneer in her craft in more ways than one, caught the Chief Executive at his matutinal ablutions. Previously he had refused to give her an interview, being prejudiced against women reporters, but when she had cornered him up to his neck in the Potomac, the hussy refused to leave until the

President spoke for publication. That was only one of the many instances of the trouble one could get into while tubbing.

But the upholders of hygiene, while admitting risks and obstacles, were making no compromises. When a young man, earnestly seeking advice, wrote: "I have been in the habit during the past winter of taking a warm bath every three weeks. Is this too often to follow the year 'round?" reformers saw him and raised him. They replied that three baths in one week, even in mid-winter, are desirable, adding that in summer once a day is not too often, and there are few, if any, bathers who would not be benefitted.

"Bathing is so inconvenient," complained the unwashed. "So are many essential things," the hydropaths sharply retorted. "But many do without bathing, and I do not see that they suffer by it," maintained an objector. To which reformers tellingly replied: "People *do* suffer by it, as well as by the prevailing practice of bathing the throat and stomach in useless and poisonous liquids."

King Alcohol was tottering on his throne. By 1838, wearers of the White Ribbon were powerful enough to push through the Massachusetts legislature a law forbidding the sale of spirituous liquors in quantities of less than fifteen gallons, "and that delivered and carried away all at one time." (That law, however, turned out to be a mistake and was repealed a year later; two-fisted drinkers had welcomed it with loud cheers.) The fervor of the Washingtonians, founded by self-redeemed drunkards,* felled thousands of apple trees, the fruits of which might otherwise—and probably would—have become hard cider. But although Mr. Graham lent his aid, abstinence from alcohol being part of his regimen, it was apparent that the White Ribboners had plenty of help. Grahamism could concentrate on other much-needed reforms.

With eloquence and enthusiasm, Mr. Graham praised hard beds, addressed young mothers with extraordinary candor, and lectured young men on chastity. He even published his chastity lecture as a book in 1842—and in Boston! He encour-

*The Alcoholics Anonymous of the day.

aged female followers who spoke on hygiene and dress reform to audiences—of their own sex, of course—and spoke with such frankness that not even pungent smelling salts could prevent wholesale swoonings. A solemn warning was uttered that women who laced themselves into hour-glass figures were in a well-advanced stage of evolution toward wasps. What bosom, so constricted, could even begin to heave? "There is," the reformers cried, "no more motion in the chest of a tightly-laced female when she breathes than there is in the towering Alps when fanned by the gentlest zephyr."

An anti-corset society was founded, its members pledging that never again would they encase themselves. In union, they discovered, there is more strength than in whalebones. One reform organization after another sprang up: The Anti-Tobacco Society, the New York Ladies' Moral Reform Society, the New York Female Benevolent Society, and the American Seventh Commandment Society. There was even—if you could believe a waggish fellow—an American Society to Prevent Children Kicking Off the Bed Clothes.

Neither Rome nor American health were built in a day, nor built without a battle. Mr. Graham was stepping hard on the toes of various vested interests. The butcher, the baker, and the ladies' staymaker. Whalers and distillers. Featherbed firms and banquet caterers. None of them heeded Mr. Graham when he protested that he had nothing to sell— (they had)— and that he was only working for the welfare of the race.

Name-calling began. "Bran-bread Graham," the Boston newspapers branded him. Even the austere Emerson in his *Journal* took a high-flown and obscure but indubitable crack at the distinguished vegetarian. "O, worthy Mr. Graham, poet of bran-bread and pumpkins," he wrote, "there is a limit to the revolutions of the pumpkin, project it along the ground with what force soever. It is not a winged orb like the Egyptian symbol of dominion, but an unfeathered, ridgy, yellow pumpkin, and will quickly come to a standstill."

Once Mr. Graham faced the martyrdom which sometimes is the lot of one who seeks to save a stubborn and stiff-necked generation in spite of itself. When in the winter of 1837 he announced a lecture at Amory Hall, Boston, local bakers rose in wrath. They threatened that any old reformer asking them for Graham bread would be given a stone. The terrified proprietor of the hall canceled the booking, and none other was available. Thereupon the owner of the New Marlborough Hotel, a temperance house, gallantly and appropriately offered Mr. Graham his dining-room for the talk and stood steadfastly by the offer even when the Mayor of Boston warned that his constables could not provide protection.

On the meeting day, bellicose bakers descended on the hotel in force. They found its first floor stoutly barricaded and upper story windows manned by a determined garrison who, being armed with shovels, might be presumed to be prepared to defend the place to the last ditch. The valiant hotel owner, taking his stand in the doorway, attempted to parley with the howling mob milling about in the street. The bakers hurled back vituperations to the effect that that fellow Graham, with his crazy demands for stale, brown loaves, was virtually taking the bread out of their mouths. Roaring and yelping, the mob surged forward to the attack. The owner waved a signal to the shovel brigade upstairs. Down on the heads of the assault cascaded a powdery mass. It looked as if the bakers were getting a dose of their own medicine in the shape of a shower of white flour. But the stuff was slacked lime. As a chronicler puts it, "the 'eyes' had it, and the rabble fled." Mr. Graham had his say on his bread.

In the 1840's Sylvester Graham's influence began to wane. Undaunted, he carried on until, as is the lot even of health reformers, his own health gave way. It is recorded that in his final illness, such accustomed restoratives as a dose of Congress water and a tepid bath failed to revive him. His death occurred in 1851.

A man ahead of his time, Sylvester Graham. Yet to dawn was the day of calories and vitamins. Medicine had still to concentrate on "lazy" colons. Fresh air and exercise were future fetishes. So were sun-tans and sacro-iliacs. Still to be exalted were the panty-girdle and the great American bath-room. But Mr. Graham, striving mightily for the well-being of mankind, had laid firm foundations.

Undeservedly, renown passed him by. His should be a more prominent pedestal * than the pantry shelf with its box of Graham crackers. Even his bread now is generally called whole-wheat. Forgotton is the commotion he caused his own lusty-living, hearty-feeding generation which might have quoted some lines from Pope for his epilogue:

> *Fame is at best an unperforming cheat;*
> *But 'tis substantial happiness to eat.*

*Graham was one of the two or three men to whom this nation might, with propriety, erect a monument—James Parton. *The Life of Horace Greeley*. New York, 1855.

FIRST BLOOD FOR YANKEE SULLIVAN

Saga of a Champion of the Prize-Ring Mid-19th Century

Oh, I killed a man, they say, so they say.
Oh, I killed a man, they say, so they say.
I beat him on the head, and I left him there for dead.
Yes, I left him there for dead, damn his eyes.

Now up the rope I go, up I go, up I go;
Yes, up the rope I go, up I go, up I go.
And those bastards down below, they'll say, "Sam, we told you so."
They'll say, "Sam, we told you so." Damn their eyes.

Anon: *Ballad of Samuel Hall*

He always fought with the Stars and Stripes bound around his mid-riff. That was why the Irishman christened James, who became an early champion of the American prize-ring, was called Yankee Sullivan. Though he was relegated to the ranks of forgotten men by a later Sullivan—the redoubtable John L.—Yankee's chronicle is an extraordinary one. Before relating it from the outset, it would be well to present a certain crucial episode, for it was this event which streaked an already checkered career with crimson and bordered it with black.

Yankee Sullivan was not in the ring as principal or second in the prize fight which took place on September 13, 1842, in Westchester County, New York, between the towns of Yonkers and Hastings. But as a chief promoter, he was deeply involved in its untoward consequences.

Early in the morning on the day of the fight six chartered steamboats slipped away from New York City docks with a certain amount of stealth. Laws prohibiting prize fighting had been passed in the States, as well as abroad, and small wonder. Its practitioners were tough 'uns, quite a few of them with criminal records. In England, set-to's of "the sweet science" had resulted in murders, free-for-all riots, rapine, and robbery. But law or not, 1,500 sports devotees boarded the steamboats, a number which would have been far larger but for

the torrents of rain which were falling. One of the vessels was reserved to Christopher Lilly, principal, and his camp; another to his opponent, Thomas McCoy.

The sun began to beam as the boats chugged up the lordly Hudson. Gentlemen in rain-bedraggled beavers, tail coats, and pantaloons dried out on deck, unfolding their morning *New York Heralds.* Yesterday had been a bad day on the stock exchange, but then that might have been expected with a presidential campaign on. Yes, even though the election was two years off. The Whigs, editorialized James Gordon Bennett the Elder, were trying to fly Henry Clay into the White House on wings of song, a device which had served well with "Tippecanoe and Tyler, Too." But Mr. Bennett, reprinting the words of "Clear the Way for Clay" (to the tune of "The Little Pigs Lay—") was sceptical. Throats ought to be wetted for singing, and a good, rousing hard cider campaign was cramped this time by the activities of all the temperance societies raising rumpuses in this year of 1842.

Readers found no advance notice of the fight, of course, but some recognizing a *Herald* reporter aboard anticipated it would be covered. Others noted that, should the fight prove disappointing, there would be fireworks at Castle Garden that evening and at the Chatham Theater a drama entitled, "Butchers of Ghent." Advertisements offered baldness panaceas, daguerreotypes, artificial teeth, flute lessons, and trusses to those who felt the need of them.

Twenty miles upriver the steamboats nosed into the shore and made fast. The crowds streamed up to a smooth expanse of turf where two ring barriers enclosed a 24-foot square. Makeshift bars did a rushing business as damp gentlemen took precautions against catching cold. Soon the greensward around the ring was covered by spectators exercising squatter's rights on places of vantage. Many glanced back curiously over their shoulders at a novel sight on the outskirts of the crowd. This exhibition of pugilism was to be graced with women patrons: the wives and daughters of Irish workmen living in the vicinity. They stood on boxes, the light of battle in their eyes bound to see this fight, and just let anybody try to stop them.

Twelve noon and Christopher Lilly appeared, accompanied by his seconds and Yankee Sullivan. With a flourish, Lilly shied his castor in an arc before him. It sailed down on to the turf and his hat was in the ring. Thomas McCoy followed suit. The two men stepped to their corners and peeled. Lilly showed a fine pair of shoulders, neck, and bust (as the male thorax was then designated). McCoy's bust was broader but his neck less sturdy. Both were in the pink and 23 years old. McCoy weighed in at 137; Lilly a trifle heavier.

At the ringside, Enoch E. Camp, reporter for the *Herald,* made ready his note book. A corking good sports writer, Camp, specialist in "The Manly Art of Modified Murder," as W. O. McGeehan would christen it some 80 years later in the *Herald Tribune.* What if neither of these fighters was first-string and the purse only $200 a side? The *Herald* man expected a real fight, and what was more, it was without the law and hot news.

Yet for a minute it looked as if there would be no fight at all. An excited gentleman pushed through the crowd, announced himself to Yankee Sullivan as a local Justice of the Peace and declared that this illegal mill must be stopped. A dirty look from Yankee and angry mutterings from the crowd persuaded the Justice it might be well to let it pass. He retired to a ringside seat with the air of one who, having done his duty, was now going to enjoy himself thoroughly.

"Time!" called the referee. "Toe the mark."

Both fighters came up cautiously to scratch. McCoy struck out. A rally. Lilly threw him. In this pre-Markis o' Queensberry era, wrestling, with cross-buttocks, chancery holds, and wrenches were all to the good. And it was bare-knuckle boxing as a matter of course. A hundred years earlier, John Broughton, the famed British bruiser, had devised "mufflers" out of regard for the "tenderness and delicacies of the frame" of pupils in his boxing school, the mufflers being gloves guaranteed to protect from "the inconveniency of black eyes, broken jaws, and bloody noses." But such were for pupils, not pugilists.

McCoy rose from his fall, with blood running from one ear.

Lilly's backers cheered, particularly his promoter. First blood for Yankee Sullivan's protégé.

Nothing daunted, McCoy defied his opponent in Round 2: "You ain't got old Murphy to deal with now." Irritated, Lilly swung on him, and Reporter Camp scribbled: "Lilly downed him with a smack in the mush trap."

Round 4. Lilly made a pass, missed and fell on his butt. Round 8—A counter by McCoy cut Lilly's smeller. The man with the broader bust was warming to his work. Bets aggregating several thousands were offered on McCoy, fewer and fewer finding takers. In Round 14, McCoy got in two good blows which Lilly returned with a smash to the dice box that rattled it. Next round Lilly landed three blows on what Camp now described as McCoy's potato trap, thus adding to the mush diet. But Lilly was bottom man when they clinched and fell.

McCoy either slipped or dropped after a body blow by Lilly in the 18th round. Yankee Sullivan, suspecting a ruse for a rest, yelled out, presuming to speak for McCoy: "What a coward I was when I fell!" The opposition retorted sarcastically. "Yes, you were!"

Lilly was going stronger by Round 21 and becoming the favorite. He tendered McCoy a slap on the snuffbox. McCoy's lips and cheeks were bleeding now, what with his adversary's persistent pounding of boxes and traps.

Up they came for Round 26. Already the fight had been in progress 30 minutes. Lilly smashed away. McCoy was hitting the turf often and being bounced on the ropes. His swelling face was a study in purple and scarlet. Lilly was unmarked.

"Ain't Chris the portrait painter!" yelped an admiring Lilly fan, and none of the opposite camp was able to retort with a remark about painting the lily.

McCoy stated in the 42nd round that he was as strong as ever, but blood was gushing from his mouth. Lilly repeatedly threw him and fell on him. "Hit him in the head, Lilly. That's the place," came advice from the ringside. Lilly obliged, and it was observed that McCoy's teeth looked loose, as well they might.

"Mac," Lilly remarked in the 53rd, "we've got a week before us. Don't be in a hurry, Tom." However, McCoy seemed to feel that matters should be expedited while he could still see, for his eyes were rapidly swelling closed. At that spectacle, shouts from the ringside grew savage and ominous.

"There's been a death in Mac's family. His shutters are closed."

"Chris, you've got the shutters up. Put a bar across."

Now McCoy was growing weaker, winded. Sullivan protested as many of the customers relented. "He's sick. Take him out. Call a doctor," came the cries. Still the courageous, incredible McCoy fought on, and in a clinch he patted Lilly on the back and actually told him, "You're game." Then he demanded, "Who's tiredest now?" in spite of the fact that he was bleeding like a harpooned porpoise by Round 84, and ringsiders were telling the referee it was a shame to let the fight go on. Yet when a Lilly second shouted in Round 106, "You've got him now!" McCoy mumbled, "Not so sure." On through Round 119 he continued to take terrific punishment. At the end of that round he staggered back to a seat on his second's knees.

A gasp from the crowd. McCoy had slid from his perch and collapsed against a corner post.

"Time!" the referee called. McCoy could not get up. The fight which had lasted two hours and 41 minutes was over. Lilly, declared the winner, jumped the ropes, amid huzzas. McCoy lay limp on the turf.

"Stand back! Give him air!" The defeated pugilist's heavy breathing slowed and stilled. His pulse grew faint, faded out. They laid his body on one of the liquor bars. Two of his brothers, who had watched the fight, carried him home on a shutter to his widowed mother on Roosevelt Street. A report spread that she had told her pugilist son that he was to come home a winner or not come home alive—with his shield or on it—but this she denied.

Excitement ran high through the city. "Brutal Murder," proclaimed the *Herald*. "We refer to our report in another column for the details of a cold-blooded murder, committed yesterday at Hastings, in this State, under the name of a prize fight. We now call upon the authorities to punish all concerned, to the full extent of the law, and put a stop to these disgraceful proceedings in this country forever."

McCoy was the first prize fighter in this country killed while actually in the ring. A coroner's jury found that his death was due to strangulation by blood from the mouth, nose, and vessels of the neck, as the result of blows and injuries received in a fight with Christopher Lilly. A hue and cry arose for the arrest and punishment of Lilly, the promoter, and seconds of the fight. The town could talk of nothing else, and the *Herald* sold like hot cakes.

The crafty Lilly circulated a report that he, too, had died from injuries. Under cover of that sensation, he escaped aboard a packet bound for England. Having fought and run away, he lived to fight another day and, as a member of the legion of the American filibuster, William Walker, to die in battle a dozen years later amid the jungles of Nicaragua.

The police net began to gather in the rest. Though the astonishing discovery was made that the revised statutes of the State of New York had failed to prohibit prize fighting, there had been a killing, and Country McCloskey, a pugilist who had served as a second, and others were given short jail sentences and paid small fines.

Finally only Yankee Sullivan, the chief promoter, was at large. Sighted cruising in the lower bay in a small boat in the hope of boarding a ship for Europe, it took two craft of the United States Navy to chase him ashore on Staten Island and a detachment of the United States Army to round him up there. He was sentenced to prison for two years.

That was not the first time James Sullivan had fallen into the clutches of the law. Born near Cork in 1813, he early drifted into pugilism. He had won three good fights and was building up a reputation when he was arrested on a larceny charge and convicted. The nature and value of the property he allegedly stole is no longer of record. It need only have been a trifle in the England of that day to have imposed upon him the heavy penalty he received—transportation to the

Australian penal colony of Botany Bay, there to serve a sentence of twenty years.

Populating one of the remoter parts of the far-flung Empire and growing up with the country failed to appeal to Sullivan. He watched his chance and blew. Aboard a bark with other convicts and ticket o' leave men, he reached the California settlement which would later become San Francisco. Gold was still to be discovered and the climate alone could not hold a fighting Irishman. He worked his way eastward overland, no mean feat *circa* 1840. Next the nervy fellow took passage from New York to Liverpool and entered the English prize-ring once more. Three more fights had been chalked up to his credit when the British police got on his trail. No more Down Under for Sullivan. He doubled back to New York.

Americanized, Old Glory bound around his middle, Yankee stepped again into the squared circle and proceeded to make himself first champion of the United States. A whirlwind fighter from the word go, it was almost always first blood for Yankee Sullivan. In one bout a smash on his mouth started his gums bleeding, but he held in the red stream until after he had tapped the claret of his opponent.

From his eminence, he was dragged by the unfortunate result of the Lilly-McCoy bout to wear New York prison stripes. Before he had served his time, he was pardoned by Governor William H. Seward, later to be Lincoln's Secretary of State. The condition of the Governor's pardon was this: Yankee must henceforth foreswear prize-fighting.

But what else could he do? There lay his quickest and easiest money. In 1841 Yankee had seconded Country McCloskey when he lost to Tom Hyer in 101 rounds, and at the finish of the fight, Yankee, champ though he was, had challenged Hyer. Now that unfulfilled engagement beckoned. Promise or no promise to His Excellency, Mr. Seward, Yankee could not resist. He and Hyer mixed it up unofficially in a brawl in a Park Row saloon. Though beaten into insensibility, Yankee publicly advertised that it had been no fair fight. Hadn't he been practically dead drunk at the time? Let Hyer meet him fair and square in the ring and take the licking that was coming to him.

Prudently avoiding New York, they were matched to fight at $5,000 a side, the bout to take place on Pool Island in Chesapeake Bay, Maryland, on February 7, 1849. Before dawn of that day, the sheriff descended on the island in a raid. Not only was he assisted by numerous deputies but by a company of militia—the second time the troops had been called out in compliment to Yankee Sullivan.

Hyer and Sullivan ducked out of rear windows of their quarters and escaped in skiffs to Rock Point. Snow had to be swept from the ring, and the pugilists, waiting for time, sat with hot bricks at their feet. Hyer stood 6 feet 2 and weighed 185; Sullivan, 5 feet 10½ and 155—a heavy handicap for Yankee.

Sports reporters for the *Herald* and *Spirit of the Times,* that premier American sporting sheet, watched them shy their castors into the ring, Sullivan's a cap of rich dark-green velvet, Hyer's a foggy felt. They peeled, shook daddles, advanced springily on their pins and raised their mawleys. Bettors thrust flimsies into the hands of stakeholders, and the fight was on.

Not first blood nor yet last this time for Yankee Sullivan. It was a fast and furious fight, but the taller, heavier Hyer knocked him flatter than a flounder in a mere sixteen rounds. Toward the last Yankee could not get his arms up. Hyer caught his head in chancery, mashed his face and sent him to a sojourn in the hospital.

Still Lady Luck had a smile for Sullivan. Not long after that fight, Hyer retired as champion and the crown reverted to Yankee. There was fight in the old frame yet. On October 12, 1853, he took on John Morrissey for $2,000 a side and the title at Long Point, Canada. He had Morrissey whipped when a wrangle started. The crowd broke into the ring and a free-for-all resulted. Yankee Sullivan, true son of Erin, joyously mingled in this impromptu Donnybrook Fair. It was a glorious scrap. A fight was a fight and let the prize-fight wait.

But it would not wait—not in the opinion of the referee,

who was a stickler for rules. In the midst of the turmoil, he called the contenders to scratch when time was up. Morrissey, who had stayed quietly in his corner, responded. Yankee, who was taking on the crowd and having heavy going, was otherwise engaged. Morrissey's fight, was the decision, and the championship. Yankee patronized another hospital.

He was 40 now—old age for a pugilist. Training between fights in New York saloons had done him no good. With his money, it had been easy come, easy go. In short, Yankee Sullivan was on the skids.

Young—and even old men were going West. The California he had known thirteen years ago took on a new lure for the Yank. In '49 it had been discovered that there was gold in them thar hills and there must still be plenty of it around.

Other men, figured Yankee Sullivan, arriving in the lively burg of San Francisco, could go grub in the earth for yellow sands. For him not the diggings but the pickings. Sydney-Town, later to be known as the Barbary Coast, was showing signs of lusty life again after the knock-out blow dealt by the Vigilantes in 1851. Ex-cons. from Australia welcomed the new arrival from the East who had once been one of their fraternity. Hoopla for red liquor, women, and high old times! They had to be financed, but Yankee Sullivan knew how to get what it took.

Not for nothing had he been a saloon owner and all-around brawler in New York. A useful hand at the polls, he had learned a trick or two in the great game of politics as played by the past masters of Tammany Hall. So he joined other graduates of that training school who were manning the San Francisco political machine run by David C. Broderick, who subsequently won a seat in the United States Senate and was killed in a duel by one of the judges of the California Supreme Court.

With the prestige of an ex-champ and the might of a strong-arm man, Yankee rose to the rank of a trusty henchman of the big boss and got his in the looting of the city of hundreds of thousands of dollars in graft.

But the carnival of crime, debauchery, and all manner of dirty work at the crossroads of the Pacific Coast could not go on. The score for 1855 was 326 murders in San Francisco alone. When two prominent and widely respected citizens were shot down in 1856 by notorious underworld leaders, the outraged decent element rose and organized the second Vigilance Committee, wresting the rule of the city from the machine and rounding up the thugs.

For the third and last time law and order laid hand on Yankee Sullivan's shoulder. He was arrested and locked up in a room in the headquarters of the Vigilantes.

Even for the hardboiled, that place was bad on the nerves. It echoed to the clatter of arms and the roar of throngs of angry, determined citizenry. Avoiding adjournment to a proper gallows, scaffolds were built out from the window sills, noosed ropes strung from overhead beams. Malefactors dropped through the scaffold traps to dangle as gruesome ornaments of the facade. And the sounds thereof were far from reassuring to prisoners awaiting a verdict—usually not one of acquittal.

Yankee Sullivan had signed a written confession, naming persons whom he accused of bribing him to stuff ballot boxes and otherwise oil the machine. He had promised to quit fighting and lay off the liquor. He would leave town, he vowed, and go back East, preferably alone and lacking company of other members of the gang who might misunderstand his penitential acts. He was ready to promise anything.

Deportation would do, they informed him, and he would not be hanged. He could not quite believe it. Awakening one night in a cold sweat, he called his guard and told him he'd had a terrible dream. Trial, conviction, and sentence to execution. The heavy footfalls of the hangman approaching his cell. The ghastly grip of hemp around his neck. The creak of the opening trap, a sudden drop, frantic feet treading on nothingness, and——

Forget it, advised the guard. But Yankee could not. There was no question that the man had guts. In scores of fights in and out of the ring, he had taken and given terrific beatings.

Their memory faded as the blackness of another night shrouded his cell.

Was it a touch of the horrors, conjuring up images in an alcohol-sodden brain? Or a conscience tortured by crimes unconfessed? Whatever the impulse, they would not hang Yankee Sullivan by the neck until he was dead, dead, dead. He seized a dull table knife. Next morning the guard found his corpse with the two large arteries of the left arm near the elbow severed.

Once more, first blood—in a way—for Yankee Sullivan.

STAGECOACH STICKUPS

There Was Gold in the Express Boxes

Mid-19th Century

Lo, here I've stood while wind and rain
Have set the trees a-sobbin',
And risked my life for that damned stage
That wasn't worth the robbin'.
                    Black Bart, the PO8

Elegant the Concord coaches
were called and so they were. Gilded curleycues ornamented
the poplar panels of the body, painted scarlet, and doors were
adorned by vistas and landscapes (no two alike), described as
gems of beauty repaying hours of study. Wheels of stout ash,
bright yellow, glistened like the gold dust in the express box
in the coach's forward boot.

At once elegant and embattled were the Concords—probably the most embattled vehicles that ever rolled in time of
peace. Those handsome pictures on the doors seldom went
long unmarred but were likely to be studded with Indian
arrows or splintered by bullets or buckshot, with the up-
holstery dyed blood-red as the exterior. For the Concord was
the chief transportation of the mining camps in the gold and
silver rush days of our West. From the 1850's into the '90's
it was the stage, in both senses of the word, for the dramatic
highway robberies that rifled mails, plundered passengers and
looted the express companies of millions in shipments of
precious metals, robberies that ranged from California back
eastward over the Emigrant Trail through Nevada, Idaho,

and Colorado, north into the Black Hills and South into Arizona.

Hub-to-hub at starting times, Concords jammed the widest street of such staging centers as Sacramento or San Francisco. Hundreds had been exported by clipper around the Horn or overland to the gold fields as well as to almost every state, territory, and province in North America, to Mexico, South America, Australia, and South Africa. Nobody else made a vehicle which could compare with this product of a firm of Yankee coachmakers, Abbot, Downing & Co., of Concord, New Hampshire. A Concord weighed 2,400 hundred pounds and cost a dollar a pound. Sturdily built, its body suspended on leather straps instead of springs, it could take everything from the terrific jolts of the wilderness roads to falls over a canyon rim and lodgment more or less intact in the branches of a projecting pine. Like the deacon's one-hoss shay, it never broke down but only wore out.

Its motive power, a six-horse team, restively champed their bits—sometimes mustangs, sometimes fine stock brought from Kentucky and Ohio, "as good as ever galloped with Her Majesty's Mail," an English traveler generously conceded. They could keep up the steady pace that enabled stagecoaches with properly spaced relays of teams to make 100 miles or more a day.

Crowned by a cream-colored 10-gallon hat, enthroned on box seat, waited the driver, holding lead, swing, and wheel spans steady with multiple reins. He could talk to each horse in his team through those ribbons and play on the foot brake as on an organ stop. With his whip lash he could flick a fly off a leader's ear or whisk a shotgun out of a bandit's grasp. A long cigar jutted from a corner of his mouth or a cheek bulged with a quid whose juice he could—and did on occasion —spit in the eye of a masked desperado.

Beside the driver—sometimes but not as often as the numerous holdups justified—sat the guard hired by the express company to protect its shipments. He was called a shotgun messenger or fortified expressman and lived up to the name.

Bret Harte, who once filled the post, celebrated him in story. Over his knees rested his double-barreled shotgun, favored for the murderous spread of its buckshot loads, but also handy was a rifle for a long range work, with revolvers in reserve. The rifle or a watch ticking in his pocket might be a token, suitably engraved, from grateful employers to testify to his readiness and accuracy in shooting it out with bandits.

Express box, mail, and baggage were loaded into the forward and rear boots, the cargo holds of the Concords. Passengers finished gulping breakfast or tossed off a last snorter at the bar: miners, American, European, Chinese—gold dust buyers—a judge or a sheriff perhaps—an occasional woman and child. Drivers bawled out the names of stops on their routes. Hangtown . . . Angel's Camp . . . Bottle Springs . . . Rough and Ready . . . Shirt Tail Canyon . . . Poker Flats . . . Piety Hill . . . Secret Diggings. The passengers climbed through those portals of adventure, the decorated doors of the Concord coaches. Whips cracked, and the stages whirled away, fanning out on their routes as they cleared town, bound to "git thar and back," accidents or holdups not barred.

On runs back from the mines, with express boxes crammed with gold dust and bullion or coach floors littered with silver ingots, the stage was set for the highwayman's entrance, and nobody could ask a more theatrical one. In a lonely spot just short of the brow of a hill he awaited his cue, the rumble of wheels and thud of hooves of a blowing team, slowed by the grade.

A shouted "Halt!" and the driver pulled up. Out into the road at the head of the team stepped a masked figure, rifle or shotgun leveled. A bandana around his face or a flour sack with eyeholes, along with duster or Indain blanket over his clothes, disguised him well. It might be Black Bart, veteran of a score of holdups, who left scraps of verse in the express box he had robbed, signing himself the "PO8." It might be Dick Fellows whose dash and enterprise was spoiled by his miserable horsemanship; his mounts always threw him, and it was impossible, in his case, declares his chronicler, "to give a man a horse he can ride." Perhaps it would be Rattlesnake Dick Barter and his gang or Tom Bell and his; Bell, Mexican War veteran and surgeon, deftly dressed the wounds of victims he winged. Or it might be some young fellow whose luck had been bad at the mines, or an eccentric amateur like the bandit of whom a newspaper reported with just scorn that "the scoundrel had his boots polished and wore a white stove-pipe hat and a silk-faced overcoat."

"Throw down that box!" the road agent commanded. Then in a split-second decision was made. The driver hauled the express chest from the boot, heaved it to the ground and was motioned to drive on by the road agent's gun muzzle. Or the shotgun messenger or some belligerent passenger blazed away, the robbers returned the fire and the battle was on.

Many a time it was the peaceful procedure. Bandits, appeased with the express box, often did not bother to take the mail sacks or line up and rob the passengers. If they did, it was conducted with a courtesy and good will that permitted the plundered to retain keepsakes and spared anyone with a plausible hard luck story. A highwayman, who felt impelled by caution to refuse a victim permission to lower his hands to scratch his nose, nevertheless kindly performed that service for the itcher, using the muzzle of his shotgun for the purpose.

Willingness to stand and deliver is understandable under the circumstances. It was easy come, easy go. The express companies, charging five per cent and higher on gold shipments, prospered mightily in spite of depredations and promptly made losses good to shippers. Well aware of this, drivers, often unprotected by guards, saw no point in arguing with a man with a gun while their hands were full of reins. No more did the earlier shotgun messengers when a road agent plainly had the drop on them. And rather than risk an indiscriminate shower of lead, most passengers readily yielded their gold. There was more where that came from.

Stagecoaches being held up could not count on rescue. It was impossible for the law to reach out into the wilderness roads when it had all and more than it could handle in the towns and roaring mining camps. Sheriffs and deputies were hard to hire at modest salaries when fortunes were being dug out of the hills and when manpower, spread thin over the vast, new territories, was so generally at a premium. When Vigilantes took over law enforcement, highway robbery was apt to increase, for they simply drove the crooks out of town and some took to road agentry. The most the express companies could hope for from the law was pursuit of the bandits after the holdup and possible recovery of the loot. And in some sections of the country the posses could obtain no information on the fleeing highwaymen from inhabitants who, resentful of the high rates charged by the companies, took a serves-'em-right attitude.

It is a curious fact that for the first few years after the discovery of gold in California in 1848, streams of treasure got through by stage, wagon, and pack mule train scot-free. The ethics of plenty prevailed, and gold was as safe in transit as in a miner's cabin. No stagecoach robbery of consequence occurred until 1852 when pioneer road agents garnered an express box yielding $7,500. In 1855 Rattlesnake Dick Barter's gang attacked Wells-Fargo & Company's mule train and made off with $80,000 in gold dust. Though half of that haul was later recovered, a realization now began to dawn upon various lazy, unlucky and unscrupulous characters. It was altogether more satisfactory to let others dig, pan, sack and ship the gold—and then step in and help yourself.

When the ranks of lawless characters from the camps were reinforced after the Civil War by soldiers mustered out of the armies, men who had learned a disregard for life and property rights as raiders and guerillas, highway robbery shifted into high.

Holdups took place with such frequency on certain roads that stagecoach teams were said to stop automatically at the customary spot. On several much-raided lines, express companies were finally compelled to stop service entirely and to close offices in towns where stagecoach robbery was becoming a local industry, with townsmen doubling as highwaymen. A driver named Baldy Green was held up so often that "Throw down that box, Baldy!" became a popular catch-line, and a song was written about him. Though he shifted to another line, robbers continued to hound him and he finally retired to become a respected justice of the peace. Only rarely did drivers turn crook and rob their own coach.

A record in non-resistance was established when a California road agent, robbing a stagecoach, was surprised but not flustered by a second and then a third drawing up behind it. He simply dealt them in and proceeded with the looting. When the road block was augmented by five freight wagons, he calmly stuck to business and borrowed the lunch carried by one of the wagon drivers. Finally an entire troop of cavalry on maneuvers trotted up. The robber included the soldiers in the covering sweep of his rifle and motioned wagon train and cavalcade on. He was obeyed without hesitation. Either he had an iron nerve or he was aware that, because of a recent shooting affray, the cavalrymen had not been issued ammunition.

Odds on a holdup became so heavy that passengers, who had on several occasions figuratively and even literally lost their shirts, turned to expressing their personal valuables and most of their cash. Those who could not conveniently shift the risk to the express companies were driven to other devices. One discouraged gold dust buyer is said to have kept three live rattlesnakes in his dust box. A much-robbed shipper of silver insured himself by sheer weight. He ran his bullion in cannonballs weighing 750 pounds each; whereupon baffled bandits sent him word they considered his method unsportsmanlike and a mean trick. To get payroll money through safely, a stage line superintendent bought an old-fashioned large bore shotgun and stuffed its barrels full of rolled currency. When he was held up as expected, the road agents laughed at him for carrying such an old and worthless gun and threw it into the bushes whence the owner later recovered it and its valuable load.

The holdup men of Idaho actually acquired a newspaper, *Idaho World,* as their house organ and campaigned in it against the Vigilantes who had been hanging robbers out of hand. Several prominent citizens were discovered to have close bandit connection including two deputy U. S. Marshals.

Highway robbery came to a pass where even women took a part. They had been useful to gangs as informers on treasure shipments and as keepers of ranch hideouts, but none actually took the road until a hard character called Dutch Kate held up a California stage to recoup a gambling loss of $2,000. The driver promptly threw down the box at her command, but it contained little of value. Her language, always lurid, was particularly memorable when she read in the paper next morning that she had passed up a passenger with a satchell holding $15,000. In Arizona a female road agent was acquitted by a gallant jury of the charge of highway robbery, though caught in the act. However she was sent to prison for having disarmed the driver which was going too far for a lady.

Highway robbery, springing up in new fields where rich gold and silver strikes were made, continued to flourish. For the most part, express companies continued to regard the road agents take as a levy of tribute, cheaper to pay than to combat. They simply took a chance on shipments going through unplundered. But they could count on help at times. Communities were spurred to action when a particularly bloody attack was made on a stagecoach, and its perpetrators seldom lasted long.

Tom Bell didn't. That surgeon gone wrong—his real name was Hodges—had a well organized gang, complete with initiation oath, password, spy system and roadhouse headquarters run by women confederates. He did well until that day in 1856 when one of his scouts reported that the Marysville, Cal., stage was carrying $1,000,000 in gold. Aboard were John Gear, the driver, Bill Dobson, the express messenger, and nine passengers but five of them were non-combatants: a Negro woman and four Chinese.

Bell and six of his henchmen swung into saddles with a plan of attack that was first-rate strategy. They would swoop down on the coach, one to the team's head and three to each flank. But it chanced that a gold dust buyer, who owed a large part of the express shipment, was preceding the coach on horseback because its swaying made him seasick. Three of the gang stopped to disarm and dismount him, and were delayed in their part of the attack when Bell and the others thundered down on the stage and shouted for a halt and hands up.

Gear reined in. The odds looked hopeless with four armed men closing in and three more galloping up. Dobson, regardless, went into action with reckless gallantry, blazing away with his armament of two shotguns and a brace of revolvers. His first shot knocked Tom Bell off his horse.

The gang's wild fusilade of lead thudded into the coach. One of its doors popped open, and the four Chinese and one white man erupted and vanished with such rapidity that they were never traced. Now Bell, only slightly wounded, was mounted and firing again. But remaining passengers had opened fire, reinforcing Dobson. The shotgun messenger's buckshot wounded another bandit. As the gang reeled back out of the road, Dobson bowled another off his horse and shouted to Gear, "Drive on!" Though wounded in one forearm, the driver yelled to his team and cracked his whip. Treasure safe but battered and blood-stained, the Concord rolled into Marysville with its casualties: one passenger shot through both legs, another's forehead furrowed, and the Negro woman, innocent bystander, dead with a shot through her brain.

Aroused citizens tracked down and wiped out most of the gang a few weeks after Dobson had received a cash reward and a suitably engraved watch for his bravery. Then a posse caught Bell, whereabouts betrayed by women of his gang. They gave him time to write a few letters, then swung him from the handiest tree limb.

Though many passengers traveled unarmed to avoid being involved in a fracas, there was a proportion ready to rally to a stage defense, as in the battle with the Bell Gang. Now and then appeared a warlike individual who would bear the whole burden himself like a certain Col. A. W. Von Schmidt, an inside passenger in a stagecoach halted by a hold-up hail.

"Don't shoot," the Colonel, gaining time, called out to the armed man at the side of the road. He got out of the coach and stepped to one side. There were women passengers aboard who must not be endangered. As he whipped out his revolver, the alarmed driver whipped up his team, removing the coach even further from the line of fire. "Drop that gun!" the Colonel now ordered and launched a solitary charge. Utterly astounded at such behavior in a passenger, the bandit dropped his shotgun and ran. Wells, Fargo, appreciating the salvage of $9,000 in the express box, presented both the Colonel and the driver with the customary watches.

Presentation of testimonial watches or weapons did little to encourage protection of shipments, as the express companies discovered when they cast up their holdup accounts. In 1875 Wells-Fargo had lost $87,000 in thirty-four California stage robberies; from 1870 to 1884 in that state alone it had been looted of a total of $927,726. Still without much help from local authorities or the Government, which allowed mails to be robbed with impunity, the express companies, notably Wells-Fargo which handled the bulk of the mining business, took measures to make the task of the highwayman harder. Boxes were strengthened and even bolted down in the front boot of the Concords. No longer could they be thrown down to be smashed open with an ax but safe-cracking tools and explosives had to be used. Cash rewards were offered for the capture of bandits, averaging $250 a head. Their most effective step was the hiring of tough hombres as shotgun messengers. Resolute and ready for anything, these men were not content to act as scarecrows on the box seat. They gave banditti a battle.

They numbered such men as John McNemer who gave up the express chest to a brigand who had him covered but dropped from the coach later, strode back, found the marauder breaking the box open and shot him dead before he could draw his gun. There was Phil Barnhart who slid off the box seat while a holdup man was distracted by the driver's conversation, sneaked around the coach and riddled the robber with buckshot. Since the frightened team had run away, Bernhard carried the safe 6 miles to the next station. No risk was ever too great for Eugene Blair. Surprised one dark night by two robbers who hailed him by name and ordered his hands up, he jumped from the box seat without delaying to grasp a weapon. Circling the coach, he flung himself on one rascal, wrenched his gun away and shot him dead with it. Then he chased the other through the brush and captured him.

Blair never hesitated at the most suicidal chances. On one occasion when he and Shotgun Jimmy Brown were messengers in charge of a large sum in payroll money, four ex-convicts laid an ambush at a relay station whose crew they bound and gagged. It was dark when the coach, lamps lit, rolled up to the seemingly deserted station. As Blair swung to the ground in front of the stable, a voice from its black doorway shouted, "Hands up!" The messenger leaped into the blackness straight for the voice and ducked. A gun roared and flamed, the bullet whizzing over his head. From the other side of the door a shotgun's twin muzzles jammed against his chest. He thrust the barrel up as the trigger was pulled. Brown out on the box took a slug that splintered the bone of one leg. Not out of action, the wounded man waited, shot-gun ready.

Now Blair was wrestling with one adversary, with the other three milling about trying to get at him. When the back of the man in Blair's grasp came into the light of the coach lamps, Brown saw his chance and let fly with his shotgun. It was close shooting but good. The robber went limp with mortal wounds from nine buckshot. The other three brigands fled but were caught next day.

So formidable were these fighting express messengers, desperados took to firing on them without warning. They only risked their own skin by asking for a surrender that was never made. Put the messenger out of action or let the stage go, became the holdup man's new motto.

Passengers who rode in a coach under guard of Mike

Tovey knew the trip would either be the safest or the most perilous they ever took. During his long career as express messenger Tovey, iron of nerve and quick on the trigger, had accounted for so many dead or captured holdup men that they shot to kill or let him pass, mostly the latter in his later years. Even so it was not wise of Tovey and Driver Raggio to allow a young schoolteacher, Anna Rodersino, to sit on the box with them during a trip when the payroll for a Calaveras County mine was aboard. She should have been inside with two other women passengers.

A double-barreled shotgun was poked around a tree trunk as the coach rolled into a lonely stretch of the road. Two blasts of buckshot swept the coach. The horses and the inside passengers were untouched, but on top the schoolteacher was killed instantly and the driver fatally wounded. Tovey, one arm crippled, caught the reins in his other hand and yelled at the milling team. The stage dashed through to safety, the young woman's body lying across Tovey's boots and the dying driver working the brake with his hands. After twenty-five years of service as a shotgun messenger, Tovey's career ended in 1893 when an assassin got him from ambush with a bullet through the back.

The professional pride of Bill Winters, a Wells-Fargo messenger, was hurt when three brigands got the drop on him. He took leave of absence and trailed them for two years, finally capturing two of them. As tenacious were the Wells, Fargo detectives such as J. B. Hume who finally tracked down the redoubtable Black Bart.

In the golden age of American stagecoach robbery, Black Bart ranks high among highwaymen. Between 1875 and 1883 he committed more than twenty-five successful holdups, always single-handed. Not once did he fire a shot—he subsequently claimed his shotgun was never loaded—and only on one occasion did anyone get a shot at him and then he was only nicked.

His disguise and technique rarely varied. Hooded by a flour sack with pierced eyeholes, a linen duster covering his suit, he leaped into the road, double-barreled shotgun leveled, half crouching to use the team as a shield. His deep bass boomed: "Throw down that box!" Having served as a first sergeant of infantry in the Civil War, he spoke with the voice of authority. No driver ever denied him nor were passengers moved to argue, for Black Bart robbed only the express and the mail. Toward passengers and women especially he was a model of courtliness. But the characteristic that spread his fame widest was his habit of leaving a token in the wrecked and robbed express box. Scribbled on the back of a waybill and signed "Black Bart, the PO8" were such bits of verse as these:

> "I've labored long and hard for bread,
>   For honor and for riches—
> But on my corns too long you've trod,
>   You fine-haired sons of bitches."

Or

> "I rob the rich to feed the poor,
>   Which hardly is a sin;
> A widow ne'er knocked at my door
>   But what I let her in.

> "So blame me not for what I've done,
>   I don't deserve your curses,
> And if for any cause I'm hung,
>   Let it be for my verses."

Black Bart picked his time and place well, avoiding shotgun messengers. Always playing a lone hand, he confided in no one. After a holdup he vanished completely. Nobody saw anything bandit-like in the middle-aged gentleman of respectable appearance and kindly manners who dropped in at a farmhouse for a meal. Nobody suspected that his traveling bag held a hood, a duster, a shotgun, broken down, and a store of stolen gold. In intervals between holdups, which sometimes ran into months, he lived quietly in San Francisco where he posed as a mining man.

He led Detective Hume a long and strenuous chase. Painstakingly Hume pieced clews together: a laundry mark on a handkerchief, a description by an observant waitress, a glimpse caught by a hunter of the bandit, unmasked, breaking open an express box. He arrested Black Bart in San Francisco and identified him as Charles E. Boles who had deserted his wife and daughter after the war. Convicted, he served a prison term and after his release disappeared. A flurry of holdups on his old stamping grounds was attributed to him but never proved. Doubtless he would have enjoyed the rumor that Wells, Fargo was saving further trouble and losses on its stagecoach lines by paying Black Bart a retirement pension.

Like Black Bart, most of the brethren of the road preferred to work the spur lines to the mines where usually they could deal with one stage at a time, free from interruption. On the overland mail's 2,700 mile route between St. Louis and San Francisco, a run which was made in 25 days, at least twelve Concords were always on the road, heading east or west. Despite the traffic, bold spirits raided the Overland, especially during the Civil War years when several gangs represented themselves as Confederate soldiers. One leader signed military receipts for the booty he took from express boxes, but it is doubtful if the Confederacy ever saw any of it.

Fourteen men of one of these bands descended on the Overland one night in 1864 and staged a holdup which might easily have reached wholesale proportions. As they were robbing one coach, a second arrived and was included; the two yielded seven bags of gold and silver bullion and a safe. The robbers withdrew without learning that thirteen other coaches were following, with the fourth carrying an extra rich treasure. However the net result for most of the gang was the same, since posses soon killed or captured eight and recovered most of the plunder.

But the Plains division of the Overland and lines through the Rockies and to the northwest and Southwest were preyed upon chiefly by another and more dreaded type of highwayman. His skin was red and the booty he sought most eagerly consisted of scalps, firearms, and horses.

Crews and passengers had to barricade themselves beneath the Concords and beat off repeated Indian attacks. There was many a running fight with rifles and revolvers blazing away from coach tops and windows, and savage horsemen closing in, firing, on both flanks of the wildly galloping team. Sometimes the coach won through. Sometimes its wreckage was found, horses dead or dying in their traces, and stripped and mutilated white bodies pinned to the prairie by lances and arrows. Strong troop escorts were the only assurance of safety and these were seldom available. Stage relay stations were frequently raided, and their tenders slaughtered and the buildings burned.

In 1863 on the Nevada Overland, Indians killed the tender and cook of Eight-Mile Station and lay in wait there for the incoming stage. It rolled toward the station with Hank Harper driving and a passenger, John Liverton, beside him on the box seat. Inside were two boys, Liverton's sons, and Judge Gordon Mott, a delegate to Congress from Nevada, asleep on the mail bags. Around the buildings several Indians loitered.

By good fortune Harper, about to pull up, caught a glimpse of the limp body of a white man sprawled across a doorsill. His whip cracked like a pistol shot, and he swung his team off the road and out across the prairie at a dead run.

But a volley of Indian bullets and arrows swept the deck of the stage before it could clear the station. Liverton gasped and crumpled down on the footboard. Harper toppled down beside him, half on the footboard and half in the cargo boot. Badly hit though he was, he clung to reins and whip. The Indians were mounted now and in hot pursuit. With all the strength of his lungs, the wounded driver shouted to Judge Mott, "Come up! Come up!"

The Judge was sixty but he managed it, crawling through

a window and up on to the box seat of the careening coach. There was no room for his feet and he was in the act of shoving Liverton's body overboard when the man groaned. Mott, somehow placed his feet, took over the reins and drove for dear life, Harper calmly coaching him on the bad turns and continuing to call to his horses and ply his whip until the Indians were outdistanced. As the team galloped into the safety of the next station, the gallant driver slumped down into the boot dead.

The Sioux and Cheyennes utterly disrupted Overland service for periods during '64 and '65. The fierce Apache competed in Arizona with white holdup men in harrying stages. Indians and outlaws are said to have cost the Overland Mail as much as all other overhead expenses combined.

Although completion of the transcontinental railroad in 1869 substituted train for stagecoach robbery on main lines, not for many years yet would the rails reach out into the hills. Concords, still essential, still embattled, rolled on. The gold and silver and payroll money in their express boxes continued to lure highwaymen. New fangled train robbery was remunerative but increasingly dangerous as express cars began to be strengthened and fortified to such an extent that they had to be breached by explosives.

The Black Hills gold rush of 1875 was grist to the mill of road agents. Their activities were steady, strenuous and largely successful. One gang provided a round of drinks for passengers it robbed and rode off wishing all a pleasant journey. A band of eight robbers, who got the drop on two shotgun messengers and made a rich haul, sportively sent word to the express company to send along some real fighting men next time and make it interesting.

Increasingly rich bullion shipments, not infrequently running as high as $100,000 and even $200,000, forced express companies to take the hint and hire messengers who would take on any odds and fight or track down highwaymen under any and all circumstances. An eight-man guard was organized for the coach which made the run from Deadwood to Sidney

with treasure from the fabulous Homestake Mine; two horsemen rode in advance, two as a rearguard, and four, heavily
armed, manned the coach which carried no passengers on the
outgoing trip. The coach itself, made into a veritable rolling
fortress with armor plating and loopholes, was dubbed "Old
Ironsides."

Escort and armament notwithstanding, a determined gang
of some five or six desperados tackled Old Ironsides one September day in 1878. They employed an Indian trick, laying
an ambush at the Canyon Springs relay station where they
shut the tenders up in a windowless room.

Somehow without its outriders that day though it was carrying $45,000 in gold bullion, the treasure coach was pro-
tected by only three messengers: young Gail Hill on top and
Scott Davis and Bill Smith inside. Gene Barnett was driving.
By special exception a telegraph operator, Hugh Campbell,
was a passenger.

The driver's "yip-yip," signal for the stock tender, echoed
as the Concord rolled to a stop in front of the log building
of the station. As Gail Hill, back to the building, lowered
himself from the box seat, a shotgun muzzle thrust through
a loophole in the building's wall. There were no gentlemen
of the road in this gang but brutal ruffians taking no chances.
The shotgun crashed and buckshot ploughed into Hill's back,
inflicting wounds from which he would eventually die. But
there was still fight in the plucky young fellow. He had
whirled and was raising his own gun when a second charge
of shot sent him reeling to collapse in a heap by the roadside.

Buckshot, riddling the Concord, put two more men out of
action. The passenger Campbell, wounded in the forehead,
struggled out and dropped to the ground. Smith, who had
been struck by a splinter from the woodwork, believed he
had been seriously injured and lay on the floor of the coach,
taking no part in the fight. The remaining messenger, Scott
Davis, had escaped from the far door and taken cover behind
a tree. From there he waved to Barnett to drive on. As the
nervy driver was gathering his team for a dash to save the
treasure, a bandit rushed from the house to the heads of the

lead pair. Davis, asking no better target, drilled him through the middle.

Plainly Davis had to be disposed of or the holdup was a fizzle. A robber circled around to take him from the flank or rear. Young Gail Hill, sorely wounded and semi-conscious, saw him. In the best tradition of the shotgun messenger, he mustered his last strength and shot the man dead.

But still Davis was forced into a retreat. The bandit leader had ordered Barnett down from the box and was approaching Davis's tree, using the driver as a shield. Davis, unable to fire, ran off through the woods to get help. Before it could arrive, the gang had made a clean getaway with the treasure.

As the arm of the law grew longer, the authorities reinforced express companies and private shippers in clamping down on the once free enterprise of stagecoach robbery. The roaring camps were civilized or replaced by large-scale mining operations. Surviving highwaymen sought other fields of endeavor or died with their boots on.

Sundry tokens remain of their life and times, stolen gold, buried by bandits who did not live to retrieve or reveal it, lies hidden in hills from which it was mined, with hoards ranging up to the $40,000 reputed to be buried on Trinity Mountain, California, and the $150,000 cached in the Jackson Hole area of Wyoming. A stagecoach stands on exhibition in the railroad station of its birthplace Concord, N. H. Another, "Old Ironsides" of the Deadwood run, reposes in the Smithsonian Institute, Washington, joined in 1945 by another embattled vehicle, the jeep.

ACKNOWLEDGMENTS

A CONSTANT impetus for this book and always on the desk before me as I wrote was an old daguerreotype of my maternal great-grandfather, Caleb Davis. It is a prim portrait, and the subject's demeanor is staid and sober but he wears a pair of pantaloons of loud and lively plaid. They persuade me he was one of my lusty forefathers.

Grateful acknowledgments also are made to the following.

Periodicals in which chapters of this book appeared: *Blue Book, Reader's Digest, Elks Magazine, Field Artillery Journal, Redbook, North American Review, Virginia Magazine of History and Biography, American Legion Magazine,* and *'47.*

Robert Frost for permission to reprint "The Runaway"; Dartmouth College for "Eleazar Wheelock."

Libraries which afforded sources for my research, and librarians whose helpfulness and courtesy greatly facilitated it:

Dartmouth College Library: Harold G. Rugg, Assistant Librarian; Miss Caroline Neef, Reference Librarian.

Colonial Williamsburg, Inc.: Mrs. Rutherfoord Goodwin, Acting Director, Department of Research.

New York Public Library: Sylvester Vigilante, Reference Assistant, American History Room; Robert W. Hill, Keeper of Manuscripts; John Tasker Howard, Curator, Americana Music Collection.

Yale University Library: James T. Babb, Librarian. G. W. Pierson, Department of History, Yale University.

New York Historical Society: Miss Dorothy Barck, Librarian.

New York Society Library: Mrs. Frederick G. King, Assistant Librarian.

Library of Congress: Miss Alice Lerch.

University Club Library, New York City: Mark Kiley, Librarian; John A. Mansfield, Assistant.

Yale Club Library, New York City: James J. Blair, Librarian.

Haverford College Library: Thomas E. Drake, Curator of the Quaker Collection.

Authorities who checked data in their fields and were of other kind assistance also:

Professor Ray Palmer Baker, Rensselaer Polytechnic Institute; Professor Dorothy Byrne Goebel, Hunter College, and Professor Julius Goebel, Jr., Columbia University; F. B. Hills, Secretary of the Morgan Horse Club; Charles S. Belsterling, Edward L. Tinker, and John T. Winterich.

Professor John A. Krout, Columbia University, whose *Origins of Prohibition* was particularly helpful, as was his advice on other sources.

Maxwell E. Perkins, Editor, and Miss S. Elizabeth Devoy, Art Director, Charles Scribner's Sons.

John C. Wonsetler, for the attractiveness and accuracy of his illustrations.

Mrs. Samuel S. Adams, my mother-in-law, for a carefully compiled index.

Mildred Adams Downey, my wife, for unsparing criticism, typing, proofreading, and other tasks, performed as devotedly for this, my eighteenth book, as for my first.

FAIRFAX DOWNEY

New York City, 1947

Bibliography

Adams, Charles Francis. *Some Phases of Sexual Morality and Church Discipline in Colonial New England.* Cambridge, Mass., 1891.

Adams, Charles Francis. *Three Episodes of Massachusetts History.* 2 vols. Boston and New York, 1892.

Adams, James Truslow. *Provincial Society, 1690-1763.* New York, 1927.

Adams, John. *The Works of John Adams.* Boston, 1850.

Album of American History. 2 vols. New York, 1944-45.

Alcott, William A., ed. *Moral Reformer and Teacher on the Human Constitution.* Vol. I, Boston, 1835.

Anburey, Thomas. *Travels Through the Interior Parts of America.* 2 vols. Boston, 1923.

American Antiquarian Society Proceedings. October, 1917.

Andrews, Charles M. *Pilgrims and Puritans.* New Haven, 1919.

Andrews, Matthew Page. *Virginia, The Old Dominion.* Garden City, N. Y., 1937.

Asbury, Herbert. *A Methodist Saint. The Life of Bishop Asbury.* New York, 1927.

Augustin, J. M. "Noted Orleans Men Fought in Duels." Article in *The New Orleans States.* September 30, 1917.

Baker, Ray Palmer. "The Poetry of Jacob Bailey." In *New England Quarterly.* January, 1929.

Banning, Capt. William and George Hugh. *Six Horses.* New York, 1930.

Battell, Joseph. *The Morgan Horse and Register.* 3 vols. Middlebury, Vt., 1894.

Bayles, W. Harrison. *Old Taverns of New York.* New York, 1915.

Belsterling, Charles Starne. *William Preston.* Philadelphia, 1934.

Benezet, Anthony. *The Mighty Destroyer Displayed.* Philadelphia, 1774.

Benton, Thomas H. *Thirty Years in the United States Senate.* 2 vols. New York, 1856.

339

Bernhard, Duke of Saxe-Weimar Eisenach. *Travels Through North America during the Years 1825 and 1826.* 2 vols. Philadelphia, 1828.

Beverley, Robert. *A True Copy of Eight Pages out of the History of the Present State of Virginia.* London, 1705.

Bladen, E. S. "Dinners of Fifty Years Ago." *In Lippincott's Monthly Magazine.* Vol. 70, p. 711.

Blaine, Delabere P. *Encyclopaedia of Rural Sports.* London, 1875.

Bliss, William Root. *Side Glimpses from the Colonial Meeting House.* Boston, 1894.

Botkin, B. A., ed. *Treasury of American Folklore.* New York, 1944.

Bradford, William. *Bradford's History of Plimoth Plantation.* Boston, 1899.

Breen, Patrick. *Diary of Patrick Breen.* In *Publication of Academy of Pacific Coast History.* Vol. I, no. 6. Berkeley, Calif., 1910.

Brillat-Savarin, J. A. *The Physiology of Taste.* New York, 1926.

Brooks, Henry M. *Olden-Time Music.* Boston, 1888.

Brooks, Van Wyck. *The World of Washington Irving.* New York, 1944.

Brown, William Robinson. *The Horse of the Desert.* New York, 1929.

Bruce, Phillip Alexander. *Economic History of Virginia in the 17th Century.* New York, 1896.

Bruce, Phillip Alexander. *Social Life in Virginia in the 17th Century.* Lynchburg, Va., 1927.

Bruce, Phillip Alexander. *The Virginia Plutarch.* 2 vols. Chapel Hill, N. C., 1929.

Bullock, Helen. *The Williamsburg Art of Cookery.* Richmond, 1939.

Calhoun, Arthur W. *A Social History of the American Family.* 3 vols. Cleveland, 1917.

Catlin, George. *Catlin's Notes of Eight Years' Travels and Residence in Europe, with his North American Indian Collection.* 2 vols. London, 1848.

Catlin, George. *Letters and Notes on the Manners, Customs, and Condition of the North American Indians, Written During Eight Years Travel amongst the Wildest Tribes of Indians in North America.* 2 vols. in 1. Philadelphia, 1859.

Catlin, George. *O-Kee-Pa: A Religious Ceremony and Other Customs of the Mandans.* Philadelphia, 1867.

Catlin, George. *An Account of an Annual Religious Ceremony Prac-*

ticed by the Mandan Tribe of North American Indians. London, 1865.

Champlain, Samuel De. *Works.* 6 vols. Toronto, 1922.

Chase, Frederick. *A History of Dartmouth College and The Town of Hanover, New Hampshire.* 2 vols. Cambridge, Mass., 1891.

Chastellux, Marquis de. *Travels in North-America, in the Years 1780, 1781, and 1782.* 2 vols. Dublin, 1786.

Child, Lydia Maria. *The Frugal Housewife.* Boston, 1829.

Church, Leslie F. *Oglethorpe: A Study of Philanthropy in England and Georgia.* London, 1932.

Cleveland, Catharine C. *The Great Revival in the West—1797-1805.* Chicago, 1916.

Cole, Henry Ellsworth. *Stagecoach and Tavern Tales of the Old Northwest.* Cleveland, 1930.

Candler, Allen D., Compiler. *Colonial Records of the State of Georgia.* 30 vols. Atlanta, 1906.

Coffin, C. C. *History of Boscawen and Webster.* Concord, N. H., 1878.

Comfort, William Wistar. *Just Among Friends.* New York, 1941.

Cook, Sherwin Lawrence. *Torchlight Parade.* New York, 1929.

Crawford, Mary Caroline. *Social Life in Old New England.* Boston, 1914.

Crevecoeur, Michel Guillaume St. Jean de. *Sketches of Eighteenth Century America.* New Haven, 1925.

Cummings, Richard Osborn. *The American and His Food.* Chicago, 1940.

Cuningham, Charles E. *Timothy Dwight.* New York, 1942.

Davidson, Rev. Robert. *History of the Presbyterian Church in the State of Kentucky.* New York, 1848.

Davis, Andrew McFarland. "The Law of Adultery and Ignominious Punishments." In *American Antiquarian Society Proc.,* Worcester, Mass., April 24, 1895.

Dayton, Abram C. *Last Days of Knickerbocker Life in New York.* New York, 1897.

Deming, Clarence. *Yale Yesterdays.* New Haven, 1915.

Dexter, Franklin Bowditch, ed. *Documentary History of Yale College. 1701-1745.* New Haven, 1916.

Dictionary of American Biography. New York, 1933.

Dictionary of American English on Historical Principles. 4 vols. Chicago, 1938.

Dictionary of American History. New York, 1940.

Donaldson, Thomas. "The George Catlin Indian Gallery in the U. S. National Museum (Smithsonian Institute)." In *Smithsonian Report.* Part V, 1886. Washington, 1887.

Doten, Dana. *The Art of Bundling.* New York, 1938.

Dow, George Francis. *Every Day Life in the Massachusetts Bay Colony.* Boston, 1935.

Drake, Samuel Adams. *Old Boston Taverns.* Boston, 1886.

Earle, Alice Morse. *Colonial Dames and Good Wives.* Boston, 1895.

Earle, Alice Morse. *Home Life in Colonial Days.* New York, 1898.

Earle, Alice Morse. *Colonial Days in Old New York.* New York, 1896.

Earle, Alice Morse. *Stage-coach and Tavern Days.* New York, 1900.

Earle, Alice Morse. *Two Centuries of Costume in America.* New York, 1903.

Earle, Alice Morse. *Customs and Fashions in Old New England.* New York, 1893.

Earle, Alice Morse. *The Sabbath in Puritan New England.* New York, 1893.

Earle, Alice Morse. "Old Colonial Drinks and Drinkers." In *National Magazine,* Vol. 16, 1892.

Edwards, Jonathan. "The Justice of God in The Damnation of Sinners, explained, illustrated and proved in a sermon upon Romans III: 19." Boston, 1788.

Elliot, Charles W. *The New England History.* 2 vols. New York, 1857.

Eberlein, Harold Donaldson, and Lippincott, Horace Mather. *The Colonial Homes of Philadelphia.* Philadelphia, 1912.

Emerson, Ralph Waldo. *Journals.* Boston and New York, 1911.

Eustis, Celestine. *Cooking in Old Creole Days.* New York, 1903.

Faulkner, Harold U. *The American Way of Life.* New York, 1941.

Field, Edward. *The Colonial Tavern.* Providence, 1897.

Fisher, Sydney George. *The Making of Pennsylvania.* Philadelphia, 1896.

Fisher, Sydney George. *Men, Women, and Manners in Colonial Times.* Philadelphia, 1898.

Fiske, John. *Old Virginia and Her Neighbours.* 2 vols. Cambridge, Mass., 1897.

Fiske, John. *The Dutch and Quaker Colonies.* 2 vols. Boston, 1899.

Foreman, Carolyn Thomas. *Indians Abroad. 1493-1938.* Norman, Okla., 1943.

Franklin, Benjamin. *Autobiography.* Boston, 1928. "Satires and Bagatelles."

Garrison, W. P. "The Isms of Forty Years Ago." In *Harper's New Monthly Magazine.* Vol. 60. January, 1880.

Gay, Julius. *Church Music in Farmington in the Olden Time.* Hartford, 1891.

Goebel, Dorothy Burne, and Goebel, Julius, Jr. *Generals in the White House.* Garden City, N. Y., 1945.

Goebel, Dorothy Burne. *William Henry Harrison.* Indianapolis, 1926.

Goebel, Julius Jr., and Naughton, T. Raymond. *Law Enforcement in Colonial New York.* New York, 1944.

Goldthwaites, Reuben, ed. *Early Western Travels, 1748-1846.* vols. 22-25. Cleveland, 1906.

Graham, Sylvester. *A Lecture to Young Men on Chastity.* Boston, 1842.

Graham, Sylvester. *A Treatise on Bread and Bread-making.* Boston, 1837.

Greene, Evarts B. *The Revolutionary Generation.* New York, 1943.

Hanscom, Ely D. *The Heart of the Puritan.* New York, 1917.

Harlow, Alvin F. *Old Waybills.* New York, 1934.

Hearn, Lafcadio. *An American Miscellany.* Collected by Albert Mordell. Vol. 2. New York, 1924.

Hone, Phlilip. *Diary.* New York, 1927.

Howard, George Elliott. *A History of Matrimonial Institutions.* 3 vols. Chicago, 1904.

Holliday, Carl. *Woman's Life in Colonial Days.* Boston, 1922.

Houghton, Eliza P. Donner. *The Expedition of the Donner Party and its Tragic Fate.* Chicago, 1911.

Hovey, Richard. *Dartmouth Lyrics.* Boston, 1924.

Indiana Quarterly Magazine of History. "A Famous Campaign Song." In Vol. 2, no. 3. September, 1906.

Jones, Charles C. Jr. *The History of Georgia.* 2 vols. Boston, 1883.

Jones, Rufus M. *The Quakers in the American Colonies.* London, 1911.

Judah, Samuel Benjamin Helbert. *Spirit of Fanaticism.* New York, 1842.

Kendall, John S. "Humors of the Duello," also "According to the Code." *Louisiana Historical Quarterly.* Vol. 23, 1940.
Kimball, Marie. *The Martha Washington Cook Book.* New York, 1940.
King, Caroline B. *Victorian Cakes.* Caldwell, Indiana, 1941.
King, Grace. *New Orleans.* New York, 1895.
Kingsley, William L., ed. *Yale College.* 2 vols. New York, 1879.
Knight, Thomas A. *Tippecanoe.* Cleveland, Ohio, 1940.
Krout, John A. *Origins of Prohibition.* New York, 1925.
Krout, John A., and Fox, D. R. *The Completion of Independence.* New York, 1944.

Langdon, W. C. *Everyday Things in American Life.* New York, 1937.
Lawrence, Henry W. *The Not-Quite Puritans.* Boston, 1928.
Lescarbot, Marc. *Nova Francia.* Trans. by P. Erondelle, London, 1928.
Lescarbot, Marc. *The History of New France.* Trans. by W. L. Grant. 3 vols. Toronto, 1914.
Linsley, Daniel Chipman. *Morgan Horses.* New York, 1857.
Log Cabin Song-book. New York, 1940.
Long, Rev. Edwin M. *Illustrated History of Hymns and Their Authors.* Philadelphia, 1876.

Massachusetts Historical Society Proceedings. Boston.
McCallum, James Dow. *Eleazar Wheelock, Founder of Dartmouth College.* Hanover, N. H. 1939.
McCallum, James Dow. *The Letters of Eleazar Wheelock's Indians.* Hanover, N. H., 1932.
McGlashan, Charles F. *History of the Donner Party.* San Francisco, 1881.
Melville, Lewis, and Hargreaves, Reginald. *Famous Duels and Assassinations.* London, 1929.
Merkel, Andrew. "The Order of Good Cheer." A Narrative Poem. Lower Granville, Nova Scotia, 1946.
Minnigerode, Meade. *The Fabulous Forties.* New York, 1924.
Monaghan, Frank, and Lowenthal, Marvin. *This Was New York.* Garden City, N. Y., 1943.

Morellet, André. *Memoires sur le Dix-huitieme Siecle.* Vol. I. Paris, 1821.

Murphy, Virginia Reed. "Across the Plains in the Donner Party." In *Century.* July, 1891.

Nevins, Allan, *American Social History as Recorded by British Travelers.* New York, 1923.

Nevins, Allan. *The Emergence of Modern America.* New York, 1927.

New England Magazine.

New Haven Colony Historical Society Papers. Vol. 7.

New Orleans City Guide. Federal Writers' Project. Boston, 1938.

New York Historical Society. Collections.

Nichols, Thomas L. *Forty Years of American Life.* London, 1874.

Norton, A. B. *The Great Revolution of 1840.* Mount Vernon, Ohio, and Dallas, Texas, 1888.

Ogg, Frederic Austin. "Builders of the Republic." *The Pageant of America.* Vol. 8. New Haven, 1927.

Parkman, Francis. *Pioneers of France in the New World.* Boston, 1870.

Parton, James. *Life of Horace Greeley.* Boston, 1893.

Paxson, Frederick L. *History of the American Frontier. 1776-1893.* Boston, 1924.

Peeke, Harrison L. *Americana Ebrietas.* New York, 1917.

Perry, William Stevens, ed. *Historical Collections Relating to the American Colonial Church.* Vol. I—*Virginia.* Hartford, 1870.

Phillips, U. B. *Life and Labor in the Old South.* Boston, 1929.

Pintard, John. *Letters from John Pintard to His Daughter, 1816-1833.* New York, 1940.

Preston, John Hyde. *Revolution, 1776.* New York, 1933.

Prime, W. C. *Along New England Roads.* New York, 1892.

Rawson, Marion N. *Candle Days.* New York, 1927.

Rawson, Marion N. *When Antiques Were Young.* New York, 1931.

Repplier, Agnes. *Philadelphia, The Place and The People.* New York, 1898.

Reynolds, James B.; Fisher, Samuel H., and Wright, Hervey B., eds. *Two Centuries of Christian Activity at Yale.* New York, 1901.

Rhys, Ernest, ed. *Memoirs of the Life and Writings of Benjamin Franklin.*

Richardson, Leon Burr. History of Dartmouth College. 2 vols. Hanover, N. H., 1932.

Rollins, Ellen C. (E. H. Ari, pseud.). *New England Bygones*. Philadelphia, 1880.

Rosenbach, A. S. W. *The All-Embracing Doctor Franklin*. Philadelphia, 1932.

Romke, Constance Mayfield. *Trumpets of Jubilee*. New York, 1927.

Saxon, Lyle. *Fabulous New Orleans*. New York, 1928.

Scudder, H. E., and Stoddard, R. H. *Men and Manners in America One Hundred Years Ago*. New York, 1876.

Sewell, Samuel. *Diary*.

Sherwood, M. E. *The Art of Entertaining*. New York, 1892.

Shryock, Richard Harrison. "Sylvester Graham and the Popular Health • Movement." In *Mississippi Valley Historical Review*. Vol. 18.

Singleton, Esther. *Social New York Under The Georges, 1714-1776*. New York, 1902.

Singleton, Esther. *Dutch New York*. New York, 1909.

Smith, Helen E. *Colonial Days and Ways*. New York, 1901.

Smith, Margaret Bayard. *The First Forty Years of Washington Society*. New York, 1906.

Sonne, Owen E. "The Donner Lake Tragedy." In *Overland Monthly*. Vol. 85, 1927.

Stanard, Mary Newton. *Colonial Virginia: Its People and Customs*. Philadelphia, 1917.

Stevens, Rev. William Bacon. *A History of Georgia*. 2 vols. New York, 1847.

Stewart, George R. *Ordeal by Hunger*. New York, 1936.

Stieff, F. P. *Eat, Drink and Be Merry in Maryland*. New York, 1932.

Stiles, Henry Reed. *Bundling. Its Origin, Progress and Decline in America*. Albany, 1871.

Stryker, W. S. *The Battle of Monmouth*. Princeton, N. J., 1927.

Stryker, W. S. *The Battles of Trenton and Princeton*. Boston, 1898.

Sweet, William Warren. *Religion on the American Frontier*. 3 vols. New York, 1931.

Sweet, William Warren. *Revivalism in America. Its Origin, Growth and Decline*. New York, 1944.

Taussig, Charles William. *Rum, Romance, and Rebellion*. New York, 1928.

Thomas, Gertrude J. *Foods of Our Forefathers*. Philadelphia, 1941.

Thompson, Mortimer M. (pseud. Q. K. Philander Doesticks). *Plu-ri-bus-tah*. New York, 1856.

Tinker, Edward Larocque. *The Palingenesis of Craps*. New York, 1933.

Towle, George Makepeace. *American Society*. 2 vols. London, 1870.

Train, Arthur Jr. *The Story of Everyday Things*. New York, 1941.

Trumbull, J. Hammond. *The Memorial History of Hartford County, Connecticut*. 2 vols. Boston, 1886.

United States Department of Agriculture. Department Circular 199. *Breeding Morgan Horses at the U. S. Morgan Horse Farm*. Washington, 1921; revised 1923.

Van Doren, Carl. *Benjamin Franklin*. New York, 1938.

Ward, Edward and "J. W." *Boston in 1682 and 1699*. Providence, R. I., 1905.

Watson, John F. *Annals of Philadelphia*. Philadelphia, 1830.

Watson, John F. *Annals of Philadelphia and Pennsylvania, in the Olden Time*. 2 vols. Philadelphia, 1856.

Weeden, William B. *Economic and Social History of New England*. 2 vols. Boston, 1890.

Wertenbaker, Thomas Jefferson. *The First Americans*. New York, 1927.

Wharton, Anne. H. *Social Life in the Early Republic*. Philadelphia, 1902.

Wheelock, Eleazar, *A plain and faithful Narrative of the Original Design, Rise, Progress and present State of the Indian Charity-School at Lebanon, in Connecticut*. Rochester Reports. Boston, 1763.

Whitney, Jane. *John Woolman, American Quaker*. Boston, 1942.

William and Mary College Quarterly.

Williamson, Jefferson. *The American Hotel*. New York, 1930.

Woodward, W. E. *The Way Our People Lived*. New York, 1944.

Wright, Richardson. *Hawkers and Walkers in Early America*. Philadelphia, 1927.

Wright, Richardson. *Forgotten Ladies*. Philadelphia, 1928.

Wright, Richardson. *Grandfather Was Queer*. Philadelphia, 1939.

Index

Fictitious characters are indicated by the symbol: *fic.*

Index

Oliver, Charles, 42
Oneida Indians, 127
Ordination Cups, 48
Oregon Trail, 282
Orleans Theatre, New Orleans, 258
Overland Mail, 331 f
Oysters, 95

Paine, Thomas, 220n
Panic of '37, 250
Paris, France, 274n
Parker, Bailiff Henry, 64
Park Row, New York City, 311
Parkins, Judge, *fic.*, 243 ff
Penn, William, 53, 81 f, 85, 87, 89
Pennsylvania, 86, 165, 178n, 241 f
Perceval, John, Earl of Egmont, 65
Philadelphia, 81 ff, 95, 168, 192, 213
Philanders (game), 111
Piedmontese Colonists, 59
Piety Hill, Cal., 321
Pilgrims, 185
Plymouth, 39
Pocahontas, 36
Poker Flats, Cal., 321
Polock, Moses, 178n
Polk, Pres. James K., 282
Pope, Alexander, quoted, 60, 302
Pool Island, 312
Port, 87, 96
Portable Soup, 188
Porter, 71, 96
Port Royal, Acadia (Nova Scotia), 29
Potomac River, 298
Poulaga, 265 ff
Presbyterians, 222
Prohibition in the United States, 61 ff
Provincial Congress, 95 f

Psalms and Sonnets and Songs of Sadness and Piety, 144
Pumpshire (Indian), 130
Punch (drink), 48, 87 f, 96, 210, 297
Punishments, 6, 43, 73, 118 ff, 314
Puritans, 137
Putnam, Gen. Israel, 97

Quadroons, 260 f
Quadroon Ball, 260 f
Quakers, 52 f, 81 ff, 168
Quaker Marriage, 81
Questing, 165

Raggio, Driver, 329
Ramble, Jack, *fic.,* 105 ff, 105n
Ramparts, New Orleans, 261
Randolph, Vt., 202 ff
Rankin (showman), 274, 277
Red-ear Kisses, 112 f
Reed, James F., 281 f, 287
Reed, Virginia, 287
Rejoice for Our Brother Deceased, 214
Religion, 220 ff
Revolution, War of the, 198, 209
Rhode Island, 52, 86
Rice, William, 202, 206
Richmond Hill, New York City, 97
Rienzi (horse), 205
River Street, Woodstock, Vt., 200
Rivington, James, 98
Rockefeller, John D., Jr., 17n
Rocky Mts., 282, 332
Rocky Nook (Watts hymn), 140
Rodersino, Anna, 329
Rogues' Harbour, Ky., 220
Rolfe, John, 36
Roosevelt Street, New York City, 309
Rosenbach, Dr. A. S., 178n